GU01019072
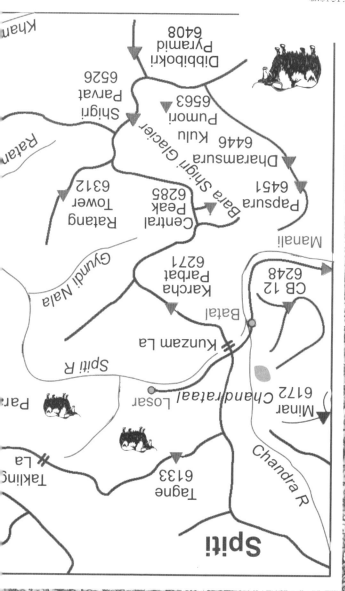

HIMALAYAN WONDERLAND

JISPA

17TH August 2011

TRAVELLING TO MANALI OVER
THE ROHTANG PASS IN A
THUNDERSTORM ON A
ROYAL ENFIELD 500cc
BIKE.

HIMALAYAN WONDERLAND

Travels in Lahaul and Spiti

Manohar Singh Gill

With Forewords by
Indira Gandhi and Sonia Gandhi

PENGUIN
VIKING

VIKING

Published by the Penguin Group

Penguin Books India Pvt. Ltd, 11 Community Centre, Panchsheel Park,
New Delhi 110 017, India

Penguin Group (USA) Inc., 375 Hudson Street, New York, New York 10014, USA

Penguin Group (Canada), 90 Eglinton Avenue East, Suite 700, Toronto,
Ontario, M4P 2Y3, Canada (a division of Pearson Penguin Canada Inc.)

Penguin Books Ltd, 80 Strand, London WC2R 0RL, England

Penguin Ireland, 25 St Stephen's Green, Dublin 2, Ireland
(a division of Penguin Books Ltd)

Penguin Group (Australia), 250 Camberwell Road, Camberwell,
Victoria 3124, Australia (a division of Pearson Australia Group Pty Ltd)

Penguin Group (NZ), 67 Apollo Drive, Rosedale, North Shore 0632, New Zealand
(a division of Pearson New Zealand Ltd)

Penguin Group (South Africa) (Pty) Ltd, 24 Sturdee Avenue, Rosebank,
Johannesburg 2196, South Africa

Penguin Books Ltd, Registered Offices: 80 Strand, London WC2R 0RL, England

First published in Viking by Penguin Books India 2010

Text and images copyright © Manohar Singh Gill 2010

All rights reserved

10 9 8 7 6 5 4 3 2 1

The views and opinions expressed in this book are the author's own and the facts are as
reported by him which have been verified to the extent possible, and the publishers are
not in any way liable for the same.

ISBN 9780670084135

Typeset in Goudy Old Style by SŪRYA, New Delhi
Printed at Replika Press Pvt. Ltd, Sonipat

This book is sold subject to the condition that it shall not, by way of trade or otherwise,
be lent, resold, hired out, or otherwise circulated without the publisher's prior written
consent in any form of binding or cover other than that in which it is published and
without a similar condition including this condition being imposed on the subsequent
purchaser and without limiting the rights under copyright reserved above, no part of this
publication may be reproduced, stored in or introduced into a retrieval system, or
transmitted in any form or by any means (electronic, mechanical, photocopying, recording
or otherwise), without the prior written permission of both the copyright owner and the
above-mentioned publisher of this book.

For the five most talented and beautiful girls in my life

Contents

Foreword to the Original Edition

There is a romantic aura about far-away places, especially if they are difficult to access. But the lives of those who inhabit our mountainous areas are far from romantic. The people are simple and sincere but every problem acquires a complexity because of the altitude, the shortage of water and the lack of communication. As one who loves the mountains, I have deep concern for the mountain people. In order to survive, they must have great faith and fortitude. They are sturdy and hard working, yet full of laughter and gaiety.

Shri Manohar Singh Gill's book has awakened old memories of my own crossing of the Rohtang with my father many years ago. I am sorry that lack of time prevented us from proceeding to Lahaul and Spiti and since then I have nursed a desire to go to this lovely part of our country. Shri Gill captures something of the majestic beauty of this area and gives us a glimpse into the lives and customs of the people and the difficulties of administration there. I hope that this book will kindle the interest of its readers and will urge them to get better acquainted with the people of Lahaul and Spiti and indeed those of all our hill areas.

New Delhi
17 July 1972

INDIRA GANDHI

Foreword to the 2010 Edition

When Shri M.S. Gill first arrived in Lahaul and Spiti as a young IAS officer nearly fifty years ago, it was still a region largely cut off from the outside world. His portrait of this land of rugged and pristine beauty and its remarkable people is rich in its accounts of history, society and folklore, and lyrical in it's descriptions of nature and landscapes. It is also brimming with excitement and the challenge of bringing the fruits of modern development to this remote district.

This new edition, which includes accounts of Shri Gill's more recent visits to Lahaul and Spiti, is enriched by his observations and reflections on the long-term effects of development on its culture and society, including the dramatically visible impact of climate change on its great glaciers.

There is much in this book to interest anthropologists and historians, mountaineers, trekkers and nature lovers. But above all, I hope it will awaken the spirit of adventure in young administrators and inspire them to take up postings in remote and so-called 'hardship' areas as Shri Gill's book so vividly demonstrates that even junior district officials, if they engage deeply and closely with the needs and problems of the people, can make a real and lasting difference and help transform lives.

New Delhi   SONIA GANDHI
9 September 2009

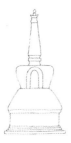

Preface to the 2010 Edition

I joined the Indian Administrative Service in 1958 and trained in the historic Metcalfe House by the Jamuna river in Delhi. During training, I went to eastern India, all the way to Dibrugarh and Digboi in Assam on what was called 'Bharat Darshan'. The highlight of my visit was Darjeeling where we got up early one morning and went to Tiger Hill to catch a glimpse of Everest in the rosy-fingered dawn. Even more exciting was a visit to the Himalayan Mountaineering Institute set up by Nehru to celebrate Tenzing's successful climb of Everest in May 1953. The institute was elegant and well located, and Sherpas in Swiss stockings and mountain boots flitted about. I was bewitched by the place and joined the Himalayan Club, even as I began to read every book on the mountains I could find.

In 1960-61, as the sub-divisional magistrate of Mahendergarh near Delhi, I kept longing for the hills, and finally ran off in March 1961 to Darjeeling to enroll in the HMI's basic mountaineering course. I spent six weeks learning mountaineering with young men from the armed forces in the glorious spring of North Sikkim, with none other than Tenzing for a teacher. In 1962, I managed to gain a posting in the border district of Lahaul and Spiti as deputy commissioner at the ripe age of twenty-six. My main qualification was stamina for hill walking and a passion to do so. Punjab was divided in 1966 and we became strangers to Lahaul and Spiti.

In 1971, I published an account of my Lahaul experience with Vikas Publishing House. It was a quickie, but still had a remarkable response. In my pursuit of a serious career, I lost interest in the book for decades. Many asked me about reprints, but I did not want one till I had re-written it extensively.

In early 2009, the urge finally came and I got down to writing. Parts of the old book have been re-written with additions drawn from my continuous association with Lahaul over the decades. My wife and I have made numerous visits there with our three girls. I am sure our affair with Lahaul will remain till the end. Tshering Dorje, the star of this book, has always been in touch with me. As Chief Election Commissioner, and now as Minister of Youth Affairs and Sports, I talk to him almost every week, whether he is in Kyelang or Kulu. I remain committed to the welfare of the people of Lahaul and Spiti, and have spared no effort in assisting them.

As a young officer in 1971, I asked Mrs Indira Gandhi, the then prime minister, with some hesitation for a foreword. It came back promptly, warmly written and with a clear expression of disappointment at not having gone to Kyelang with Nehru, who loved the mountains and always tried to steal a few days of rest there. Indira Gandhi did the same and the habit continued with Rajiv. I remember when I took a mountaineering team from Punjab to meet him, he seemed excited yet pensive that he could not go on a trip to the hills.

After re-writing this book, I sent a draft to Mrs Sonia Gandhi and asked her if she could write a second foreword for me. She responded promptly and graciously. I can see from the last paragraph of her foreword that Mrs Sonia Gandhi read through my draft—her clear expression that young administrators should look to take adventurous postings in India's remarkably varied landscape obviously refers to my strongly-held view in this book. The fact is that most of our public servants, even in their early youth, look not for challenges but to the opportunity to water their careers and quickly reach urban flesh pots, and if possible, the World Bank.

I am grateful to Mrs Sonia Gandhi for her foreword and I do hope that my book will be read by the young and adventurous. My warm thanks to an old friend, Harish Kapadia, for his valued assistance. I also must thank Gurvinder Singh Randhawa, Jasbir Singh Chopra, and George Varghese for their valuable assistance. Finally, I wish to thank my publishers, Penguin Books India.

Willingdon Crescent,   MANOHAR SINGH GILL
New Delhi
16 November 2009

Preface to the Original Edition

This book is my account of nearly a year's stay in a little known valley in the inner Himalayas near the Indo-Tibetan border. Lahaul lies in the north-western part of India beyond the Great Himalayan Divide. To be exact, it is situated between north latitude 32°8' and 32°59', and east longitude 76°48' and 77°47'. It comprises a vast mountainous area of 2,255 square miles lying south of Ladakh. The Great Himalayan Divide separates it from the district of Kulu. The mountain range is almost uniformly 18,000 feet or higher, and the sole access to Lahaul lies over the 13,050-feet-high Rohtang pass. To the west lies Chamba, and Jammu province. Spiti in the east is separated from Lahaul by a high mountain rib running north from the main Himalayan range. The two valleys have a tenuous link over the Kunzam pass (15,055 feet).

Lahaul has a central mass of high mountains and vast glaciers. Peaks of 20,000 feet or more abound. The Chandra and Bhaga rivers rise on either side of the Baralacha pass (16,047 feet), and flow through narrow valleys on opposite sides of the central ridge to meet at Tandi, giving birth to the Chandrabhaga, which in the Punjab plains becomes the Chenab river. The Chandra and Bhaga valleys are largely desolate in their upper reaches.

Near the confluence there is cultivation on flats above the rivers, and there are many picturesque villages. The Pattan valley beyond the confluence, on account of its reduced elevation, is richer both in crops and population.

These rugged valleys lie at a height of 10,000 feet to 16,000 feet above sea level. The summers are pleasant, with rich crops, lush green meadows and masses of alpine flowers; not so the long winters. From the first snowfall in October–November to the month of May, the valley is continuously under snow.

Kyelang gets about twenty feet of snow in the winter. The temperature falls to -13°C or even lower. The Rohtang pass is then closed to the outside world, and the valley must live on its own resources. Living is hard, with limited fuel, and no fresh fruits and vegetables. But the people have a cheerful happy attitude to life. They have achieved complete harmony with their harsh environment, and display a wonderful contentment.

Since independence, the Punjab government has done much to improve the lot of these fine people. Roads have been built, water supply schemes laid, and hospitals and schools opened. Lahaul-Spiti is now a separate district with headquarters at Kyelang. A council chosen by the people advises the administration on welfare and development schemes.* All this is in sharp contrast to the British period when the valley was left to fend for itself.

I had always wanted to visit this strange and romantic land. Hikers and mountaineers spoke in glowing terms of its clear summers, massive glaciers, and challenging peaks—most of them unclimbed. Fortunately, the Government of Punjab gave me an

---

*The credit for this goes primarily to the dynamic leadership of the late Sardar Partap Singh Kairon, who, in spite of his indifferent health, personally visited these remote valleys, travelling long distances on foot and horseback. After the reorganization of the Punjab, beginning 1 November 1966, the district forms part of the state of Himachal Pradesh.

opportunity to live for a year in this fascinating Shangrila. I was appointed deputy commissioner of Lahaul-Spiti in 1962, the second officer to be so posted since the creation of the district in 1960–61. Many officers and others have visited the valley in summer. Hardly any spent the winter there, and certainly none have written of a winter in Lahaul. With no contact with Chandigarh save a wireless set, and no work within the snow-bound valley, I was rich in time. This I invested in a study of the people placed under my charge. I took part in their festivals and fairs, and tried to identify myself with their lives and longings.

All this I did primarily for the pleasure of it, but I had another motive too. The setting up of a district administration with concentrated work on community development, health and education was bound to have an impact on the people very soon. Apart from raising the standard of living and reducing the harshness of existence, such contact was likely to change and modify the social values and customs ·of the people. Time-honoured traditions and values would soon crumble under the bulldozer effect of new cultural influences. I wanted to record and preserve something of the life and values of the people of Lahaul before this finally happened.

The people of Lahaul-Spiti have been kind and hospitable to me beyond measure. This book is an effort to pay back a little of that debt. I have tried to record everything as I saw it, without any attempt to make comparisons. I believe that the social system of a people is, to a large extent, the result of their environmental needs. It evolves out of collective experience. There is an old Lahaul saying that no custom is bad if it leads a people to happiness. The Lahaulas have been well served by their customs and beliefs.

The first draft of the book was written in 1967. Over the years, whenever I could arouse my interest in the manuscript, I attempted to improve and re-write it. In this I have had valuable counsel from Dr M.S. Randhawa, who is ever willing, and even anxious, to help the new writer or the unknown artist. To Tshering Dorje, I owe more than I would care to admit! Major Haripal Singh Ahluwalia, the Everest hero, and Jo Bradley of Cambridge University Press, both in their own ways, have been of immense help. I must acknowledge gratefully the valuable secretarial services of Sardar Chanan Singh, Shri T.R. Vij, and Shri Attar Singh.

Chandigarh   MANOHAR SINGH GILL
18 July 1972

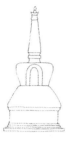

A Beginning

Afoot and light-hearted, I take to the open road,
Healthy, free, the world before me,
The long brown path before me, leading wherever I choose.

—Walt Whitman

It all began one August morning with a summons from the Chief Secretary, Punjab. As Under Secretary, Labour, I sat in an eighth-storey room in Le Corbusier's elegant Secretariat, looking out over his other fantasies, the High Court and the State Parliament building. The Chandigarh lake shimmered in the distance. All morning I plodded through numerous memoranda from labour unions, preparing summaries for the deputy secretary (DS). It was all so tiresome, more so on a sultry August day. The telephone rang and I was told the chief secretary (CS) would like to see me. Wondering what it could be about, I walked down to his fourth-floor office over thick piled carpets, past a Le Corbusier tapestry on the wall and humming air conditioners. The chief secretary, E.N. Mangat Rai, stood at the far end looking at a huge map of the Punjab on the wall, pipe in hand.

Without turning around he asked in his gruff voice, 'How are you making out in Labour?'

'Not too badly, Sir.'

'Would you like a change?'

'If I can get out of the Secretariat, yes.'

'The hills or the desert? I can give you a choice.'

'Any time, the hills.'

'It will have to be the high hills, not the Kangra or Kulu districts with their pleasant wooded valleys, the trout, and the tourists.'

I knew what he meant. In the Punjab of 1961, with no Haryana and a pocket-sized Himachal Pradesh, Punjab stretched from the districts of Mahendergarh and Gurgaon in the south-east, to Lahaul-Spiti in the north, the high Himalayan valleys beyond Kulu and the 13,050-feet-high Rohtang pass. I had started life as a sub-divisional magistrate (SDM) in the desert district of Mahendergarh, bordering Rajasthan. The visionary Punjab chief minister, Sardar Partap Singh Kairon, made sure that young entrants to the administrative service started with the rough areas and worked for the development of New India. I was posted at Mahendergarh. With my trunk and hold-all, I had taken the shuttle train from Delhi to my new posting, Mahendergarh, a small station on the Jaipur route. I was met at the station at an unearthly hour by my peon, and subsequent aide-de-camp, Shadilal, a slim man with a fierce curling moustache and a stylish Rajasthani turban with a long *shamla* at the back. Erect and soldierly, with a twinkle of welcome in his eyes, he represented the best of the desert.

Next to the station was a *mandi* or market with the grain traders' modest shops below and households above. The government had built a small house for the SDM there. It had no electricity and the water came from Matadin's well nearby. I spent the next fifteen months there, cycling to the little fort to hold court and taking camel rides around the villages, fighting locust swarms in the desert summer heat.* In the house, my furniture consisted of a borrowed bed, and a table and chair from the office. In the great summer heat, during the evenings, desperate for a cool breeze, I slept out in my sandy compound. My night suit was a pair of shorts and my air conditioner a small hand towel kept under my pillow to wipe the sweat away. There was only a low mud compound wall. So the magistrate's 'palace' was open at night to the merchants' donkeys and the mandi's pie-dogs. The dogs spent all night howling and chasing each other around the yard. They had a tendency to chase the weak one as a pack and attack him. One summer night, a dozen of them were after one unfortunate weakling. He raced across the sand, and got under my bed, obviously being fully aware of his constitutional rights and the duty of the magistrate to protect him! I woke with a start and found a dozen snarling wolves at my bedside! Needless to say, I did my magisterial duty and did not run away. Occasionally, the donkeys turned out in the evening 'to graze in Commons', shuffling about for a blade of grass in the sand. They would often end up standing around my bed. Suddenly, one of them would start an almighty braying next to my ear for whatever reasons donkeys do so! The effect can be imagined! Nevertheless, I enjoyed my time in the desert. But the summer dust storms and heat could not be ignored.

During my training, I had for the first time travelled to eastern India on what we called Bharat Darshan. In Darjeeling, that glorious hill town, I had my first glimpse of Mount Everest from Tiger Hill. But the event that impacted my mind was a meeting with Tenzing Norgay at the Himalayan Mountaineering Institute

---

*Locusts are all gone now, but in the 1960s, Rajasthan and southern Punjab used to face regular locust attacks with swarms flying across from the Middle East. My Block Development Officer and I often ran around in the hot sun shepherding the locust swarms into the ditches which we had dug. Once they were in, we quickly closed the ditch. But there would be more on the trees.

(HMI). Everest had been climbed for the first time in May 1953 by Hillary and Tenzing. Nehru, perceptive as ever, had set up the HMI—with Tenzing as Director of Training—as an adventure school for the youth of a new independent India. He dreamt that our people too would pitch themselves against the highest ramparts of the world, risking their lives in high adventure, being thus trained for the leadership of a free India able to compete with the best of the world. Brigadier Gyansingh, who subsequently led the first Indian attempt on Everest in 1960, was the principal of the institute. Set in sylvan surroundings, the HMI had a dream campus—the ever-smiling Tenzing in colourful Swiss stockings, plus-fours and mountain boots, a rakish beret on his head, was a hero there above and beyond all film stars. The library was stocked full of books by great mountaineers. As soon as I returned from Darjeeling, I became a life member of the Himalayan Club set up in 1928. Needless to say, my visit to Darjeeling and my meeting with Tenzing had a lasting impact on me.

Sitting in the desert sands of Mahendergarh, I also had for a boss a slightly mad deputy commissioner (DC). M was a middle-aged man, promoted through the ranks and totally insecure, having served as an under secretary in the newly-created Punjab Vigilance Bureau. He had become so nervous after his experience as a thief-catcher that he was a bundle of doubts and diffidence. He would clear no file, take no decision and lived in a perpetual funk. In such a situation, my thoughts turned to the HMI, and one morning, I wrote a simple postcard to the CS, E.N. Mangat Rai, asking if I could be sent for mountain training to Darjeeling. I broke all civil service channels by writing directly to the CS and this was a punishable act. Mangat Rai, fortunately, was a chief secretary of the unconventional British school. A brilliant graduate of Government College, Lahore, he had dabbled in writing, sports, and anything that came to his mind. As CS in independent India, he followed very unconventional ways. In the evenings, he welcomed young officers home, offered a proper drink to the thirsty, and sat long hours in equal argument over the political issues of the day. He did not pull rank and was happy to be called 'Bunchie' by his deputy secretaries outside the office; but in office, the next morning, he was grim and gruff, demanding the highest standards of performance and offering no liberties to subordinates.

As the weeks passed with no response from the CS, I waited apprehensively. Suddenly, one March afternoon, I got a telegram from the chief secretary: 'Reference your letter, if willing, report to HMI Darjeeling immediately.'

I was desperate to go. Nehru's school, unfortunately, was being patronized only by young officers from the armed forces. No one from the civil services ever dreamt of going there. They were not the adventurous men of the British Indian Civil Service. They were career-driven Indians, all determined to end as cabinet secretaries. If I could go, I would be the first civil services officer there. In my letter to the CS, I had argued that India had a long border with Tibet, where the Chinese were aggressive and active since 1959, perhaps earlier. The issue had started disturbing Parliament and the people of India. Kairon, the perceptive chief minister of Punjab, had broken up the huge Kangra district of 10,000 square kilometres to create the new district of Lahaul-Spiti on the frontier in order to effectively administer the region and show an Indian presence on the border. Most officers avoided such difficult postings in isolated remote areas. They still do! I suggested that the government needed to encourage young officers to take to mountaineering so that a cadre could be built up of willing volunteers. I had made my offer to the CS, who had accepted it.

Now I knew the DC would not allow me to go; over his dead body! So I wrote a vague note to him, sent it by slow camel post to Narnaul, the district headquarters that was twenty miles away, and left for Delhi and on to Calcutta by the night train. By the time the DC got my epistle, I was trekking through the glorious tea gardens around Darjeeling in spring weather, down to the Rangeet river. The DC searched high and low in the Punjab and beyond, but never found me till I decided to come home two months later. The ten-day trek through the tea gardens up the Teesta river to the mountains of western Sikkim, just below the great 24,000-feet-high Kabru Dome, remains the most valuable of my memories. We camped by the river, got up every morning at five and were given *aloo parathas* in round cane baskets, after which we walked in glorious weather through deep forests laden with lichen and moss. Every variety of Himalayan bird flitted about. We walked in the shade the whole day through the thick dark, mysterious forests. Occasionally, we came across a small Buddhist shrine on a lonely ridge with a beautifully painted Bodhisattva, festooned with silk scarves left by worshipping hill folk. One night, we camped outside the great Pemayangtse monastery and sought the blessings of the lamas. In later life, I have gone up the same route with sadness gripping my heart. Roads have been built, the forest cut and the hill slopes vandalized. Now there is no shade and no birds sing. There is only the pitiless glare of the sun, reflecting the shale and rubble of road construction.

At Yoksam village, the last green oasis, we camped next to the mountain hut of the HMI. It was a pleasant site with green fields, alpine trees and little rills of water going down the slopes. Village children, happy, laughing Mongoloid faces, gathered to gawk at us. The evening was spent drinking *chhaang* in bamboo cups, singing folk songs and telling stories around the camp fire.

The next day, we began climbing up the sheer Dzongri Ridge— I, Hari Ahluwalia, and Gombu, who both subsequently climbed Everest in 1965, competing in a race to the top. The murderous climb almost killed me. Gombu, Tenzing's nephew, of course won the race to the top. Then we walked along the top of the ridge through a forest of rhododendron, a splash of every colour shining in the spring light. We got lost in the rhododendron forest. Its myriad branches were intertwined like snakes in the hair of the Furies. It took hours to get out of the grip of those rhododendron branches. Finally, we came down to the proper path. At the ridge line, we stopped to admire a fantastic sight. Spread out below us was a huge bowl-shaped valley. At the far end, a host of Himalayan peaks led by the Kabru Dome (24,000 feet) pierced the sky in a vast panorama. We rested, feasting on this amazing vista and taking panoramic photographs. We then took the long walk down and up again to the other side of the valley to our camp at Chauri Khiang that nestled in the shadow of the great Kabru Dome.

We spent three weeks at Chauri Khiang at a height of 16,500 feet, learning snow and ice craft. I was the only civilian in a bunch of fine young army, navy and air force officers. The March weather was tempestuous, with occasional nights of heavy snow. The little tents we slept in would get buried under. We were taught to come out in the bitter night cold to clear the snow. Nobody would! I can never forget Tenzing, the great hero, walking around at midnight, shaking our tents to get rid of the snow. He mothered us. I shared my little mountain tent with Colonel Jaiswal of the Indian Army, an older man who was being trained to be a future principal. At 16,500 feet, we all suffered from the lack of oxygen, and Jaiswal often put his considerable nose out of the tent flap at night to suck in more oxygen. One evening, he even complained to me that I was monopolizing the little oxygen in the tent! We climbed to about 18,000 feet during training. On the way back to Darjeeling, we had a night of fun at Yoksam village, drinking chhaang in bamboo cups with reed straws and bathing in hot springs by the river, our Sherpani porters in one pool and us in another close by. To be sure, we never looked their way!

Nehru came to our graduation. He used to visit the school regularly, accompanied by his friend Dr B.C. Roy, the great chief minister of West Bengal. It was Nehru who pinned on our silver graduation ice axes. Indira Gandhi and Rajiv Gandhi were present there. Incidentally, Nehru's practice was followed by both of them. Subsequent prime ministers, though still the presidents of the HMI, rarely went. Now, the defence minister of India is the president of the HMI, and the graduation is no longer attended by the prime minister, the defence minister and the chief minister of West Bengal. When I see the current political problems in the Darjeeling hills, I do feel that the Nehruvian policy of warm and intimate contact with the hill people was the correct one and has unfortunately been allowed to fade away into a mere formal relationship.

I returned to Mahendergarh with some apprehension, but survived the DC's ire thanks to the support of the unconventional Mangat Rai. Two years later, I ran away from another boss in Chandigarh to climb for two months in the Parbati valley of Kulu. That time, Kairon, the perceptive chief minister, saved my bacon from an equally irate Registrar of Cooperatives.

The CS obviously remembered my desires—to get away from M and the desert. He had not forgotten my successful but rule-breaking adventure in the HMI Darjeeling, and so his offer to me to be the deputy commissioner of Lahaul-Spiti was a test and a challenge. With more than five thousand square miles of high mountains, glaciers and deep-cut valleys, none less than ten thousand feet high, Lahaul-Spiti is wedged between Tibet in the east, Ladakh in the north and Kulu in the south. The district is composed of two distinct valleys—the Lahaul and the Spiti valleys.

The Lahaul valley starts from the Baralacha pass (16,000 feet) in the north bordering Ladakh in the state of Jammu and Kashmir. In the centre of the valley is a mass of high mountains, 20,000 feet or higher, known as the Mulkila group of peaks. Two small rivers start from the Baralacha pass, and flank the eastern and western sides of the Mulkila mountains. The western river Bhaga flows through the well populated Lahaul valley; the eastern one called the Chandra flows through the totally desolate eastern valley. Both meet a few miles below Kyelang, the district headquarters, at the village of Tandi. From the Tandi confluence, the combined streams are known as the Chandrabhaga and it flows through a narrow gorge south-eastward through Doda and Bhadarwah, till it debouches near Jammu as the great Chenab river of the Punjab. It enters Pakistan, a short distance beyond Jammu, on its way to the sea.

The Spiti valley is cut off from Lahaul by a north–south ridge, which can only be crossed over the Kunzam pass (15,000 feet). One has to go from Khoksar, the first village down the northern slope of the Rohtang, up the Chandra valley, in an eastward swing, then climb to the Kunzam and drop down to the first Spiti village called Losar. Beyond Losar, there was no road and one had to walk to Kaza, the sub-divisional headquarters, crossing the fast-flowing Spiti river by a rickety, narrow, swaying footbridge strung high above the river. The Spiti river ultimately pours into the Sutlej, south of the Shipki pass. Thus, the Lahaul waters end up in the Chenab, going south-westwards, and the Spiti waters go eastwards into the Sutlej. Both rivers meet south of Multan in Pakistan at the Panchnad, where the four Punjab rivers join Father Indus. The connection between the Lahaul and Spiti valleys only lasts for a few months in the summer.

The districts' sole precarious link with the Punjab lay over the Rohtang, 13,050 feet high, snow-bound for six months or more, and with a murderous reputation. Life was harsh and primitive, but exciting. A modest jeep track had been cut up the steep Rohtang ridge from Rahla. It went up in a zigzag, over rocks and stones, and a jeep was barely able to bounce and groan up the steep phase. The road, if it could be so called, was open only after May, and would often close with the early snow in September. The steady piling up of snow locked the valley in an icy grip. There was no way to come out in the winter. Daring locals did one or two dangerous winter crossings of the pass, walking all the way from Kyelang to Manali, a distance of 80–100 kilometres, braving avalanches in the snow-choked valley. They would walk for some hours in the dark early mornings when the snow was firm, and camp in a village for the rest of the day, when the avalanches started thundering down the mountains. To cross the pass in the winter was to take a chance with one's life. In Kyelang village, the DC's headquarters, there was no medical aid whatsoever. The civil surgeon was somebody on a punishment posting and would happily kill the DC since he could not lay his hands on the Director of Health! With no hospital, no operating theatre, no electricity, and no helicopters, one could die of a burst appendix or pneumonia. The link with Chandigarh was only a wireless set and the night life was a radio, on which we heard Amin Sayani and the *Binaca Geet Mala* on Radio Ceylon, which was the rage in the India of the 1960s. The winter excitement of three bachelors in Kyelang consisted of sending mischievous song requests to Radio Ceylon dedicated to an unnamed beautiful girl in Sector 16, Chandigarh, where all our IAS bosses lived.

The nearness of Tibet and China added zest to living, and urgency to one's work. The country was full of concern for the Chinese push on our borders. The chief minister was anxious to provide rapid development, particularly health, education and agriculture to the people of these border valleys, and had developed a personal interest in this remote district. Though asthmatic, he travelled every summer to Lahaul, and even Spiti, dragging his chief secretary, finance secretary and all principal officers with him. Meetings were held in the valley. Young officers were given a hearing and final decisions taken in favour of the field officers' views on the spot. There was to be no tedious file noting in Chandigarh and references to the Departments and the Cabinet. What was decided on a windy afternoon in a tent in the Lahaul valley was the final decision of the Punjab government and had to be implemented promptly by all Chandigarh babus, in peril of punishment for any dilatory behaviour. Incentives were also given to those who served in these high mountains. Only Kairon could dream up such a system of governance for these remote corners. Sometimes I think, if only Delhi mandarins had followed his example, India would not have had the permanent problems with our eastern citizens.

I jumped at the offer to give up the miserable dispute files of the Labour Department, and be the king of 5,000 square miles of high mountains and glaciers, with a population of barely 20,000 people, with villages of five or ten hamlets at heights of 15,000 feet or more. It was an offer I simply could not refuse. As I thought later, for once my pleasure became my duty. How many men can say this in life?

I knew something of Lahaul-Spiti already, having read Justice G.D. Khosla's book *Himalayan Circuit*, published in the early 1960s. Khosla, an ICS judge of the Lahore and later Punjab High Courts, was fond of trekking and had gone on a six-week walking tour of Lahaul and Spiti in the 1950s with Srinegesh, the commissioner of Jalandhar, and Bachitter Singh, the magistrate of Kulu. His lordship's ostensible reason for this one-month tour to Spiti and Lahaul was the urgent need to inspect the Kaza magistrate's court. In a crime-free tribal valley of genial people, there was, however, not much to inspect.

They trekked all over Spiti, then went up the Chandra valley, and came back to Kyelang, via the Baralacha pass. Khosla left an exciting travelogue, which revived my interest in the high Himalayas. A year later, I went in early spring by jeep from Pathankot with my HMI course-mate, Hari Ahluwalia, up the Kangra valley to Manali for the first time in my life. The broad Beas valley beyond Nurpur, with the high snowy Dharamsala ramparts in the west, and the rich gently sloping valley, going down to the Beas river in the east, was a revelation. We travelled in the early morning through a land favoured by the gods. As the sun came up over the low eastern hills, I remembered Shakespeare's lines:

But, look, the morn, in russet mantle clad,
Walks o'er the dew of yon high eastward hill.

The road was empty in those days and we drove on up to Palampur, a delightful station of pine trees, sloping hills, and well-manicured Kangra tea-gardens. The historic town of Mandi was a delight. The Raja's palace across the Beas river was impressive and on a ledge above the road was a gurdwara commemorating Guru Gobind Singh, who used to come here often to visit his friend, the Raja. On the river bank, in the sand and stones, was a huge boulder with a yellow Sikh flag on it. It is said that the Guru often sat there, contemplating the green waters of the Beas. Beyond Mandi, we entered the gorge, which led to Kulu. The river, on its furious way to the plains of the Punjab, occupies most of it. The British-cut road was only a twelve-foot ledge on its right bank. It was an exciting sight with every kind of vegetation clinging to the steep rocks.

Incidentally, as I write now, I see the vandalization of this gorge by the so-called development of later decades. Many years after my Lahaul adventure, the Beas river was totally tamed and bound hand and foot. A dam was built at Pandoh beyond Mandi, and the gorge, one of nature's wonders, was submerged in a lake. The Pandoh waters were taken in long tunnels across the Sundernagar valley to the Sutlej river to augment the waters of the great Bhakra dam. This may have pleased the builders and the development czars, but it destroyed the Beas river.* Now, it is almost dry at Mandi town and all the way down to Nurpur. The green *mahseer*-laden waters are gone and the rocky bones of the sacred river lie exposed to all and sundry. The road has been taken in zigzag cuts up the right bank slope. Its entry into Kulu, through numerous tunnels, is a sad experience for someone like me, who once saw the river in its glory and beauty.

Finally, Hari and I emerged out of the gorge into a huge open green valley, with snow mountains at its northern end. The paradise of Kulu was before us. We drove through apple orchards in full bloom, tended to by beautiful women. Kashmir is beautiful, but the Kulu valley is no less. No wonder many of the British, the Banons and Johnsons, married pretty local lasses and settled here. Why would they go back to wet and misty Albion? Beyond Kulu, the valley rapidly gained height till we came into the pine forests of Manali. We drove to the top end and into the beautiful compound of the forest rest house built by the British. It was in a thick pine grove, protected from being cut by a British commissioner who had declared it an archaeological monument, thus forbidding the entry of the forest contractors! Nehru made this rest house famous in 1956, when he spent a week of rest here, going through his boxes of correspondence with the world's greats, which were put together in his book *A Bunch of Old Letters*. We spent a few restful days in the historic rest house, walking to the Vashisht hot springs across the river for a dip. With the advent of spring, the Kangra Gaddis were already taking their flocks of sheep to the Lahaul valley for summer

---

*I also have to say with sadness that the pristine Sundernagar valley has suffered at the hands of engineers and lately, cement manufacturers.

grazing. Writing now, after many decades, with time having flitted by, I still vividly recall the beautiful grey-eyed Gaddi girl I had photographed then. We went one day to Rahla (9,000 feet), the foot of the Rohtang Pass, and attempted a walk up the sheer face, Hathi Matha, to test our muscles and our training. The Harambha Devi temple in the shade of dark pines was a compelling mystery. The sulphur-laden hot springs in Vashisht village across the river were a soothing attraction. We spent much time soaking in the hot water. The Kulu-Manali visit had left rich memories in my mind and I longed to see what lay beyond the Rohtang.

E.N. Mangat Rai was in an expansive mood. Over a cup of tea, he talked of Lahaul. 'I hope you know the difficulties. The valley is snowbound and cut off all through a long and severe winter. No communication, not even letters then. Not much in the nature of creature comforts or medical aid. You have to live like the locals.'

I thought it all heavenly. I dreamt of being cut off from Chandigarh and its meaningless government circulars, its tedious routine and petty intrigues. E.N. talked on, 'But you will like it—particularly the hiking and the climbing. Most wonderful area for mountaineering. No monsoon. Fine weather all through the summer. Glaciers and mountains of twenty thousand feet at your doorstep. Take an interest in the people. There is much work for an amateur anthropologist. Be in sympathy and harmony with them. Be aware of your surroundings and the people, and you will never be lonely.' E.N. was clearly of the Verrier Elwin school of tribal administrators.

'When can you leave?'

'Within three days, if you like, Sir.' I wanted to put some distance between me and the labour unions at the earliest.

'Well good luck to you, and keep me informed.' At the door, E.N. softened a little and confided, 'I think I envy you. I wish I were younger, and able to get away from these concrete walls . . .'

Two days were spent in hectic activity, collecting tinned food, cameras, mountain boots, sleeping bags and a thousand other odds and ends. Finally, one fine morning, I found myself at Chandigarh's fledgling airport waiting for the Dakota flight from Delhi to Manali. These vintage specimens of World War II still do yeomen service in India, flying mainly on faith!

As we lifted over the airfield and gained height, Le Corbusier's brain-child fell into clear geometric patterns; sector and sub-sector, all dotted with neatly built cubes of white and grey. We swung away to the north, flying over the low Shiwalik hills. After about twenty minutes we cleared the crest of this range and flew into the broad Sundernagar valley, heading for Mandi. From Mandi, the fun began. Turning sharply, we entered the Beas valley. Now the plane flew low, hemmed in on both sides by steep mountains. The valley was so narrow that the sides seemed within touching distance of the wing tips! The plane turned and twisted like a car in a traffic jam. There was no scope for turning back. I think most passengers prayed; the tourist guide in Delhi had evidently told them only of the beauties of Kulu, not its hazards!

After another ten minutes the valley broadened out and we flew low over the Beas river, which tumbled and rumbled down the boulder-strewn valley in its mad rush to the plains. Soon, we were skimming over the water and then, with a bump or two, we came to rest in a small grassy patch on the water's edge. The sole and proud representative of Indian Airlines came forward accompanied by all the local urchins. Together, they put up a rickety ladder and we stepped out to a perfect salesman's smile from Mr Airlines and cheers from the children. We deserved the ovation. The flight to Kulu is basically an affirmation of one's faith in God and the machine age!

The plane was tied up in a corner of the field, the luggage and passengers loaded on to a bus that rivalled the Dakota in age, and the wind sleeve hauled down and stowed away. Mr Airlines adjusted his peak cap at a rakish angle, took the front seat, and we rumbled away in a groan of gears. Kulu airport was closed for the day!

At Manali, I was sorting out my boxes and crates from the tourists' luggage, when I heard a soft voice at my elbow. 'Mr. Gill, Sir.' I swung around and found myself looking at a tall, well-built man of about thirty, with Mongoloid features and a perpetual twinkle in his eyes. A handsome man, except for the silly little Lenin peak cap on his head, which gave him a slightly comic look. He might have been a young Mao Tse Tung in another life. 'Sir I am Tshering Dorje, Bhoti teacher, come with the jeep from Kyelang,' he said.

I had heard much about Dorje, a young Lahaula, extremely intelligent, tough, and with a most interesting and chequered past. In his youth, he had travelled widely over western Tibet and Ladakh. He joined the monastery of Tholing near Taklakot in Tibet, spending the summers there and the winters in Lahaul. But his restless spirit found the lamaistic discipline and confinement irksome. He ran away and got married. Now he teaches Bhoti to new district officers in Lahaul. All spoke of him as a virtual Jeeves.

Dorje stepped aside and introduced the jeep driver Fauja Singh, literally meaning 'Army lion'. Fauja Singh was true to his name. A powerful, bush-bearded Sikh, he had seen service with the Fourteenth Army in Burma. A veteran of the Tiddim road, he now delighted in roaring down the mule tracks that did duty for roads in Lahaul.

Both men were Lahaul characters and their fame had filtered down to Chandigarh. I looked forward to working with them. Quickly and efficiently, they sorted out my packages and loaded them. The jeep swung away across the suspension bridge over the Beas, the road rising in a series of serpentine curves. On our left was the river, and in front the magnificent ice walls of the Himalayan divide separating Kulu from Lahaul. On either side, beautiful pine forests raced down the mountain slopes to the water's edge. We gained height quickly and the valley got narrower, the Beas now pounding down a deep gorge.

Another bend in the road and the valley came to an abrupt end. Wedged in front of us like a giant dam was a mountain mass bare of all vegetation. It rose sharply in a series of rock buttresses and grassy slopes. I had to throw my head back to look at it. The pine forests came down the side slopes and then stopped abruptly at the foot of the pass like hesitant maidens. A few tea shops, some road builders' huts and scattered stores marked Rahla at the foot of the Rohtang pass. No wonder the local people called this sheer rocky face in front of us Hathi Matha.

A short halt for tea and we were off again. Now the real climb started. The road rose in a series of steep zigzags up the sheer face. In fact, it was hardly a road; I might better describe it as a boulder strewn ledge cut along the mountain side. After every two or three hundred yards, it took a sharp hairpin bend. The jeep bounced along, groaning in low gears. It had no grip on account of the loose stones, and I half expected it to bounce off the edge. Fauja Singh drove on serenely. He particularly delighted in demonstrating his virtuosity on the U-turns. He would cut sharply, then back the jeep over the abyss, without so much as looking back, to complete the turn. The toes he kept on the brake, in case the jeep rolled back over the edge; the heel on the accelerator as a cut engine could be equally fatal. He was an artist and he knew it. I sat quietly, trying to renew my faith in destiny and God. I dared not do otherwise. I had been told about a commissioner touring Lahaul with Fauja Singh. At a particularly dangerous section, the commissioner thought discretion the better part of valour and decided to get off. He asked Fauja Singh to drive on and wait a little distance away; he and his German wife would walk, stretching their legs, and all that! Fauja Singh stopped the jeep, saluted, and said, 'Sir, I also have a wife and children. If you walk, I walk!' The commissioner meekly got back into the jeep and they drove on. Fauja Singh did not, of course, hear the rebuke from the commissioner's German wife, 'R, you really deserved that!'

Sanity returned slowly to the slope. The groaning of the jeep ceased and soon we were on top of the saddle. A small stone shelter for travellers caught in a Rohtang hurricane, a little board saying 'Height: Thirteen Thousand Fifty Feet', and some prayer flags marked the pass. The view was magnificent. Looking back, we could see heavily forested ridges stretching back to the snow covered peaks around Manali. In front lay the Chandra valley of Lahaul, a barren land of rock and snow. Gephan peak, abode of Gephan *devta*, the presiding deity of Lahaul, stood directly opposite the pass. Head uplifted and beautiful fluted sides covered with a mantle of snow, it was a mountaineer's dream. In 1912, Captain Todd and the Swiss guide in General Bruce's party got to within twenty feet of the top. They were almost blown off by the fierce gale from the Rohtang and retreated.*

---

*'Fuhrer reports it to have been extremely hard work, but very fine climbing—ice and snow, with occasional bits of outcropping rock, their only trouble being that, owing to the heavy cornicing of the ridge, they occasionally had to take to the face. However, when they had passed all difficulties, and when not more, he says, than twenty minutes from the top, they were suddenly caught in a regular *ourmente*, which nearly took them off the mountain, and without stopping a moment, they fled.' (Lt. Col. C.G. Bruce, *Kulu and Lahoul* (London: Edward Arnold, 1914)

On either side of the pass were two peaks of sixteen thousand feet or more, like the horns on a saddle.

For once, there was no gale on top of the pass. It was exceptionally calm. We sat down near the stone hut and opened a thermos of tea. Tshering Dorje talked of Rohtang and its legends. The Kulu people have an interesting story about its origin.

It is said that at one time, there was no gap in the great mountain barrier separating Lahaul from Kulu. The people of Lahaul were very sad as the winds and birds had told them of another world rich in trade across the mountain barrier. They tried again and again to discover a way, but there was none. Disappointed, they thought that perhaps the Lord of Creation did not wish them to go beyond the mountains. But again they remembered what the winds and the birds had told them about the wonderful opportunities of trade in the south. So they decided to approach Lord Shiva to help them find a way over the mountain barrier.

The priests sacrificed a young virgin as in those days it was considered an honourable and good thing to sacrifice, and even to be the one sacrificed. Besides, this was the only way to get in touch with Lord Shiva. The priests went into a trance to speak to Lord Shiva and begged that the people of Lahaul be allowed to cross the barrier. But Lord Shiva was angry as the people had turned to him only after they had failed to find a way themselves. So he refused to answer. The priests and the people were greatly distressed, as men in those days were pious and it was not good that Lord Shiva should be angry. Another boy as well as a second virgin were sacrificed, and the priests asked again for an answer. Lord Shiva got over his anger when he saw these simple and good people entreating his help and said, 'Yes, you and your people may go beyond the barrier.'

One of the priests replied, 'O Lord, there is no way. We have searched much but found none. How shall we go?' Lord Shiva answered, 'Indeed, you have been wicked to look for a way yourself. Nevertheless, I will give you a path to the plains.' And the priests and the people prostrated and gave thanks to the lord. 'But beware,' Lord Shiva said, 'of the winds which my whip will unleash when I strike down the barrier. These winds will be sudden and fierce, and will last for all time to come. Beware, lest you get caught in them and perish.'

The priests thanked Lord Shiva and informed the people about Shiva's boon. Lord Shiva sent messengers to warn the people to the south. Everyone in Lahaul and Kulu hid, lest they should be stricken by the awful might and majesty of Lord Shiva. Taking his whip, Lord Shiva smote the mountains again and again. There was a terrible crashing and fierce and strong winds, such that the mountains swayed before them. Huge rocks fell from the mountains. Finally, there was a great silence and darkness fell over the land as all birds, animals, and even the rocks and the sun stood still before the majesty of Lord Shiva.

After some time, the people recovered their courage and came out, and lo and behold—there was the Rohtang pass! The people of Lahaul rushed to the top, but when they got there, they were afraid, as there was no way to get down to the valley on the other side. Disguised as a mortal, Lord Shiva appeared again to show them the way. Telling the people to watch, he gave a mighty leap, and as he went through the air, a path sprang up below him on the ground. This path led to Manali. But Lord Shiva apparently miscalculated the spring, and landed head first near Manali village. To this day, the earth there has a bruise and a swelling, and that is the hillock above Manali. There is also a rock to commemorate the landing of the Lord. The people of Manali built a temple around the rock in praise of Shiva, for they got much trade from Lahaul. Lord Shiva, however, went away with a broken head. Many people hurried over the new path in both directions. But some in their foolishness forgot Shiva's warning about the wind. The pass seemed so safe and easy. Because of their carelessness, many died on its treacherous top, frozen by the wind. To this day, almost every year, some people pay the supreme price for their recklessness on the Rohtang. The people of Kulu vividly recall a clear and sunny October day in 1869 when some of their men returning from Lahaul were caught in a sudden wind storm on the pass and seventy of them perished. Within a month of my arrival, I was to experience in dramatic fashion the truth of this legend.

The Lahaul people have a different story about the making of the Rohtang pass. It is said that long ago, there ruled in western Tibet a king by the name of Gyapo Gyaser. He was a very powerful ruler and had conquered many kingdoms around Tibet.

Once, he came to Lahaul on his horse named Thuru Kyangmo. This horse was also well known and could fly like Pegasus. The king was accompanied by a goddess named Ane Gurnam Gyamo. The king travelled through Lahaul, conquering the land as he went. At last he came to the great mountain barrier near Khoksar. At that time, there was no Rohtang pass, and the high mountains extended in a continuous chain between Kulu and Lahaul. Thus the people of Lahaul were completely cut off from the south, and had no contact with Kulu. The king was very keen to go across this mountain barrier and see the new lands on the other side. He, therefore, gave a powerful blow with his magic hunting crop and created a great dent in the mountain chain above Khoksar. He was about to give another blow, but the *devi* restrained him saying, 'If you make the pass too low and easy, the Buddhist people of Lahaul will mingle with the people of Kulu and the plains. This will not be good.' The king then passed over to the other side.

Travelling down he came to Rahla, where he met a very

beautiful and bewitching *rakshasani*. He fell in love with her and stopped there. Forgetting his own kingdom, he began to spend all his time in pleasant dalliance with the rakshasani. Meanwhile, his own kingdom in Tibet was attacked by a neighbouring king. His armies were defeated, his cities ravaged, and his queen carried away by the victor. The people were in great distress and they constantly prayed for the return of their king. The prime minister, who was a very wise old man, decided to send a message to the king. He wrote a letter which he tied to the wing of a *thung thung* (Saras crane), and asked the bird to carry it to the king across the mountains. For many days, the thung thung flew looking for the king, until it came to Rahla, and saw him playing chess with a beautiful lady. The king, on seeing the bird, was reminded of his country and of the long interval he had been away from it. He thought to himself, if the bird sits on my right, the news will be good, but if it comes to my left, it will be bad. The thung thung alighted to his left. The king saw the message tied to the wing and took it. He was greatly distressed to read of the ravages suffered by his kingdom and of the loss of his queen. He decided to go back immediately.

When he broke the news to the rakshasani, she began to cry, and said that she wanted to go with him. Perplexed, the king consulted the goddess, who declared it impossible to carry the rakshasani to their country, for their own gods would be displeased. The goddess said it would be best to kill her by a stratagem: she asked him to suggest to the rakshasani that since the horse could not carry two people, she should hold on to the tail when the horse flew off. The king gave this suggestion to the rakshasani and she agreed. Everything was readied, and the king mounted the horse. But as the rakshasani caught it by the tail, the horse, Thuru Kyangmo, gave her a mighty kick. The rakshasani was hurled with great force against a nearby cliff and killed. So great was the force that the outline of a woman was impressed into the rock, and can be seen to this day. The king flew off to his own country, accompanied by the goddess. The dent made by the king with his magic hunting crop ultimately came to be known as the Rohtang pass and became the main route between Lahaul and Kulu.

Tshering Dorje paused. We had dallied long enough on the pass, bewitched by the surrounding beauty and the tales of gods and demons. It was getting late and we still had forty miles to go to Kyelang. Quickly, we rolled down to Khoksar, Fauja Singh showing complete mastery over his home road. Khoksar is a desolate place, marked only by a small rest house and a suspension bridge over the Chandra river. It is important, however, as a road junction. Upstream from here, the road goes along the Chandra river to the Kunzam pass and into the Spiti valley, downstream to the Tandi confluence, and then up the Bhaga river to Kyelang, the district capital. Beyond Kyelang, the route leads over the Baralacha pass to Leh, the capital of Ladakh.

After crossing the suspension bridge, we drove along the right bank of the Chandra river. The road was dusty, the hills barren. The river water was a muddy brown and the banks were strewn with loose boulders and scree, the result of winter avalanches from the surrounding slopes. Except for a few fields of barley at Khoksar, there was no vegetation. We drove through such a desolate landscape for about ten miles, till we came to Sissu. What a change! The village is situated on a broad flat above the river. On the hill slopes were plantations of willow, poplar and alfa. The fields around the village were full of lush green barley and buckwheat. There appeared to be no shortage of water. It flowed in abundance down the slopes and through the fields in little channels. In Lahaul, people have perfected the technique of bringing water from the high glaciers to the villages below in channels cut along the contours of the rock face. Sometimes these water channels, known as *kuhls*, run for miles and are cut along cliff edges.

Water had made all the difference to Sissu. Rich crops, lovely trees and a mass of summer flowers surrounded the village. Along the water channels, I found every colour and specie of alpine flowers, and the hill slopes were covered with white, pink and yellow wild roses. Sissu is typical of Lahaul scenery. From the green valley, one looked across the river and up the mountain at a massive glacier wedged in a narrow gorge, topped by a beautiful peak of twenty thousand feet. All this one could take in at a single glance!

Sissu is important to the spiritual welfare of the people of Lahaul. Behind the ridge on which the village nestles, towers the peak of Gephan, abode of the presiding lord of Lahaul. The peak is visible from both ends of Lahaul, from the Baralacha and the Rohtang passes. On a clear day, it can even be seen from Simla. Other mountains in Lahaul may be higher, but none excites the imagination more. There is a temple of Gephan in the village, and in summer, a festival is held here.

It is said that the Gephan devta* came to Lahaul from Ladakh, across the Baralacha pass. He was accompanied by his mother and a retinue of lesser devtas. At that time, there lived some *rakshasa*s near the Baralacha pass. They were keen that the Gephan devta should not cross into Lahaul; it was their private preserve. To hinder the devta's progress, they raised a severe snow storm. It snowed continuously for many days and the pass

---

*'Temples to devtas and devis and to snake-gods are frequent in Pattan though almost entirely wanting in Gara and Rangoli. An exception in Rangoli is the temple at Sissu to Gyephan, the god of the Snowy Cone mountain of the same name; he is the brother of Jamlu, the god of Malana in Kulu, and as at the temple of the latter so also sheep sacrificed to Gyephan are slain by having their bellies slit open and the gall extracted while they are still alive.' (*Kangra District Gazetteer*, 1897)

was deep under snow. In spite of the soft snow, Gephan devta crossed the pass with his followers. On the way, his mother was buried under an avalanche. The party pressed on till it reached Zing Zing Bar in Lahaul. After six days, Gephan devta went back to the top of the pass, dug out his mother, and brought her safely down. The devta passed through Lahaul and ultimately settled at Sissu. He is said to live on top of the Gephan peak. The mother, who was named Zangdul, settled at a place called Kewak, about two miles from Sissu towards Khoksar.

The Gephan devta is also reputed to have brought various food grains to the valley of Lahaul. It is said that before his coming, the valley was ruled over by rakshasas who only ate meat. When the devta was coming to Lahaul, he decided to bring seeds of various grains. To hide them from the rakshasas, he and his companions filled their mouths with a little of each variety of seed. During the fight at the Lingti plains, beyond the Baralacha, one of the rakshasas smote Gephan on the cheek with his fist. The devta lost many of the seeds in his mouth there, along with a few teeth! Only a few barley, wheat and buckwheat seeds remained in his mouth. Even today, there are little mounds on the Lingti plains, which are said to be heaps of the grain knocked out of Gephan's mouth by some particularly belligerent rakshasa. The three main crops grown in Lahaul are barley, wheat and buckwheat—the result of the few seeds which the devta managed to smuggle in. No wonder the people of Lahaul hold the Gephan devta in such awe and respect.

The rest house at Sissu is situated in a fine grove of willows overlooking the river. After a welcome cup of tea with the engineer working on the road, we drove on. At Gondhla, the next important village, Thakur Duni Chand welcomed us.* One

---

*The thakurs are the gentry and quondam rulers of the valley. They are more or less pure Botias or Mongolians by blood, but have begun, as the natural sequence to the Hinduising tendency already described to assert a Rajput origin. Three families of thakurs retain in modern times a

of the hereditary families of Lahaul, Duni Chand has a small castle with an ancient tower which is worth exploring. But Gondhla and the Thakur's tower are overshadowed by the Gondhla peaks. Across the river, they rise sheer for thousands of feet, with ice walls to match the Eiger's north face, and so much more.* In fact, I think Lahaul is a mountaineer's paradise. Nowhere else can one drive in a matter of hours to the base camp of a twenty thousand-feet-high mountain. The weather is fine all through the year. There is no monsoon as the clouds cannot cross the mountain barrier and precipitate themselves on the Manali side of the range. Tough porters, as good as the Nepali Sherpas, are available. For a small, cheap expedition out to have fun, Lahaul is the place.

We descended to the Tandi confluence. The slope of both the Chandra and Bhaga valleys ease here, and the rivers meet in a gentle embrace. The confluence is overlooked by the Goshal Cone, a *lingam*-like peak of about twenty thousand feet. There is a sandy beach and a beautiful *chorten* at the confluence triangle. I walked down to the water's edge and heard the gentle murmur of the two streams united again after a long separation.

---

status of importance as jagirdars—that of Hari Chand Negi of Lahaul who holds his village of Kolong in jagir, that of Devi Chand who holds Gumrang, and that of Hem Chand who holds Gondla.' (*Kangra District Gazetteer*, 1897)

*'I have seldom seen such imposing and hopeless precipices, a magnificent piece of mountain sculpture, but not for the foot of man; some eight thousand feet of gigantic pitches, every little valley being filled up with hanging glacier at the steepest angle, from whose ends broke off continual small ice avalanches. The upper ridges seemed equally uncompromising, all of the boldest and steepest scale.' (Bruce, *Kulu and Lahoul*)

The Tandi confluence of the Chandra and Bhaga rivers is sacred both to the Hindus and the Buddhists. There is an interesting story connected with this place: it is said that the son of the Sun god and the daughter of the Moon fell in love with each other. They decided to get married and alighted on top of the Baralacha pass. For some obscure reason, they went off in opposite directions, planning to meet at Tandi for the marriage. Chandra, the daughter of the Moon, found an easy way through the valley, down from the north-eastern slope of the Baralacha pass, and arrived quickly at Tandi. Bhaga, the son of the Sun god, had to cut his way through a very narrow and difficult valley, and could not keep his rendezvous. Chandra waited at Tandi for some time, and worried, came up the valley to Beeling near Kyelang. Here she met the prince, and together they went down to Tandi and were married.

The sadhus who come from the plains to visit the temple of Triloknath beyond Thirot, and to bathe at the Tandi confluence, have another story to tell. It is said that long ago, Lahaul was the abode of the rishis. They used to come here in large numbers for meditation. In those days, these two rivers ran full of milk. They did not tumble through narrow gorges, but on the contrary, flowed gently through pleasant grassy meadows. The rishis, who had their ashrams on the banks, would sit in *samadhi*, and every morning, before opening their eyes, drink a little milk from the river.

The rakshasas who got to know of this wonderful land were jealous and one day, they killed and threw animals and men into both the streams at the two ends of the Baralacha pass. In the morning, the rishis, without opening their eyes, took a drink from the rivers. When they opened their eyes, they found that the rivers were running blood. Having drunk from the polluted waters, the rishis were defiled and had to leave these valleys. In anger, they laid a permanent curse on the two rivers, saying that henceforth, they would flow deep in narrow channels, and no men would be able to drink from them, or use their water for water-mills.

The road crossed the Bhaga over a newly-built bridge and began to climb up the right bank of the Bhaga river. The valley was narrow and rose sharply. On our left were sharp cliffs, on the right, little flats full of barley and buckwheat. After about four miles, around a bend, we suddenly came upon the village of Beeling, clustered together at one end of the village fields. The village is perched overlooking the deep Beeling *nullah*, which separates it from Kyelang. We drove across a little bridge, up the opposite slope, and found ourselves in Kyelang, a compact cluster of square-built houses bunched together on the flats above the Bhaga river. The slope around the village was covered with green fields of barley and buckwheat, interspersed with groves of willow and poplar. Magnificent snow peaks dominated this pleasant oasis in a wilderness of rocks and glaciers.

A welcome party awaited us—Lama Dumbaji, abbot of the Shashur monastery above Kyelang with his lama band, which immediately began to play vigorously. School children, men and women from the village, and a host of curious giggling girls who were waiting their turn at the water tap, all shyly smiled at me. The headman of Kyelang, Kalzan, a small man with an infectious grin, stepped forward and welcomed me. I immediately christened him Mayor Kalzan, boss of my little capital.

I was escorted down to my house. Thanking them, I bade them goodbye. Though the elders went away, a lot of happy-faced curious children hung around my veranda. The house was lovely . . . five rooms, a loft and a beautiful veranda—all in excellent wood. It was the residence of the Moravian missionaries who were in Lahaul from 1854 to 1940.

The Moravian mission among the Tibetans and Lahaulas was started in 1856 by Reverend A.W. Heyde and a friend, Mr Pagell. From the beginning, it was run on practical as well as spiritual lines, and they entered into the agricultural life of the peasants. They were soon joined by Mr Jasckbe, an able linguist who gathered his intimate knowledge of the Tibetan tongue from his long periods of residence with the country people. He compiled a dictionary, framed a grammar, and translated the New Testament into classical Tibetan. Rev Heyde and his wife, also scholars, translated the New Testament into colloquial Tibetan.

The story of Mr Pagell and his wife, who also came out as a young bride, is a stirring one. They started the centre at a place in the upper Sutlej valley called Pooh in 1856. For eighteen years, they worked there, often terribly depressed but persevering in the face of all difficulties, and they had many converts. One winter, they both fell ill, and convinced that they could not recover, had their coffins and shrouds prepared.

Mr Pagell died on a cold January day. Fortunately, the poor wife only survived her husband by three days. Feeling her own end was near she laid herself in her coffin and died peacefully. They were buried by their converts and the headman of the village at once sealed up their effects. When, in answer to an appeal from the Tibetan Christians, a member of the mission was able to push through to Pooh the following May, he found all the Pagells' belongings in perfect order.

When the Moravians left in 1940, they sold the house to a local landlord, Thakur Pratap Chand, who has now rented it out to the government. A small compound with yellow wild rose bushes completed the picture. The missionaries gave much to Lahaul—internal heating, ventilation with windows and glass panes, the growing of vegetables, and the knitting of socks and pullovers. They also gave of themselves—many old and young lay buried below the DC's house in a clump of willows.* I was told that the house was haunted, and on certain nights, an old lady could be seen walking about with a stick in the rose garden. If the poor lady existed, she never bothered me in the least. The mission did not, however, have much success in the conversion of locals to Christianity. The number of the faithful stood at twenty-nine only, including children, in 1897.†

As the sun went down, I stood on the veranda having a last look around. Below and around me lay the village, quiet and serene in the evening shadows, smoke rising from chimneys all along the slope. Looking down the valley, I could see the snow lingam of the Goshal Cone, glowing with the last flush of sunlight. On the opposite side of the valley, Karding and its monastery nestled in the shadow of the Dilburi peak. As twilight came on, all was quiet, save for the occasional gruff barking of a dog and the muffled roar of the Bhaga river in its cavernous passage. And then, the shrill haunting notes of the *gyadung* began to float down from the monastery. I was home at last.

---

*'The pathos of these isolated lives struck me very forcibly as I walked from the willow-shaded path leading from the house to the God's acre below. For, enclosed within stone walls and entered by a gate from the lower garden was the little cemetery, full of graves. Under the protecting branches of willows and poplars rested the bodies of two children of this family, as well as those of several other small boys and girls. There are memorial tablets to some adults, too, but the greater proportion are to young children.' (Lady Bruce, quoted in Bruce, *Kulu and Lahoul*)

†'The very tolerance of the Boti race in religious matters will, I think, [be] one obstacle to their conversion. In the Sunday services of the mission house, I saw an old and learned lama, who lives there to assist Mr Jeschke in his Tibetan studies, join in the hymns and responses with great zeal and fervour. I do not think that either he or his friends saw anything inconsistent in his so doing, though he had not the least intention of becoming a convert to Christianity. All worship is good, seemed to be his motto.' (Sir James Lyall writing in 1868, quoted in the *Kangra District Gazetteer*, 1897)

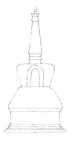

The Land

For lust of knowing what should not be known,
We take the Golden Road to Samarkand.

—James Elroy Flecker

Turning west a little, he speered for the green hills of Kulu and sought Kailung under the glaciers. 'For thither came I in the old, old days. From Leh I came, over the Baralachi.'

'Yes, yes; we know it,' said the far-faring people of Shamlegh.

'And I slept two nights with the priests of Kailung. These are the hills of my delight! Shadows blessed above all other shadows! There my eyes opened on this world; there my eyes opening to this world; there I found Enlightenment; and there I girt my loins for my Search. Out of the Hills I came—the high Hills and the strong winds. Oh, just is the Wheel!' He blessed them in detail—the great glaciers, the naked rocks, the piled moraines and tumbled shale; dry upland, hidden salt-lake, age-old timber and fruitful water-shot valley one after the other, as a dying man blesses his flock, and Kim marvelled at his passion.

—Kim by Rudyard Kipling

Where is this fabled Shangrila, which drove the lama in Rudyard Kipling's Kim to such poetic ecstasies of description?

The valleys of Lahaul and Spiti lie deep in the lap of the inner Himalayas, far beyond the tourist resorts of Kulu and Manali in Himachal Pradesh. The Rohtang pass, which lies astride the route from Manali to Lahaul, and the Kunzam pass (15,000 feet), which separates Lahaul from Spiti, still manage to protect these remote valleys from the mundane and the commonplace, and preserve much of their mystery and romance.

Lahaul lies in the north-west part of India, beyond the Great Himalayan Divide. It comprises a vast mountainous area of 5,760 square kilometres south of Ladakh. The Great Divide effectively separates it from the districts of Kulu and Chamba in the south. Spiti—pronounced 'Piti'—lies to the east of Lahaul, and is separated from it by a high mountain ridge, running north from the great Himalayan range. The Kunzam pass provides a brief and tenuous link between the two valleys in the short summers.

Lahaul may be divided into four distinct parts—the Chandra river valley, locally known as Rangloi; the Bhaga river valley, known as Gara; the Pattan valley through which flows the Chandrabhaga river; and lastly, the tongue of land of 260 square kilometres lying to the north, beyond the Baralacha pass bordering Ladakh, known as the Lingti plains, which is at an elevation of about 13,700 feet. Uncultivated and uninhabited, the Lingti plains form a kind of no-man's land between Lahaul-Spiti and Ladakh.

The great triangle formed by the looping Chandra and Bhaga streams is one mass of high mountains and vast glaciers. The peaks rise to heights of more than 19,000 feet, and the numerous valleys amongst them are filled with glaciers. It is one great ice belt, broken here and there by lofty heights and ridges of impossible rocks and snow. The most well-known, though not the highest peak in the area, is Gephan, abode of Gephan devta, the presiding deity of Lahaul.

The Spiti valley too is completely hidden by lofty mountain

ranges with an average elevation of 19,500 feet or more. These effectively cut it off from the Kinnaur and Kulu districts in the south, Tibet in the east, Ladakh in the north, and Lahaul in the west. High mountain passes, such as the Kunzam la, provide a tenuous link with the outside world. The Spiti river rises in snow beds at a height of about 15,700 feet on the eastern side of the Kunzam pass, not far from the source of the Chandrabhaga at the Baralacha. It tumbles rapidly into the broad Spiti valley, down which it has scoured for itself a deep flowing bed, almost sixty metres lower than the original level of the valley. In its race down the 160 kilometres-long Spiti valley, the river picks up important tributaries such as the Pin, Gyundi, Lungze and Mamdang on its right bank, and the Shila, Hanse, Tagling, Tabo, Gimdo, Lingti and Parechu on the left. The frenzied race of the Spiti ends near the Shipki pass, where it batters its way through a narrow gorge and finds solace in the bosom of the Sutlej river. Even at this point, the Spiti valley is more than 10,800 feet high.

The mountain rib running north from the Kunzam pass is the watershed between the Sutlej and Chenab rivers. Interestingly, the crest of the ridge on the north bank of the Chenab, which has an elevation of about 17,700 feet, forms the watershed between the Chenab and Indus rivers, while the Beas and the Ravi rivers rise to the south of the Great Himalayan Divide, which separates Lahaul from the Kulu and Chamba districts. The Beas is formed by the glacier streams slightly to the east of the Rohtang Pass, while the Ravi's source is in Bara Banghal, beyond the Dhauladhar range, south of the Kugti pass. The Lahaul-Spiti district and the area surrounding it is thus the root of all the great rivers of the Punjab, barring the Jhelum, which rises at Kukkar Naag, beyond the Banihaal pass in the Kashmir valley.

Till 30 June 1960, Lahaul-Spiti formed part of the district of Kangra in old Punjab. In order to give an impetus to the development of these remote valleys and in view of the Chinese pressure on our northern border through Tibet, the Punjab government created the new district of Lahaul-Spiti. Lahaul-Spiti, comprising a vast area of high mountains, massive glaciers, and rugged valleys, is probably one of the most fascinating parts of our country. The district headquarters lies at Kyelang, which is a small village situated in the upper portion of the Bhaga river valley, at a height of approximately 10,300 feet. The village consists of a cluster of square-built houses bunched together on the flats above the right bank of the Bhaga river. Surrounded by green fields of barley and buckwheat, interspersed with groves of poplar and willow, and dominated by magnificent snow peaks, Kyelang is a pleasant oasis in a wilderness of rocks and glaciers. Lady Bruce, who spent an enchanting summer in the valley at the turn of the century, described the beauty of Kyelang thus: 'Kyelang is like a barbaric jewel—a roughly cut emerald in a bronze and silver setting. In plain words, it is an oasis of green fields and willow-planted watercourses surrounded with brown hills and snowy heights.'

But Kyelang is only representative of the beauty and charm of the Lahaul valley. With the height varying from about 2,700 to 3,300 metres, the valley has pleasant summers with rich crops, lush green meadows, and a mass of alpine flowers. Lady Bruce had this to say of the flowers on the Rohtang and beyond:

> The long grass banks were covered with mauve primulas, and irises of many shades of purple and blue. Anemones and Asters, Gentians and Daisies, and the famous blue poppy grew in mixed bouquets as gaily mixed as any child's bunch of flowers, but with longer stalks. We left the richly wooded hills, and pleasant paths of Kulu, and took to open downs and stony roads. Now and then we made a shortcut, through grass thick with flowers, and then joining the path again, wound round rocky corners, and found ourselves held up by an impasse of old avalanche snow.

It is a land of perpetual sunshine. The heavy monsoon clouds are unable to cross the Great Himalayan Divide, and therefore, even in the months of July and August, there is no rain. The melting winter snows cover the hillsides with lush blue grass, the favourite of Gaddi shepherds and sheep from Kangra. Wild roses of every hue and colour and masses of alpine flowers splash colours over the hill sides, which are only accentuated by the outline of the snowy ridges. Of the wild roses in the Himalayas, Lady Bruce has this to say:

> From April onward, it was roses, roses, all the way, from Abbottabad to far Lahaul. They varied, of course, from the petted garden ones, with all in their favour, to the tough, prickly bushes, covered with bloom, which battled for existence, in bare, rocky corners, where one would swear no rose could grow. The rose is the kindest of wild Indian flowers, and one of the most bare and arid spots one could find on the Frontier, the stony Samana, is redeemed by roses; and the hill fort of historic Saragarhi, is called Gulistan.

The winters are long, with the entire valley buried under metres of snow. The temperature falls sharply below freezing point. But the beauty of the landscape still remains. The snow-covered valley, the distant peaks and blue sky, the forests of blue pine on the hillsides, and the charming three storied cube-like habitations of man, in this heart of elemental nature, present a never-to-be-erased picture.

Spiti is harsh, with nature at its cruellest. The vast open valley is dry and barren—not a tree, not a bush, to break the harsh contours of the painted mountains of Spiti, which soar high into the blue in uninterrupted lines from the river bed. The barren wind-scoured mountains pour myriad coloured scree down the slopes in every shade known to nature and man. This is a landscape where one might experience the moon without having had the chance to be there. Tiny villages cling to little patches of green on the flats above the Spiti river. Water is scarce and fuel even more so. In the day time, the heat and glare from the rock and shale is tremendous; at night, the temperature falls sharply since it is a Himalayan desert. A strong demonic wind howls through the valley, like a rakshasa in agony. The Spiti valley overpowers one with a sense of space and eternity. A master craftsman, Rudyard Kipling, has better described this feeling of awful loneliness thus:

> At last they entered a world within a world—a valley of leagues where the high hills were fashioned of the mere rubble and refuse from off the knees of the mountains. Here one day's march carried them no farther, it seemed, than a dreamer's clogged pace bears him in a nightmare. They skirted a shoulder painfully for hours, and, behold, it was but an outlying boss in an outlying buttress of the main pile! A rounded meadow revealed itself, when they had reached it, for a vast tableland, running far into the valley. Three days later, it was a dim fold in the earth to the southward.
>
> 'Surely the gods live here!' said Kim, beaten down by the silence and the appalling sweep and dispersal of the cloud-shadows after the rain. 'This is no place for men!'

Spiti had a population of about 6,000 odd souls for its area of approximately 7,680 square kilometres of glaciers and high valleys. The lowest point of the valley is about 10,800 feet, and some villages lie as high as 13,700 feet. Kibber, north of Kaza on the way to the Parang la, is at over 14,500 feet. Though rich in space—2.5 square kilometres to every citizen—Spiti is poor in cultivable land. Over the centuries, man and yak have scratched out 1,200 hectares in isolated patches on the flats above the river. There is plenty of water in the river below and the snow peaks above, but the searing, stone strewn flats are as dry as the valleys of the moon. There is no rain in summer as the mountain barriers keep the monsoon away. The winter snow is also light and it cannot be retained once the summer sun begins to scorch the valley. With great ingenuity, the Spitians have here and there brought water from the high glaciers to soak their precious fields on the valley floor. On these they grow a harvest of barley, buckwheat, peas and rape seed in the short summer season. There are almost no trees in the valley. The dry harsh climate and the height of the valley prevent their easy growth. Women have to climb as high as 15,700 feet to collect dwarf juniper branches and furze for fuel. Fuel is gold and is hoarded as such. Life is hard in the extreme. In winter, the snowfall is far lower than in Lahaul, but a terrible, biting wind, which howls down from the steppes of Siberia, makes living a test of physical and mental stamina. The Spitian is in a constant Promethean conflict with the gods. King Lear's heath was not half as cruel and cold as the Spiti valley in winter.

HISTORY

Lahaul

The district of Lahaul finds historic mention as early as the seventh century of our era. Hiuen Tsang, the Chinese pilgrim, mentions it as a district to the north-east of Kulu called Le-hu-le—clearly the Lhe-yul of the Tibetans and the Lahaul of the people of Kulu. It is probable that the country was from the earliest times closely linked to Tibet, its population being mainly of Tibetan origin. When the Tibetan empire was broken up in the tenth century, Lahaul was probably included in the kingdom of Ladakh formed out of the wreck by a chieftain named Palgi Gan.

Subsequently, in the second consolidation of the Ladakh kingdom under Thsewang Namgyal, which took place in about AD 1580-1600, according to documents preserved by the lamas and seen by Joseph Davey Cunningham for his book on the history of the Sikhs, Lahaul is clearly omitted in the areas held by the Ladakh kings, though Zanskar and Spiti are shown as part of the kingdom. It is probable that in the confusion prevailing at that time, Lahaul became independent and remained for a short time governed by thakurs, or the petty barons of small clusters of villages. Four or five of these families survived through the British rule and held their original territories as *jagirs* on payment of tribute.

Spiti

After the first formation of the kingdom of Ladakh, Spiti appears to have now and again been separated from it for a time. It was perhaps independent for some time, as it is mentioned in the records procured from the lamas by Cunningham, but was conquered by Singhi Namgyal, king of Ladakh, in about AD 1630, and was allotted with Zanskar to his third son, Tenchog, in about AD 1660. Soon after, it was incorporated in the Guge principality, which lay to the east, and was not restored to Ladakh till about AD 1720, when the king of Ladakh, at the conclusion of a war with Guge, married the daughter of the Lhasa commander and took Spiti as her dowry. After this, Spiti remained a province of Ladakh, but because of its remote and inaccessible situation, the country was always left very much to govern itself. An official was sent from Leh as *garpon*, but he generally disappeared after harvest time, and left the real administration to be carried on by the wazir and other hereditary officers of Spiti, who again were completely controlled by the parliament of *gatpos* or *lambardars* of villages and *tappas*. This is the state of affairs in the early nineteenth century, as described by Cunningham, who drew from Moorcroft's notes on his travels in Ladakh.

Spiti was always liable to be worried by forays. Gerard mentions that in AD 1776 or thereabouts, the Basharis held the fort of Dankhar for two years; and in Moorcroft's notes, Trebeck gives an account of a foray, which had been made just before his visit, by a large body of armed men from Kulu. The Spiti people were not a war-like race and paid tribute or protection money to all the surrounding states in order to escape being plundered. After the Sikhs had annexed Kulu in 1841, they sent up a force to plunder Spiti. The Spiti men, according to their usual tactics, retreated into the high uplands, leaving their houses in the valley and the monasteries to be plundered and burnt. A few straggling plunderers in the Sikh force, who ventured up too high were surprised and killed. The Sikhs retired, and did not attempt either to annex the country to Kulu or separate it from Ladakh. The separation from Ladakh was done by the British in 1846 on the occasion of the settlement of the trans-Sutlej states after the First Sikh War, in order to secure a road to the pashmina wool district of Chang Thang. In the autumn of 1846, Captain Cunningham and Van-Agnew fixed the boundary between Spiti and Ladakh.

For the first three years, the collection of revenue was farmed out to Mansukh Dass, wazir of the Raja of Bashahar. In the autumn of 1849, Major Hay, assistant commissioner of Kulu, went to Spiti and took charge. He spent the best part of the winter there in Dankhar fort and submitted a valuable report, which was printed by the government. The report contained a full description of the Spiti area by Egerton, Deputy Commissioner of Kangra, who toured the area in 1846.

RELIGION

The people of Lahaul-Spiti follow the Buddhist faith. As the traveller approaches any village in this area, he will pass long walls, on which stones with carved prayers are put by travellers going on long journeys. On entering a village, one must keep the sacred wall of prayer-stones to the right. The outskirts of every village are dotted with beautifully built chortens, which are tall pyramidical monuments, often containing relics of some holy lama. The high ridges above the villages and the valleys often have Shangrila-like monasteries, perched precariously on ledges along the cliffs. These white-painted, golden-pinnacled *gompas* command spectacular views of the valleys and the snow peaks.

According to General Cunningham, Buddhism was introduced to Ladakh in about 240 BC, and was firmly established there by 100 BC. There is no doubt that it was introduced into Lahaul and Spiti from Ladakh. Both the prominent sects of Buddhism—the Drugpa or red-hats and the Gelukpa or yellow-hats—are found in Lahaul-Spiti. The Lahaul valley belongs entirely to the red-hats, who have a somewhat easier code of conduct. The lamas are allowed to marry and carry on worldly affairs. In fact, the Kyelang lamas manage their farms and businesses during the summer months down in the villages. In the winters, they retire to cells in the monasteries for long periods of prayers and meditation. Many of them spend weeks and months in solitary retreat. Thus they seem to have found an ideal balance between the temporal and the spiritual. In Lahaul, nuns are allowed to live in the monasteries on an equal footing with the monks. The Gelukpa or yellow-hats of Spiti are however far more rigid. Monks are bound to celibacy and the Gelukpa do not recognize the institution of nuns. Nuns in Spiti may live in houses in the village, but certainly not in the monasteries.

The people of these valleys have an intimate relationship with their religion and their monasteries. Nearly every village has a gompa on the ridge above the village. During the long winter months, the lamas are invited to the homes for long sessions of prayers, at which they are generously entertained at considerable expense. Boys and girls trudge up through the winter snow to the Karding and Sha-shur monasteries, 1,500 feet above the village, to bring down the sacred hand printed texts bound between heavy wooden slabs. At home, in the main room, ten to fifteen lamas led by the abbot will sit on carpets around a heated samovar of tea, and read the prayers as do the Sikhs the *Granth Sahib* in an *akhand path*—the continuous reading of the holy book. When reading, the lamas sound like a disturbed swarm of bees.

In the summers, *chham* or dance festivals are held at the monasteries, and are known to us as devil dances. These are nothing but morality plays acted out in open-air theatres, in the shadow of the snows. The abbots and the senior lamas sit on a raised platform on one side, along with the monastery band. Actors, who are monks of the monastery, dress in rich silken costumes and beautifully-painted masks, and act out the age old conflict between good and evil in the form of dance and mime. Like the Ramleela in the plains of north India, these legends of tyrant kings and the brave struggles of well-known heroes against evil are watched by the people with avid interest. These festivals also provide an occasion for everyone to have some fun in the fine summer weather. The Sha-shur monastery has a beautiful amphitheatre in a hollow below the monastery, surrounded by blue pines. With snow peaks all around, it is one of the most idyllic theatre spaces that I know.

Of the monasteries of Lahaul, one might mention the Sha-shur, Karding and the Guru Ghantal around Kyelang; and the Kye and Tabo in Spiti. Sha-shur is the church for Kyelang and is situated in a pleasant pine forest, 1,500 feet above the village. Guru Ghantal, perched on a cliff above the Tandi confluence of the Chandra and Bhaga rivers, is perhaps the oldest monastery in the Lahaul valley. It is said to have been built by Padma Sambhava* when he visited Lahaul. Covering the pinnacle of a volcanic cone, a few kilometres from Kaza in the Spiti valley, the Kye monastery has a spectacular appearance, like the famous Potala Palace in Lhasa. This monastery rises in terraces along the sides of the volcanic cone. It has probably the finest collection of *thankas* (scroll paintings) in the entire district. Tabo, situated lower down the Spiti valley, is the oldest gompa in the Spiti sub-division and has very beautiful murals.

---

*Padma Sambhava is said to have brought tantrik Buddhism to Tibet and Bhutan in AD eight century.

A visit to any of these monasteries brings one face-to-face with the Shangrila-like atmosphere of these romantic valleys. Nestling in the shadow of the snow peaks, far removed from modern man and his mundane doings, these serene sanctuaries of the red-robed lamas and the gompas truly remind one of James Hilton's Shangrila.

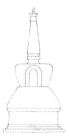

Surely the Gods Live Here!

The real voyage of discovery consists not in seeking new landscapes,
but in having new eyes.

—Marcel Proust

I was in charge of two distinct areas, Lahaul and Spiti. Though
administratively one, they were geographically separate entities.
Lahaul consists of the valleys of the Chandra and Bhaga rivers,
along with the mountain mass they clasp between their extended
arms. Below Tandi, the two join to form the Chenab, one of the
Punjab's great rivers. To reach Spiti, one goes up the Chandra
valley from Khoksar. About two marches short of the Chandra
river's source at the Baralacha, the path climbs steeply up the
ridge on the left bank to the 15,055 feet high Kunzam la. From
this watershed, the Spiti river flows down a broad valley till
almost a hundred miles later, it batters its way through a fearful
gorge and seeks sanctuary in the Sutlej. Two separate drainage
systems flow in opposite directions from the Kunzam ridge and
end in two of the great Punjab rivers.

Chance had placed them in one administrative division, but
the rule of Kyelang lay lightly on Spiti. Nature ensured that the
Kunzam opened even later in the summer than the Rohtang

because of the deep piled snow in the upper Chandra valley. One was lucky to get across in mid-June. Mid-September generally saw the first snowfall and the gate to the Spiti valley was locked. For the rest of the year, the DC's authority depended on a tenuous wireless link, which did not help much. An even younger vice-regent in the valley, in the shape of an imperious assistant commissioner, generally considered the Lahaul viceroy 'an old bore', and preferred not to hear the cackle from Kyelang. The wireless set could always go out of order! Following a time-honoured civil services tradition, the Spiti deputy invariably felt the Kyelang overlord to be ignorant of and insensitive to the problems of the Spiti citizens. While hotly denying any such possibility, the Kyelang man usually felt the same about the drones in the Chandigarh Secretariat! Occasionally, like Aurangzeb in his dotage, the DC felt his fair province of Spiti slipping away from the empire under an obstreperous governor. Strident orders sizzled out over the wireless, but to no avail.

On one occasion, the hint of open rebellion came over the wires. The Spiti subedar accused the boss of seeing problems through rose-tinted glasses, and had the temerity to advise him to get rid of them! Kyelang hummed with rumours of a coup for the wireless operators kept the town fully supplied with gossip. Aurangzeb had, in such cases, to literally cool his heels during the long winters and console himself with dreams of a summer expedition to quell all rebellion in his fief. The summer reunion quickly resolved the disputed points of theology, generally arguments on the interpretation of revenue law! All differences were buried in pots of tea in Kaza, the Spiti capital. Aurangzeb came home and immediately got into the next argument, which naturally lasted the new winter! Part of the problem lay in the fact that the DC would be twenty-seven or twenty-eight years old, and the SDM at Kyelang and Kaza, two years younger. I was just past twenty-six, when I became the DC of Lahaul-Spiti. My Kaza deputy was my former class fellow!

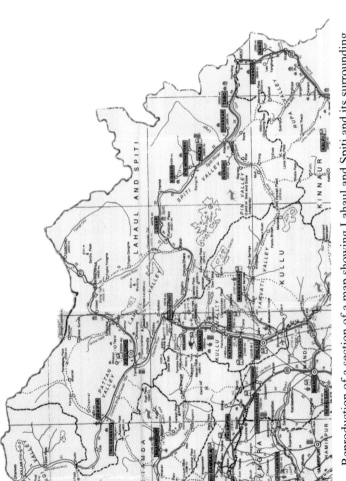

Reproduction of a section of a map showing Lahaul and Spiti and its surrounding districts in Himachal Pradesh, courtesy Himachal Tourism.

A house in Lahaul in the evening sun.

Fields with crops during summer in Tandi village,
across the Chandrabhagha river.

Poplars in autumn.

A Kyelang house with the hay
stacked on the roof in summer.

Summer in Kyelang.

A thanka in Kye gompa.

A thanka in Kye gompa.

A mural in Jispa.

A Jispa fresco.

A statue of Aviloketeshwara

Looking north from
Kyelang.

Harvesting potatoes in
Pattan valley.

Threshing barley in autumn.

Lahaul mountains from the air.

Tshering Dorje on the way to the
Sha-shur monastery in winter.

The Deputy Commissioner
with his staff in winter.

Vinnie and me at Chandrataal.

Vinnie at Kunzam pass before walking down to Chandrataal.

Fearful of losing half my kingdom with the approaching winter, and even more afraid of being accused of passing orders in ignorance of local conditions, I decided to go for a quick tour of the valley before the snows came. I had just three weeks for a journey of 170 miles and back, a great deal of it to be done on foot, at heights varying from eleven to fifteen thousand feet.

In the last days of August, I motored back to Khoksar with Fauja Singh. After a night in the tiny dak bungalow, we started early the next morning for the Kunzam pass. Above Khoksar, the Chandra valley winds its desolate way up to the snowfields of the Baralacha. The old mule track was in the process of being made jeepable. Only the odd government jeep braved the way to Losar across the Kunzam pass. We climbed all the way to the Rohtang pass and then pulled away eastwards along the ridge towards Spiti. For a while there were some pleasant patches of grass soaked in little mountain rills, and even a few *bhojpatra* trees, but soon the valley bared its true visage. The Chandra crashed down the boulder-strewn valley with a tremendous roar, like some giant beast in agony. Like a man in a fearful hurry, it battered itself against the massive boulders, rather than pick a careful way around them. Perhaps it was already dreaming of the pleasant wooded valleys of Chamba; and the limpid wandering ways of the Punjab, lined with fields of ripe sugarcane, young wheat and mustard, through which came young maidens to dip their earthen pots in its placid inviting water. From the river, the valley rose in steep slopes to the battlements of the giants and their snowy peaks.

The track was dusty. The inner Himalayas get no moisture, little snow and no rain. The winter snow and avalanches only help to break up the surface of the mountains and bring down stones and rubble. As everywhere else, the jeep brought the inevitable cloud of dust in its wake. It seemed such an intrusion in this valley of pure mountain air and clear summer skies. Traffic was at its peak since it was the fag end of the short summer. Every now and then, we passed mule trains heavily loaded with grain, salt, kerosene and sugar. The valley has to be stocked with all necessities before the long winter sets in. Surprisingly, a large part of the transport in these forbidding valleys is organized by men from the plains district of Hoshiarpur. For centuries, intrepid men, clad only in thin cottons, have braved the fierce passes of the high Himalayas to carry goods to Ladakh, Tibet and distant Kashgar and Khotan. These plains Punjabis used to go regularly over the Baralacha, through Leh, past Doulet Beg, Auldi, and over the great Karakoram pass, to the Central Asian marts, carrying sugar, salt and grain, and bringing back wool, silk and dried fruits. This historic route over the Karakoram pass is littered with the bones of these brave men and their mule caravans. This great silk route trade was suddenly strangled by the Chinese after they manned our Tibetan frontiers.

After some time, the road wound down to the valley floor and we came to the camping ground of Chhetru, a patch of blue grass on the water's edge. Some muleteers were cooking their simple fare while the animals grazed nearby. A tiny two-room hut did service as a dak bungalow. I now had a sandwich and some tea. We crossed a new suspension bridge to the right bank of the river and drove on our dusty way.

The journey was becoming tedious; mile upon mile of a hot sandy track along a crazy river. The snow peaks which gave one hope had also receded behind the nearer ridges. Occasionally, we passed encampments of Tibetan labour. Work on roads was in full swing. The little tents pitched on the flats above the river looked so vulnerable in this vast wilderness. The children played along the roadside; the smaller ones slept blissfully on home-made hammocks in the shadow of the giant rocks. The elders toiled in the sun. Our jeep broke the monotony of their lives and they rushed across to look at us, smile as only hill people can—without reservation—and shout 'Juley!' Not all were so easily distracted from their sorrows. While passing a group of workers breaking stones, I spied a girl of terrifying beauty. She stood alone, outside the pale of their cheerfulness. As we came near, she looked at me. I flinched under the weight of her many griefs and looked away. I knew then that I had seen a Ruth 'amid the alien corn'. The picture of a personal sorrow against a background of the mighty, impersonal, unfeeling giants of creation is engraved in my memory. The apparition haunts me even now and my mind flies back over the years to that group of refugees from another land, and the sorrowful figure in their midst.

The journey continued. Even the normally loquacious Fauja Singh fell silent. And then, around yet another shoulder of another rocky ridge, we came face to face with the gods, in the shape of the Bara Shigri glacier. From the top of its 21,000 feet peaks, it poured down the mountain flank in one awe-inspiring mass of snow, ice, rubble, and rocks. The 1897 *Kangra District Gazetteer* describes it thus:

> The most noted glacier in Lahaul is that known as the Bara Shigri, at the bend of the Chandra, on its South Side. It is nearly two miles wide, and runs right down to the river; the marks are still to be seen throughout Lahaul, of the destruction caused many years ago, by a portion of the glacier having fallen across the river, and dammed up the water, until the melting of the ice, released the pent up flood.

Captain Harcourt, who visited Lahaul in 1869, said this of the Bara Shigri: 'In the early morning, when the sun has little power to melt the ice, the passage of the glacier is comparatively easy, though I doubt whether it would ever be possible to ride over it, for every step has to be scanned over, and, as I counted 3648 of these when I walked over it in 1869, it might be safe to put the width of the Shigri at nearly two miles.'

Like an arrested apocalypse, it seemed about to roar down any minute into the Chandra river. Yet, like the gods, it held its destructive self in check, satisfied with the contemplation of its

Jovian powers. We stopped to gaze at its battle-scarred face, with its furrows of a million years of sun and snow. In the summer, groups of young scientists come to the Shigri glacier and its circle of great peaks, known to every mountaineer. At the top of the glacier, these beautiful fluted, sculptured giants of nature stand in a semi-circle around a great snow amphitheatre. The geologists look for uranium and other rare metals, and I met them many times later, including once in a moment of crisis.

This was in 1961. Four decades later, as I revise this account, I ponder on the world's environmental crisis. Long after I left Lahaul-Spiti, got married and had children, I kept making regular visits to the valleys. As time has passed, the Shigri, far from falling into the Chandra, has receded towards the upper edges of the amphitheatre. The great slope now shows only weather-beaten boulders, shale and rubble. My personal observation of a lifetime shows a severe recession in the Himalayan glaciers. Scientists who visit the Shigri every year to measure its receding phase report their grave findings with alarm. A report in the *Hindustan Times* of 4 November 2007 quotes the scientists of the National Institute of Hydrology, Roorkee, and points to global warming having led to a 0.74°C rise in temperature, and a 17 cm rise in sea levels in the twentieth century alone. The Indian Space Research Organisation (ISRO), after a study of 446 glaciers in India, found a 21 per cent glacial retreat—from 2,077 square kilometres in 1962 to 1,628 square kilometres at present. The glacial melt in the Himalayas will increase flooding and rock avalanches. It will affect water resources in the next three to five decades and will put the lives of 500 million people across the subcontinent, from Pakistan to Bangladesh, in jeopardy. As I write, I get reports from Lahaul-Spiti that apples are now being grown in both valleys while the apple harvest of the lower Kulu valley is falling—a clear indicator of increasing temperatures.

But in August 1961, the Shigri was a truly impressive sight. I had to tear myself away from the spot; this intensely physical symbol of eternity had me enthralled! Fauja Singh was unimpressed. The old warrior gently admonished me, 'Sahib, let us go. There is nothing in these mountains. If you stop every time you see a glacier, we will never get to Spiti. There is little else in this land, except snow and rocks.'

The rest of the journey to Batal was an anticlimax. Batal was a small tea shop by the side of the suspension bridge, attended to by a Tibetan refugee. Over a cup of heavily sugared tea, I inquired how business was. Alas! Even in this god-forsaken valley, the man was not beyond the reach of the all pervasive trader! He had been set up by a Manali shopkeeper, who had him by the throat. I looked into the tent, which contained the usual bundles of cigarettes, tea, salt and sugar, luxuries in a land wilder than the wildest of the American West! Apparently, the attendant also ran a kind of beer bar. Chhaang,* the Lahaul barley beer, could be had in plenty. No wonder Fauja Singh had complained of fatigue as we approached Batal! He certainly knew all the right places for a thirsty man in the Western Himalayas. After a while, a well-built Khampa stumbled out of the back of the tent. He carried the famous knife of his people and seemed quite happy with the world. The chhaang seemed good! I asked him about the Khampa rebellion and the fighting he had done. In answer, he just took off his shirt and showed me his muscular body covered with bullet scars.

Tea over, we once again crossed over to the left bank. The bridge was wedged between steep escarpments, and across it, Fauja Singh had to do some tricky manoeuvring on a narrow ledge overhanging the river. He went across with total sang froid. Afraid, but not wanting to show it, I wished I too had taken a glass or two of chhaang. The road climbed steadily for about five

---

*'It is for the manufacture of beer (chhaang), that wheat is generally brewed; another sort of chhaang is brewed from rice and barley, and a sort of whisky is also distilled, from barley which is drunk in the rawest form, and is never allowed time to mature.' (*Kangra District Gazetteer*, 1897)

miles in successive loops till the slope suddenly eased and we were on the Kunzam saddle. The usual cairn with prayer flags and carved stones proclaimed yet another Himalayan pass. Looking down, I could see the silver ribbon that was the Chandra river. Across the river, and opposite us, towered the peaks of the central Lahaul mountains with Mulkila, the highest, in the centre. Had we been magic mountaineers, we might have climbed the Mulkila ridge, dropped to the Milang glacier on the other side and come out fifteen miles above Kyelang in the Bhaga valley. The Kunzam ridge running north-south, divides the watersheds of the Chenab and Sutlej rivers. The Chandra river rises at the Baralacha pass, swings around the central mass of Lahaul mountains and goes south-westwards, acquiring the Bhaga river at Tandi, after which it goes on to Jammu and into Pakistan. The waters on the eastern side of the Kunzam trickle down, slowly forming the Spiti river, which rushes past Kaza, in a powerful torrent and swings away, south-eastwards, falling into the Sutlej below the Sumdo flats. From the Kunzam, it is possible to trek in an angled walk downwards, for about six kilometres on the west face of the Kunzam ridge to the beautiful, out of this world Chandrataal lake that nestles in the shadow of the Mulkila group of mountains.

I stood a while, drinking tea, taking pictures, and above all, filming the magic scene with Wordsworth's 'inward eye' for future bliss. But we could not linger. One last longing look and we turned our backs on Lahaul. Spiti awaited us below. As the jeep rolled down, I could see a sunny valley flanked by red, yellow and ochre-coloured mountains, with myriad pastel shades in between. Spiti has a population of a few thousands for an area of approximately 3,000 square miles of mountains, glaciers and high valleys. However, though rich in space, a square mile to every citizen, Spiti is poor in cultivable land. Our men in Spiti consider it the true frontier. The people of Lahaul appear to them to be living in the softest of fleshpots! I think they are right.

In the late afternoon, we arrived at Losar, the first village in the valley, nestling at a height of 14,000 feet! I received what vanity might describe as a tumultuous welcome. The entire population of a couple of hundred people had turned out to inspect me! The lama band made noises appropriate to the occasion. The *sarpanch* offered the traditional white scarves and we adjourned to his house for tea. Ducking into a tiny door, I found myself in a dark, mud-walled room. I could hardly stand erect and felt like some absurd giant in a mountainous Lilliput. Spiti houses are flat mud-walled structures with low roofs. There are no windows and the completely enclosed space keeps in the warmth during the bitter winter. We sat on Tibetan rugs against the wall. Tea was served in painted cups on low lacquered tables. But alas! Branded biscuits had conquered this outpost also! The citizens, particularly the women, took turns peering in at the single door. My host was the essence of politeness and courtesy. We talked whatever people talk on such occasions. Then, accompanied by all the curious onlookers, we walked down to my camp on the river bank.

The time was late afternoon, almost evening, and the dying sun was playing its golden light on the fort-like escarpments across the river. The Spiti mountains are totally bereft of vegetation. The erosion of wind, sun and snow over the centuries has peeled off their skin and bared their raw flesh in all its gory visage of veins and criss-crossed arteries. Hanuman had opened his chest to show his true heart to the divine Ramchandra. The Spiti mountains have attempted something similar. I have never seen such a display of raw colours. If the earth could show its guts, it has done it here. The slate and scree slopes came down in smooth curves from the pinnacles to the valley floor, the colours blending as if painted by some giant brush. These desolate empty valleys, with these painted mountains, might well be the mountains of the moon.

I sat outside the tent and soaked in the dying Roerich

scene.* The village children watched from a distance. Suddenly the local *patwari* materialized at my side. He was carrying a beautiful grey-brown bird in his arms. 'Sir, I have caught a snow cock!' he said.

'How on earth?' I asked.

'Huzoor, it was being chased by an eagle, and was driven down from the ridge. They live at 17,000 feet or more. It was so tired that it flew in here, and took shelter in one of our tents.'

In the history of the civil service, all kinds of people have been known to throw themselves at the mercy of the district officer. This must surely be the first snow cock to do so! Sadly, my hunger overcame my sense of honour and the bird found its way into the cooking pot. Today, many many decades later, as I read this, I recollect the scene and I am overcome by a powerful sense of regret. The snow cock is long gone, and I have little time to linger, but the regret for the wrong I once did remains. My thoughts go back often to the lines from Coleridge's *The Rime of the Ancient Mariner*, which I had learnt in school:

God save thee, ancient Mariner,
From the fiends that plague thee thus!—
Why look'st thou so?—'With my crossbow
I shot the Albatross.'

---

*Nicholas Roerich, the famous Russian painter, left Russia when the Soviets took over, and settled in India. He lived for long in a cottage close to the historic Nagar castle in the Kulu valley. In the 1920s, he used to go regularly to Lahaul and spend many months there, camping and creating his remarkable paintings. His son Svetoslav, who married the great Indian actress Devika Rani, followed in his footsteps and became an outstanding painter himself. A fascinating collection of their paintings is housed in a museum in Bangalore. Some years back, when I went to New York, I heard of a private collection of Roerich's paintings. I managed to view these paintings and what really touched me was that the room was full of paintings of Lahaul and villages like Gondhla and Sissu.

Like the ancient mariner, I wonder if the Almighty has finally absolved me too.

The road ended at Losar. Road cutting was underway on an alignment to Kaza. Early next morning, we set out on the next stage. Sibal, the assistant commissioner, and Jasbir Singh the *tehsildar* accompanied me. A short walk took us to Hansa: a few houses huddled together in the middle of a forest of stones and rubble. I visited the primary school, and distributed sweets to the somewhat surprised children. The local forest ranger wanted to show me his plantation. We marched out a couple of hundred yards till we came to a small stone enclosure. Inside, I found a few wilting eucalyptus trees in a grim battle with the stony soil and the elements. I saw the mark of death on them and turned away, feeling sorry for these beautiful plants and the poor forest ranger. We maintained a forest range in the district, and Sarbans Singh was its energetic head. He struggled and struggled with the elements to grow a few scraggy blue pines.

After a cup of tea with the panchayat, we continued our walk. Over the ages, the river has cut for itself a bed at least a couple of hundred feet below the valley floor. Wind and water have eroded the banks of stone, sand and scree, and left the most weirdly carved pillars and promontories. High above the river, they look like carved giants from some past heroic age. We went down the slope to the stream-bed, and crossed it by a new bridge. I marvelled at the men who had carried each girder up the Rohtang and across the Kunzam to build these bridges. I hope someday, when an account of the building of modern India is written, someone will take time off from the worship of political heroes to add a footnote on these gallant but unknown men who struggled with the Himalayan heights to give us access to these remote lands. Slowly, we climbed up to the flat on the opposite bank. By now, the sun was truly up and the heat and glare from the rock and shale was tremendous. The Spiti valley overpowers one with the sense of space and eternity. Plodding along in single file down the never ending flats, with the giant peaks for company, we might have been the first men on the moon.

Near Keoto, our halt for the day, I saw some women heating a brass vessel in the fields. On inquiring, I was told they were distilling liquor! There were no excise laws in the tribal areas. We went over to have a look. The women were amused and offered us a sip. Unfortunately, the liquor was still hot!

The next morning, we left early as we wanted to cover two stages and reach Kaza. All morning, we continued our monotonous walk across the valley. Outside a village, we suddenly came across a single beautiful tree, daringly splendid in its isolation. Underneath it sat a holy lama, around whom villagers crowded for his benediction. So immersed were they in matters of the spirit that they totally ignored the DC's presence. It was a chastening experience and I felt like a minor Alexander in the presence of a Diogenes. We too paid our obeisance to the lama and continued on our way. Late afternoon saw us in Rangrik, perhaps the biggest village in the valley. Situated on the right bank of the Spiti river on a large flat, the village boasts a fair amount of cultivable land and a school. Kaza, the seat of the government, lay across the river on another flat.

Opposite Rangrik, the Spiti passed for a short distance through a narrow gorge, an obvious site for a bridge. Louis Dane, then Assistant Commissioner, Kulu, and later Governor of the Punjab, had built the first one in 1883. Timber was brought in with great difficulty from the Sutlej valley forests. The technique used was simple. Heavy logs were anchored in stone abutments on the cliffs, and pushed out over the river. The narrow gap that remained was spanned by boards nailed to a pair of shaky planks. As we approached the bridge, my heart missed a beat. It was the flimsiest of structures. The wooden beams and the sleepers in the middle had probably not been changed since the time of Sir Louis! There was no railing to lend moral support.

In a cool, casual voice, I inquired why it had not been repaired. 'Oh Sir, we are soon going to have a new jeepable Bailey bridge,' replied Jasbir Singh, the tehsildar. Well, I thought to myself, there is no reason for someone to get wet in the meantime! Someone had wisely provided a wire rope-*jhula* as a standby, and for a fleeting moment, I was tempted to throw away my pride and meekly sit in its bucket. Maybe it was Jasbir Singh's way of testing me. Without even looking over the shoulder or bothering to ask me, he boldly thumped his way over the bridge. The frail bridge, shivered and swayed, but like a good sailor, Jasbir held his balance. Jasbir was a Gurdaspur Majha Sikh, as difficult as they come in that area. Standing on the other side, he coolly watched, perhaps amused at my predicament. Many are the cups a district officer has to drink; let this be another, I thought to myself, and stepped on. I did not look down. I saw only the rocky cliff opposite. As the middle swayed in the wind, I almost grabbed for the non-existent railing, but my balance held, and I passed the tehsildar's test.

Kaza must surely be one of the most barren outposts in the country. A few scattered houses on a rocky slope with a patch of green by the river was all it had to show for human endeavour. The houses were really hovels, short window-less camel-coloured mud cubes, each with one small door. The assistant commissioner lived in a room of about twelve square feet. I had to duck through a five-feet-high door. Inside, it was pitch dark. In the harsh winter, it was best to lock the single door against the blizzards and hibernate. A bed on the mud floor in one corner, a pile of tinned provisions, a steel trunk, and a kerosene lamp completed the assistant commissioner's worldly goods. In one corner, a hole had been made through the wall; here, occasionally, the great man poured a bucket of water over himself. Calls of a more pressing nature, he answered in a neighbouring house, using the usual system of dropping the load through a hole in the ceiling into a room below. The neighbours encouraged the use of their facilities, since it added to their stock of fertilizer for the summer!

Kaza, in those days, had no rest house, not even a single-roomed one. We faced a piquant situation. Virender Sibal, the eldest brother of the Human Resources Development minister, was my class fellow in Government College, Ludhiana. He entered the Indian Administrative Service two years after I did. Here we were in a remote Himalayan valley, boss and deputy, expected to maintain a British formalness as we slept on the floor, under a giant quilt, me snoring towards the east and Sibal towards the west. In the morning, he took a walk outside in the dust, while I poured my bucket of water over myself. His cook was a local boy, who could make a rough paratha. Furniture, there was none; in any case, sitting on a chair in that room, one would hit the ceiling. Breakfast, we had sitting cross-legged on the quilt. We then emerged in solemn dignity to walk the village street to his little office, to talk to the few officials, and visit the primary school.

I spent a couple of days in Kaza. It was good to relax for a while in the pleasant autumn weather, to soak my blistered feet in salt water, and to prepare for the next part of the journey. I also had to go through the motions of inspecting the assistant commissioner's court. The people of Spiti are free of crime and the civil officers hardly have any court cases to deal with. But the time-honoured ritual has to be kept up, and we wasted half a summer's day looking through musty files. Since the crop was still in the fields, we walked in solemn procession to check the *patwari's girdawari* of the crops. With the utmost gravity, I went over the ownership and the state of the crop in the few patches of green that Kaza possessed. The Spitians seemed amused by our somewhat futile exertions, but we had to keep up the rigid, century-old requirements of the British and Raja Todermal's revenue system.

One morning, I took time off to visit the nono of Spiti, the traditional head of the area. The nono is an ancient office from centuries past, which the British maintained to exercise administrative authority over this remote valley. The office is an amalgam of a petty raja and village headman. The present nono, a young school boy, lives across the river in Kuiling village. Rather than go back to the rickety bridge near Rangrik, we chose to swim the river on our horses. It is best to attempt this early in the morning, when the snows have not melted, and the water is still low. Even at such a time it is risky. G.D. Kholsa, in his book *Himalayan Circuit*, describes how one of his muleteers, nearly lost his life in attempting a crossing at Kaza. The man was miraculously saved, but the horse was swept away. Sir Louis Dane also recorded the loss of three porters in August 1884, while trying to ford the river, in order to avoid the extra walk to Rangrik bridge! With the porters, he lost three loads, all his money, and the Government funds for the journey!

We left early and walked our horses down to the river. A couple of Spiti men took each horse by the bridle and pulled it into the water. The poor beasts had great difficulty in finding footholds because of the slippery stones on the river bed. In the middle, the water was so deep, that for a while man and horse had to swim against the current. We passed over safely. The nono was a youngster who studied in the Manali School. I missed his colourful father, who figured so prominently in Khosla's book. The nono gave us tea served out of a beautiful Chinese silver kettle and richly-sugared flour pudding in Tibetan porcelain cups. Conversation centred mainly on the successful completion of the nono's high school studies! By the time we returned, the river was in a bad mood and we had the greatest difficulty crossing back.

Another morning, we took time off to visit the Kye monastery, the biggest and most spectacular in the valley. The Kye gompa sits on a volcanic cone, high above the Spiti valley. Covering the slopes of the volcanic cone, a few miles from Kaza, it could be anyone's idea of a Shangrila. The monks' cells rise tier upon tier, till one's gaze reaches the main building on the pinnacle. In some ways, it has the same architectural impact on the onlooker as the Potala Palace in Lhasa has. The monks met us at the foot of the hill. After a presentation of ceremonial scarves, we walked in solemn procession up the winding path. The incarnation lama, a young boy, was unfortunately held up in Tibet, where he had been sent for theological studies. The regent, a tall, thin, sad-faced man with a drooping moustache, who might have been Harold Macmillan in another birth, met us at the entrance to the main chapel.

The Kye gompa, dating to about the fourteenth century, is one of the oldest in the valley. It possesses a most fabulous collection of thankas, traditional Chinese scroll paintings of the Buddha's life and other sacred icons on silk cloth. We were taken to a room on top of the monastery, where out of a battered wooden trunk, the lamas took out the most amazing artistic treasures. One after the other, the thankas were unrolled in the bright sun for our inspection. Looking at the scrolls of dirty muslin, we hardly suspected that these contained such richly-painted scenes of gods and goddesses, the colours as fresh today as when they were when first painted centuries ago. I could only gaze in awe at this collection. There was an ironic contrast between the modest mud walled monastery, the shabbily dressed and somewhat seedy-looking lamas, and this 'treasure beyond price'! The Kye gompa, like all monasteries in the two valleys, also had a collection of fine bronze icons. From its roof, we got a marvellous view of the Spiti river valley, with little green villages on the high flats above its banks, snaking its away south-eastwards to the Sutlej river.

After I had been to almost all the important gompas of Lahaul-Spiti, Tshering Dorje told me in Kyelang that an 'art lover' had come to the valleys once, inspected a lot of thankas and bronzes, and then persuaded these innocent lamas to let him take them away for an exhibition in Europe. When the treasures did not come back, the lamas led by Dorje, the only educated man amongst them aware of the value of these pieces, made a mighty fuss. Finally, Dorje took a group of lamas to Delhi, where they met the collector and were offered some items to take back. As Dorje complained to me, they always felt they had been cheated of many of their rare and precious religious icons.

We repaired to the regent's chamber for tea. Over cups of hot and salted yak-butter tea, we spoke about Spiti and its social system. The main Spiti monasteries of Kye, Dankhar and Tabo belong to the celibate Gelukpa or yellow-hat sect. The Spiti monastic system seemed to have solved the valley's social needs arising out of the problem of a limited population. The eldest son in each family inherits the land and settles on it after marriage. The younger sons join the local monastery and become monks. Each family, therefore, maintains a cell in the nearby monastery where all the monks of the family—uncles, nephews and brothers—may be found living together. They are supported by the family who send a part of the produce of the land to them. Apart from this, they share the earnings of the monastery from religious ceremonies. At harvest time, parties of monks go out on begging expeditions. They go around from house to house and stand in a row to chant certain verses that say, 'We men have given up the world; give us in charity the means of life; by so doing you will please God whose servants we are.'

'As soon as the eldest son marries, he succeeds to the family lands and dwellings. The father immediately retires to a smaller house called khang-chung, kept for this purpose. He receives a piece of land for his upkeep, and henceforth has nothing to do with the family estate and its produce. The younger brothers are sent to the local monastery. Monks in Spiti, however, do not necessarily give up all hopes of savouring the pleasures of the flesh. If the head of the family dies leaving a young widow, the younger brother almost always elects to leave the monastery. He is then considered his brother's widow's husband. She cannot object nor is any ceremony necessary. Another possibility is that when the head of the family begets only daughters, he decides at some stage to marry off one of them and take a son-in-law into the family as his heir. In such a situation, the younger brother often objects and leaves the priesthood in order to accomplish what his elder brother had failed to do: beget a son. His right to do so is usually allowed. He will marry and put his elder brother in the khang-chung. Sometimes, by agreement, and to the eternal shame of the elder brother, he will cohabit with his sister-in-law and produce a son. A monk who throws off his frock has to pay a small fine to his monastery, and I am sure this is one fine which is paid with alacrity! Monogamy is thus the general rule in Spiti and the population is kept down by this interesting custom of primogeniture.

The Kye gompa regent was considered a fortune teller of some standing in the area. After tea, one of the assistant commissioner's local deputies delicately put before the regent the anxieties of two young bachelors locked away in a somewhat unpromising marriage market! The regent gravely considered the matter, scribbled some calculations, and made a pronouncement which, to put it mildly, was extremely encouraging. Never have a deputy commissioner and his assistant gone down from Kye to Kaza with a lighter step!

At Kaza, we were joined by Chhibber of the Punjab Police and his wife Malathi. Chhibber was inspecting the police in the valley and Malathi had bravely elected to go along with him. After the Chhibbers had formally called on him, the assistant commissioner had no alternative but to host a dinner at his official residence. We sat around a kerosene lamp in Sibal's one-room apartment, while his major-domo caused something of a gastronomic sensation by actually producing green vegetables! These high valleys produce very few vegetables. In the short summers, cauliflower introduced by the Moravian missionaries is grown. At the start of the winter, it is buried in the soil, and the snow and negative winter temperature keeps the cauliflower preserved, to be eaten during the long winters.

We left early the next morning. The Chhibbers promised to follow. We walked along the left bank of the Spiti, picking our way among the fantastically eroded towers and columns, some with huge stones perched precariously on their heads. It was a dull and dusty walk, which finally brought us to the fields below the village of Dankhar. Even these were dry and empty since the barley had been cut. The fort of Dankhar could be seen 1,500 feet above us on the ridge line. The village was out of sight. Dankhar had been the traditional capital of Spiti in the past and Major Hay, the first assistant commissioner of Kulu, spent a winter in this fort in 1846. It was also notorious for a dungeon, in which the nono used to lock up malefactors, leaving it to the complainant to feed the convicted! We did not have the heart to climb up to have a look and left it for another day. The Chhibbers soon arrived, with Malathi complaining of blisters. Hot, salted foot baths were produced and amity restored. The Himalayan desert that it is, the valley cooled sharply as soon as the sun went down. The night was filled with a superb, enchanting silence, save for the distant murmur of the river.

The following morning, we again made an early start. The monotonous walk down the valley continued. Once the sun came up, it became terribly hot and dry. The glare was so intense that I had to tie a cotton jacket over my face, with just enough of a slit to see through. The Chhibbers suffered considerably. They had no peak caps to protect their faces. In desperation, they tied office files on their heads for protection! At about ten, we reached Tabo. Clouds had formed already and it was cool. The whole village came out to welcome us, and we marched in a ragtag procession to the monastery on the edge of the village. Tabo is perhaps the oldest monastery in the valley, and the only one not located at a commanding height. It stood on the flats near the village and might have been mistaken for a house. I inspected its dim interior with a torch. It had the usual statues and books, but what amazed me was a wall mural of the Buddha, which might have come straight from Ajanta. I examined the four walls around the central chorten, which held the relics of a long dead *rimpoche*. In the poor light, I saw these panels, unknown to the culture czars of the government in Delhi. When I came back to Kyelang, I wrote a long letter to the Government of India, pointing out the beauties of Tabo and the need to recognize and preserve them. Sadly, I neither got an answer nor an acknowledgement from the Government of India. If I recollect correctly, Professor Tucci, the great Italian-born Himalayan explorer, had seen and recognized the worth of Tabo. Today, in this new century, I find with amusement that Tabo is considered a Himalayan treasure, and is now internationally recognized and lauded. I was happy to find an expensive coffee table volume on the Tabo monastery in a bookshop in Zurich.

A dance was performed for us. Heavily-jewelled women formed a line and did a three-step dance to a peculiar hissing sound. The entire village had collected for the occasion and everyone had great fun. After some tea, we continued on our way and halted for the night at the village of Lari, a veritable oasis in this dry valley. There was a lovely stream to pitch one's tent by, and some marvellous poplars to look at. The village maidens came out to our camp and examined us with unabashed curiosity. Sibal and I were sure that the Kye regent's 'third eye' was working and that the fulfilment of his prediction was near at hand! Alas, we left the next morning unsolicited.

The Chhibbers and Sibal were keen bridge fans. I was ignorant of the game, but the nearest candidate to make a 'four' must have been hundreds of miles away across the mountains. The three of them eyed me as a potential victim. After much private confabulations, I was invited to be the fourth in a game of bridge; as if they had a choice. I was of course helped with the bidding, and someone invariably chose to play my hand! The expert that he was, Chhibber could not help telling his wife where she had gone wrong. 'Darling why didn't you lead with the ace?' he would ask. The argument would go on long into the night! Sometimes, next morning, they walked apart in this desolate valley, each cocooned in isolated resentment. Chhibber, a young deputy superintendent of police, newly married, did not seem to understand the art of submitting to a lady's superior judgment!

The next day, we walked to Hurling, the Punjab Armed Police base camp. Starved of visitors, they gave us a warm welcome with the luxuries of hot baths and beds in bunkers to sleep in. In the morning, Sibal and I went off to visit the village of Gue in a neighbouring valley. We promised to join the Chhibbers at Kaurik. We climbed up out of the Spiti valley and walked over bare scree mountain slopes.

The village of Gue boasts of a few houses and a primary school. Grave-faced little children sat in their Sunday best, in complete awe of the first-ever inspection by a visitor from far away Kyelang. The school master was a bright-faced Lahaul young man. Having shown the flag and after distributing sweets to the children, we continued on our way to Kaurik. We had to climb some steep slopes of loose scree, and for a while, it was tricky work. On that lonely ridge, completely bereft of any other presence, we suddenly came face to face with a young man in a most beautiful Chinese silk gown, with a Tibetan conical fur hat on his head. The hat cone had gold and silver snakes running around it. Around his neck, he had a most beautiful necklace of a variety of precious stones found only in these Himalayan regions, and equally impressive long earrings. He had a Tenzing-like smile that stretched from ear to ear, with warm crinkled eyes. Obviously, he was a Spiti Beau Brummel. He was off to a wedding somewhere over the mountain he said.

After walking around numerous mountain folds, we finally came to the ridge line. A few bunkers on the saddle and a pillar proclaimed yet another gateway into Tibet. We had arrived at Kaurik. The height must have been above 15,000 feet. The Chhibbers had arrived earlier and we found mugs of strongly sugared hot tea awaiting us. This was to be our last evening together as the next day, the Chhibbers were to continue on to the Sutlej valley, and return to Chandigarh via Simla. We would walk back to Kaza. The bridge fans were keen on a farewell game. A petromax was produced and we played on late into the night till Chhibber asked the inevitable question of his wife, 'Darling why did you not lead with the ace?' The game broke up, leaving me richer by two rupees! The Chhibbers, undoubtedly continued their bridge discussions up to Simla.

As usual, Sibal and I started early the next morning on our long walk back. The novelty had worn off and the monotony remained. We were determined to do the fifty-six miles to Kaza in quick time. We both felt fit and acclimatized and walking long distances at heights of over 11,000 feet no longer seemed to tire us. After a short halt and a meal at Hurling, we continued on to Lari. We reached Lari late at night with the village asleep, and the shaggy hill dogs growling at us. We spent the night in the sarpanch's house since we had left our tents behind. We started again long before dawn as we were determined to walk the thirty-odd miles to Kaza before nightfall. We walked all day.

Himalayan valleys, even at this height, are hot in the day and the direct rays of the sun hurt. The dusty valley, with not a green leaf in sight, was tiresome to the body and the spirit. We plodded on hour after hour in a dutiful trance of determination, sharing no conversation, wrapped in our own silences. We saw Kaza like Everest, a distant goal that had to be achieved. The sun set in a blaze of colour. After a while, the moon came up around the mountain peaks. The valley was full of soft lights and dark shadows. The silence was overpowering. The spirits and elves of this mysterious valley were undoubtedly out. I could feel their presence. We were so tired that all conversation had dried up. I plodded on thinking only of Kaza, like some 'fair valley of Avilion'. The last miles, beyond the turn to Kaza, in the looming threatening shadow of Dankhar fort, high on the ridge, were a torture. I felt like lying down, but knew that come what may, Kaza had to be reached. There was no turning back with the mountain peak so near. It was almost midnight when we stumbled into a sleeping Kaza. We had done fifty-six miles from Kaurik in two days!

It was a joy to laze in the sun the next morning. Our feet were blistered and our muscles were sore. A day's rest made me feel better. But I still had to cover a long walk to Losar before I could take the jeep home to Kyelang. I decided to go via Kibber. Long strides took me past Kye gompa and up the slopes to Kibber. It lies on rolling, bare mountain tops at more than 14,000 feet and looks like the grasslands of Tibet. A farmer was ploughing his tiny holding with a pair of yaks. A little girl led the pair around by the nose, while the farmer held down a most primitive wooden plough. A beautiful snow dome that seemed so near invited ascent. In the school there, the children sat around a tandoor fire. Winter seemed on the way and the short summer was already a memory. From Kibber, it was downhill to Kiato, and I went as fast as I could, trying to kill the long mountain miles. I was alone with my orderly. The journey seemed interminable. Great was my surprise when on going down to the new Bailey bridge on the Spiti below Hansa, I spied a jeep on the other side. Fauja Singh stood grinning by its side. Taking pity on me, he had forced his jeep over the still half-built road to save me many miles of walking. I could have hugged him for this kindness. Fauja Singh produced some tea as I collapsed with relief into the front seat. After a short rest, we headed for home. The road was now familiar and held no terrors. Fauja Singh sped on at a merry pace, revelling in activity after three weeks of a lotus-eater's life in Losar. I dozed in the front seat. Every now and then, Fauja Singh tried to start a conversation. I could see that something was worrying him. Ultimately, he asked, 'Sahib, why do you go walking all these miles in this dusty, god-forsaken valley? It does not become a deputy commissioner. What will people in Chandigarh say if they knew?!'

I had no answer to his question and pretended to sleep as the mountains slid by.

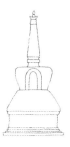

Avalanche!

Come, my friends, 'Tis not too late to seek a newer world.
Push off, and sitting well in order smite
The sounding furrows; for my purpose holds
To sail beyond the sunset, and the baths
Of all the western stars, until I die . . .

—Lord Alfred Tennyson

On 18 September 1962, I returned to Kyelang after a hurried tour of Spiti. The previous night, there had been light snowfall on the higher peaks surrounding Kaza. But the eighteenth morning was fine and sunny. We drove all day over the Kunzam pass, down the Chandra valley to Tandi, and were home as dusk settled over Kyelang. During the night, a light snowfall started, and it went on intermittently. By the next morning, Kyelang and the surrounding hills were covered with a thin white film a few inches deep. Given the light snowfall in Kyelang, there was sure to be a heavy one on the Kunzam pass. Had I dallied a day more at Kaza, I would have been trapped in the Spiti valley, unable to cross the Kunzam back to Kyelang. I would then have had to walk a very long way down to the Simla road beyond Spiti, and come right around via Chandigarh, Manali, and over the Rohtang to my headquarters. I had made it to Kyelang just in time.

For the next two days, snow, hail and rain fell in irregular showers. This was not altogether unexpected as there had been recorded reports of snowfall in early September in Lahaul. The commissioner of the Jalandhar division, who was on a tour of the valley, postponed his departure by a couple of days. The weather had improved when we saw off the commissioner and party. Reports had come in that landslides had blocked the road and there had been slips of retaining walls in places. Since winter was so close, repairs could be carried out during the next summer only. The jeep road was closed and therefore the party was to stay the night in Gondhla, then walk to Khoksar and across the Rohtang pass to Manali.

The next morning, I was sitting in my veranda having breakfast when a runner came from Khoksar with a cryptic message from the Public Works engineer: 'Very heavy snowfall in Khoksar, Rohtang top, and in Chandra valley. Continuing. Large force of labour still working on road trapped between Khoksar and Kunzam pass. Many deaths reported due to Shigri glacier fall. Request immediate help.'

I questioned the messenger, a road labourer. He reported continuous and heavy snowfall at Khoksar for about five days. Khoksar, he said, was in utter confusion with hundreds of labourers camping there. Others had begun struggling in to Kyelang. There were wild rumours of numerous deaths; of the Shigri glacier having fallen; an avalanche during the night having swept a whole camp into the Chandra river; of there being no food and shelter in Khoksar.

The situation appeared to be bad. I decided to go and see things for myself. Packing a few clothes and a sleeping bag, I left immediately for Khoksar. Communications with Chandigarh and Kyelang would be vital. I asked my portable police wireless set to follow on a mule. We left Kyelang in sunshine, but soon ran into light rain. It came on and off at intervals. Being thoroughly acclimatized, we kept up a steady pace. In Lahaul-Spiti, men from the plains have performed prodigious feats of walking. I personally know of individuals who have walked fifty miles in a day, at heights of over ten thousand feet. Punjab Police personnel at Kaurik were reported to regularly walk from Kaurik to Manali over the Rohtang pass, with only a night halt on the way. These constables performed this amazing trek to save time from their precious short leave for visiting their families. To walk thirty or forty miles in a single day is not considered exceptional. It just shows the possibilities if one is properly acclimatized.

After a couple of hours, we reached Gondhla, and Thakur Duni Chand was there to welcome us. Duni Chand lived in an interesting ancient castle, with a high watch tower at one end. The building is now a heritage landmark. A little rest over tea and biscuits, and we were off again. As we approached Sissu, the weather got worse. A heavy gale began to blow. Rain came in showers mixed with hail stones that stung our faces. The sky was dull and overcast. We had to lean into the wind to walk. My clothes were soon soaked in spite of the wind proof jacket. One of my orderlies tried to use an umbrella, but the wind would not allow it.

With relief we saw the Sissu rest house loom out of the mist. The room was open and we quickly got in, out of the sleet and rain. The two-room rest house was on a pleasant grassy slope with poplars all around. In front of the rest house, across the Chandra river, tower the giant Nilghar peaks—sheer snow-covered cliffs of twenty thousand feet. Glaciers hung in rocky clefts. My orderly looked around for the keeper so that we could try for a cup of tea, but he was nowhere to be seen. We waited for some time, but in vain. It was getting dark, and we had ten miles to go. The worst of the weather was apparently before us. We thought it best to push on. These last ten miles were a real trial.

Steady rain and sharp hailstorms dogged us all the way, if anything, getting worse as we neared Khoksar. Darkness came fast, and visibility was extremely poor. We tried using a torch, but it was not of much help. Little streams of rain water fell on the road from the cliffs along its side. Occasionally, loose stones rolled down; these were more dangerous.

With evening, the cold also came on. Distances in the hills are always deceptive. As we turned each bend in the road, we expected to see the Khoksar suspension bridge. But every bend disappointed us till we got weary of looking and just plodded on. We finally made it to Khoksar in the middle of a raging snowstorm. A week ago, when I had passed through here, I had seen a rock strewn, dusty, windswept Khoksar, dry as a desert. Now, we plodded through soft, new fallen snow to the rest house. The hills and rocks were all covered with a white mantle of snow. Khoksar had changed completely.

In a long day of walking, we had covered 54 kilometres through rain and sleet. A quick change, a hot cup of tea, and a seat near the fire soon made me forget the day's tribulations. I called for the engineers and asked for facts. They were grim enough. The Public Works Department (PWD) had about two thousand road labourers, along with their women and children in the Chandra valley, working on the road to Spiti. The labour and the PWD officials usually withdrew to their base in Kulu by the end of September—well before the first heavy winter snowfall. They did not, therefore, come prepared with arrangements to combat snow or severe winter conditions. Their camps were strung out all along the hundred miles to Spiti when the first snowfall began on 18 September. They thought it to be a light, off-season precipitation and waited for the sky to clear. It did not. The snowfall became heavy and continuous. Within twenty-four hours, many feet of snow had fallen in the valley and more was falling. The labour had single fly tents, most of which collapsed. None, not even the officers, had warm clothes, shoes, and snow goggles. During the day, the glare from the snow was tremendous and many people had become snow blind.

Near Chhetru, half way up the Chandra valley, during the night an avalanche had hit a camp that was on an exposed slope and had swept many people into the river. Wild estimates of casualties were given, but no one was sure. A government party carrying money for the treasury in Spiti was also reported to be somewhere in the valley. No one knew what had happened to it. There were many other parties of travellers, traders and government officials in the area. Now everyone was hurrying back to Khoksar to try and get over the Rohtang pass to safety. The commissioner of Jalandhar had to walk to Khoksar with his wife and was now camped in one of the rooms of the tiny rest house there, waiting to find his way over the pass. The pass by now had many feet of snow and was closed to vehicles for the winter.

One could dare it on foot only. The Gaddi shepherds from Kangra, who have traditional grazing rights for their sheep in the high pastures of Lahaul, come in the summer and return to Gaddi land before the start of winter. Many of them were also trapped on the Khoksar side of the Rohtang with their sheep and lambs.*

My first concern was the people pouring into Khoksar after a harrowing march through soft snow, without food, clothing and shelter on the way. There were only two tiny, one-room rest

---

*The Gaddis have to live their entire lives in the high mountains with their sheep flocks; in the winters, they have to come down snowy slopes. They are great experts at glissading. They form human trains, with the elders in front, and women and children in the middle, all holding on to each other. In this manner, they go glissading down all grades of slopes, using sticks with metal points as brakes. The stick is dug into the snow to come to a halt. There is excitement and even danger in this, for one can always shoot over a cliff edge, if careless. But the Gaddis do not worry. They will risk a slide, even on the most dangerous slope.

houses in all of Chandra valley—one at Chhetru and the other at Batal at the foot of the Kunzam pass. Even Khoksar had nothing beyond the little rest house. We assessed our resources and realized that luckily, the PWD had plenty of stores of food and tents at Khoksar. First thing in the morning, I ordered that free kitchens be started to feed all who passed through. A little above Khoksar, there is a piece of flat ground called Gramphoo. We pitched tents there and started a camp to house all refugees from the valley. I summoned a team of doctors from Kyelang to assist the lone PWD doctor stationed at Khoksar.

I met many of those who had come through to try and get reliable information. They were all exhausted from walking for many days in soft snow, in places waist deep. Most had snow burns, and many had snow blindness. Women had thrown their long hair over their faces to get some protection from the snow's glare. Some had frost bite. Very few had adequate clothing and shoes. The Chandra valley had suddenly become a death trap. There was no shelter, water or food all along its hundred-mile length to Khoksar. Even the jeep road had disappeared and the stragglers had to make a new path along the hillside—always in danger of soft snow avalanches.

My wireless set arrived, and I got in touch with Chandigarh. The government was most worried. The national press had picked up the tragic story and blazoned it across the country on banner headlines. The *Tribune* of Ambala wrote, 'TWO THOUSAND AND FIVE HUNDRED PWD MEN TRAPPED IN SPITI, LOCATION STILL UNKNOWN, AIR FORCE AND ARMY HELP SOUGHT, DEATHS CAUSED BY SLIDING OF GLACIER.' The *Hindustan Times* in New Delhi reported, 'TWO THOUSAND AND FIVE HUNDRED TRAPPED BY GLACIER, WEATHER THWARTS SEARCH BID, NO CONTACT WITH TRAPPED PARTY; DEATH TOLL IS FIFTY, NEW BID TO AIRDROP SUPPLIES FOR TRAPPED MEN IN SPITI FAILS.'

A large group of correspondents from Delhi and elsewhere collected in Manali to follow the story. Unable to cross the

Rohtang, they collected every scrap of information trickling into Manali and wrote dramatic, though somewhat exaggerated, stories. Most of the newspapers proclaimed that the Shigri glacier had fallen and caused all the trouble. The glacier is on the left bank of the Chandra river, while the road to Spiti is well away on the right bank. The poor Shigri was hardly to blame. Reports of deaths were also conjectural and exaggerated. I tried, as best I could over the wireless, to correct the picture.

I asked for medicines, particularly for frost bite, to be sent up from Manali. I also summoned some Sherpa instructors from the Western Himalayan Mountaineering Institute, Manali, to help us with ground reconnaissance of the Chandra valley, and to assist in rescue work, if necessary.

The Manali mountaineering school was set up by Kairon. It was the second such institute after the HMI. Kairon had made me the Director of Sports of Punjab state, a position which only he could imagine and create. I was the first person who held such a position in the country. It looked odd to us at the time, but the chief minister knew better. He set up the first sports school in Jalandhar, where the best talent of the state was kept in boarding at state expense, to be educated and coached in various sports. Almost all of India's best atheletes in the 1960s were from that nursery.

But, to come back to the Manali mountaineering school, Mr Fletcher, ICS, was my boss for this endeavour. The school was housed in a modest bungalow near the Vashisht hot springs. Harnam Singh, a botany professor from Hamirpur, who had trained in the HMI with me, was the principal. We worked hard to make the school a success, and brought Sherpas from Darjeeling to be instructors at the school. Fletcher's original idea was to house the institute in the historic Nagar castle, but Harnam preferred to live in Manali, which had a little bazaar and therefore, some life. Fletcher raved and ranted often, but Harnam had a short line to the chief minister in Chandigarh through his mother-in-law, a leading Congresswoman of the hill areas.

To add to my troubles, two flash messages came from Chandigarh. A Films Division party of the Government of India had come to Spiti to make a documentary. They were lost somewhere between the Baralacha pass and Spiti. We had to find them. And, another party of geologists had been high up on the Shigri glacier on their annual expedition searching for uranium. What had become of them?

As the national press took up the story of the disaster, the government got increasingly worried in Chandigarh. Messages flew back and forth till my battery-operated wireless set nearly collapsed. For some time, we remained out of contact with the country and the world. A party of state ministers, anxious to be seen as doing something in the crisis, established camp at Kulu. They tried repeatedly, with the help of Indian Air Force planes, to reconnoitre the valley. But Lahaul remained completely covered by a thick cloud blanket. Occasionally we heard the drone of planes, high above the valley. We never saw one.

We soon had the camp running smoothly. Shelter, food and medical aid were given promptly to all those struggling in from the Chandra valley. They came in a steady stream. After a day's rest, these parties pushed on over the pass in batches, escorted by local men. The Rohtang top had many feet of snow, but it had settled somewhat, and the pass could be crossed, though with considerable difficulty. At Rahla on the Kulu side, another relief camp was opened. Exhausted parties trekking across were given hot food and then taken by bus to rest camps at Manali.

The commissioner, who was held up at Khoksar, also decided to cross after the first few parties had gone over. I accompanied him to see things and get a little exercise. A part of the way was clear, but soon the soft snow started. It became more and more exhausting to trek as we gained height. Not everyone in the party was fit, and we had to stop frequently for rest. All along the way, we found abandoned baggage and dead mules sticking out of the snow. Numerous sheep lay dead or dying. The shepherds from

Kangra had been caught on the wrong side of the pass by the sudden snowfall. The sheep just could not walk through soft snow, and hundreds had died on Rohtang. Near the top, there were some frozen travellers. The scene was one of total havoc. An enterprising reporter from the *Hindustan Times*, who managed to see things for himself, wrote:

Heavy snowfall and raging blizzards, unusually early this year, brought death and tragedy to the Chandra, Lahaul, and Spiti valleys, sending hundreds of labourers, and local peasantry working in road gangs fleeing to the safety of Manali. The retreat and the only route of relief along the Rohtang pass, thirteen thousand and fifty feet, was cut, and the pass turned into a veritable death trap. Even as the story unfolds, our staff photographer, Kishore Parekh, trekking to the treacherous pass and beyond, found grim reminders of the ordeal. A Rahla peasant, one of the road gang, lay huddled in an ice-cave, in which he had sought refuge, but never awoke to see another day. Scattered all along the desolate snow carpeted pass, were the belongings, which the exhausted and panic-stricken labourers abandoned as they fled. Beyond Rahla, the track was more forbidding; a caravan of mules laden with blankets, medicines and food for the trapped labourers turned back as the animals sank deep in the snow. Stragglers from the first road gangs to cross the pass brought more harrowing tales of men sinking waist deep, of a mother abandoning a dying child and of an entire group of people swept off their feet and to their death by high winds.

The tortuous bridle path, down the south side of the mountain range, is marked by strings of prayer flags, stressing in the wind, tokens of man's gratefulness for deliverance from what had appeared to be certain death in the snow-swept valley.

The route we took bore the marks of an exodus—abandoned shoes, strips of old clothing and broken pieces of bamboo staves. A copy of a recent issue of the Indian Concrete Association's journal told of technical personnel who had trekked to safety that way.

We were still fifteen hundred feet below the pass when the

commissioner decided to call it a day! Well past his youth, having lived in the plains, and not fit or acclimatized, he simply could not walk and climb in the snow and slush. We turned back. On the way, the commissioner's vigilant eye spotted an abandoned lamb. We carried it down and had our first fresh meat meal after many days, cooked and served by the great man himself to pass the idle hours. After a satisfying meal of lamb curry with some local chhaang, the commissioner felt distinctly more cheerful. The party finally crossed a week later when the weather had improved.

In answer to my urgent summons, a party of Sherpa instructors—friends of many pleasant days in the mountains—soon arrived. I immediately sent them on a ground reconnaissance of the Chandra valley. They were to go all the way to Batal at the foot of the Kunzam pass, to render aid to people on the way, and to come back quickly to give me a correct assessment. I also asked them to make specific enquiries about the geologists on the Shigri glacier.

The fate of the Films Division party, which had come to Lahaul, was also worrying me. Headed by Mr Thapa, himself a hill man, they had spent a pleasant week in Kyelang filming the documentary. I had attached Tshering Dorje with them for local assistance. They planned to go over the Baralacha pass, down the Chandra valley, and on to Spiti over the Kunzam pass. By our estimates, they would have been just over the Baralacha pass when the snowfall came. What became of them, no one knew. I asked my assistant in Kyelang to send a search party to the Baralacha. After two days, the reply came. So heavy was the snow around the Baralacha that the party could not even approach the foot of the pass. I told Chandigarh of this and a flight was arranged to look for the missing party. But the clouds persisted and the aircraft had to go back. There seemed no way out. We waited for the weather to clear. I continued to hope that Tshering Dorje would see them through, though things seemed rather bleak for them.

A couple more days passed in waiting. And then one morning, a bunch of bearded, sun-burnt young men burst into my rest house room. The lost geologists! Were we glad to see them! They were all plainsmen, headed by Srikanth, a young south Indian. None of them had any experience of mountaineering. Over cups of hot tea, the leader related their story:

All three of us were in our high camp at about eighteen thousand feet on the Shigri glacier when the snowfall started. It was not too heavy on the first day, and we thought the spell of bad weather might blow over. During the night, however, it snowed very heavily. I gave orders to retreat to base camp. Carrying all our valuable equipment, we started out at about 5 a.m. It took us the best part of the day to climb down and cover the distance. The soft snow made progress difficult. We had to be particularly wary of hidden crevasses, which abound on the steep, broken Shigri face.

For three days, we remained confined to our tents at base camp. It continued to snow off and on, and we had to clear our sagging tents during the nights. Avalanches thundered down the Shigri face, but luckily our camp was not too exposed. In any case, we were in no position shift camp. We prayed and hoped for the best.

With the weather continuing to get bad, I realized that we had to get out fast. Our supplies and strength were both running out. Our main problem was the swollen Chandra river. We had to cross it. We packed our valuable equipment, and stowed it carefully in the tents, to be retrieved later. Carrying rucksacks full of essentials only, we left at 4 a.m., so as to reach the river bank early–well before the snow melts, and makes the river unfordable. The journey over the broken, boulder strewn snout of the glacier was a nightmare. Those who have been on a glacier would know.

Opposite the Shigri glacier, the Chandra river breaks up into a number of separate streams, and is fordable. But even among these, many channels are fast and tricky. Luckily, we had Panchhi Ram, our Lahaula orderly in the party. He guided us. Holding hands to form a human chain, we waded into the icy water. The current was fast, and it swirled about us, reaching the chest in the deepest parts. We swayed and leaned into the current and the chain held. Once across the river, we knew we would pull through to safety. By evening, we struggled into Chhetru rest house, tired and hungry, but alive!

I marvelled at the pluck of these youngsters. Marooned high on the Shigri glacier, with the river barring their way, they had been in extreme danger. Their courage had saved them. After a couple of days rest, they left for Manali. Within ten days, they were back to retrieve their equipment! The Geological Survey of India, created in the nineteenth century by the British, has done and continues to do yeomen service for the nation. They spend entire summers high in the mountains, risking their lives on steep glaciers, prospecting for rare metals. They deserve the country's acclaim.

The geologists gave me more good news. They had learnt at Chhetru that the Films Division party had reached Batal at the foot of the Kunzam pass. My Sherpas had gone on to confirm the news. Other parties coming into Khoksar had also met the group along the way. They were said to be making their way to Khoksar rather slowly, and some of them were totally exhausted. I passed on the happy news to Delhi. We could relax a little now. The evacuation was proceeding smoothly. The lost people had been located. News had also come in that the treasury party was safe at Chhetru with their treasure. They had, however, lost most of their mules and therefore could not bring the chests of money back. A special labour force of forty Lahaulas was recruited and sent to their rescue.

Thapa and company straggled into Khoksar in ones and twos, escorted by the Sherpas. They were lean, terribly sunburnt and heavily bearded. We could hardly recognize them as the smart Bombaywallahs who had left Kyelang two weeks back. Tshering Dorje was as fit as ever, except for the sunburn. They received a warm welcome from our little headquarters, and deserved it too.

For them, it had been a miracle of survival. They were on top of the Baralacha pass when the weather deteriorated. Tshering Dorje knew the signs only too well. They could not turn back. He urged them to push on quickly, and get as far below the pass as possible into the Chandra valley before the snow storm came.* At night, there was a tremendous snowfall. By morning, the camp was many feet deep in snow. The mules were miserable with nothing to eat and they could hardly walk in deep soft snow. Apart from Thapa, the leader, the other two members of the team, raw youths from Kashmir and Madras, having their first look at the high mountains, were completely disheartened. Dorje himself was worried. The nearest human habitation was many marches away at Batal. Travel through the snow filled, desolate, upper reaches of the Chandra valley would not be easy. They could count on no assistance, except their own stamina and resolve. Luckily, Dorje had an able ally in Thapa, the leader of the group. A tough and courageous hill man from Garhwal, Thapa faced the situation bravely.

But Dorje was the flame that burnt the brightest. To a Lahaula used to long journeys to Tibet across the highest mountains in the world, such situations are not new. And Dorje was one of the very best. Each morning, he forced the members out of camp, rolled the tents, loaded the animals, and pushed the party on. If the snow was soft, he made the way; if the muleteers grumbled, he cajoled and threatened them; if a member was tired, he carried his pack; and if anyone lost heart, he

---

*'The source of the Chandra is a huge snow bed, more than sixteen thousand feet above the sea, on the south-east slopes of the Baralacha pass. From its very commencement a considerable stream, it becomes quite unfordable a mile from its source. For the first fifty miles, the valley of the Chandra is entirely uninhabited; the hills sweep down wild and barren to the river, and end in broken cliffs, the base of which is choked with the debris of decomposing rock. Above, the scene is equally desolate.' (*Kangra District Gazetteer*, 1897)

reasoned with him. Dorje was like a human dynamo. When all were tired, he cheerfully set up camp single handedly, cooked and forced food on reluctant eaters. He even carried and dragged mule loads into camp when some poor animal, exhausted by the soft deep snow, stopped and refused to budge. When they lost the way, Dorje found it. He was on his home ground and in his element.

A number of mules died. They were forced to abandon luggage, including valuable films and cameras. Dorje stored them all in a cave near the Chandrataal, used by shepherds in summer.* After many days of torture, they stumbled into the tiny Batal rest house. They were still many marches away from Khoksar, but they knew they had survived. In Batal, the group found a roof over their heads and other human faces around them. That was enough. The Sherpa party also caught up with them and then everyone really relaxed. Their loads were shared and each member was fussed over in so many little ways. At Khoksar, the party indulged themselves in an orgy of eating and sleeping. Not so for Dorje. After a couple of days' rest, he collected a party of Lahaulas, and went off to collect the abandoned cameras!

Another few days and my work was really over. All the labourers had left. Perhaps a few stragglers remained at Khoksar. The engineers could look after these and other minor matters, such as closing the camps. I prepared to return to Kyelang.

---

*'The Chandra Taal is a favourite halting place for the shepherds. The lake is three quarters of a mile or more in length, and of considerable width. It is fed by springs and melting snows, and the surplus water runs by an outlet into the Chandra river.' (*Kangra District Gazetteer*, 1897)

The Chandrataal was a magical lake facing the Mulkila group of high snow peaks. Siberian ducks camped here on their way to the Indian plains, safe from disturbance. Sadly, during recent times, the Indian zeal for development has cut a road to the lake. The silence of this solitary lake has been violated.

The sky also cleared at last, and the sun shone out of a clear blue sky.

We were standing out in the rest house courtyard when we heard the drone of plane. Soon a Dakota aircraft appeared and the sky blossomed with parachutes. An invasion? No. Supplies of food and clothing for the trapped labour! I suppose the drop was just for the record. Men were sent out to collect the packages and put them in the store. I took one last look around Khoksar, the scene of such feverish activity in the last ten days, and headed for home. Summer had gone and we were approaching autumn. Soon, the leaves of the Sissu poplars would turn yellow then russet and finally fall, and the long winter would be upon us. The last of the outsiders had gone. The valley seemed so quiet and peaceful. The mountains stood still and silent, as we strolled down the sunny road to Kyelang.

Karding Monastery

Strange, is it not? That of myriads who
Before us pass'd the door of darkness through
    Not one returns to tell us of the Road,
Which to discover we must travel too.

—Omar Khayyam

The unseasonal September snowfall had left a permanent crust of ice on top of the Rohtang pass. Vehicular traffic had stopped completely. A few people, mostly locals, still continued to cross, but the rush of visitors from the plains had gone with the last of the jeeps in early September. The valley began to prepare for the long winter ahead. Supplies of dry rations, tinned food and other necessities were stored. Some of us brought eggs and fresh apples from Manali. As part of the development effort, poultry had been carried across the Rohtang in crates on mules and distributed to the local households. They looked after them, and in the winter fed them indoors. Some eggs were produced in the village in winter and I used to have the luxury of buying a few everyday. The *churus*, a cross between a yak and a cow, produce some milk in the barren winters. Tara, my kitchen boy, used to get me a glass of fresh milk every morning. This was also a luxury.

The temperature in Kyelang is so low during the winter that fruits and vegetables do not perish. The valley becomes a giant freezer during the many winter months. My Moravian mission-built house with thick mud walls and a wooden floor was reasonably comfortable. At night, we lighted the round *chulha* for some warmth. These chulhas, designed by the missionaries, were round tin vessels with a hole that could be closed in the top, through which pieces of wood could be thrown in. At the bottom was a side door for the ash to be cleared in the morning. The vessel had an air pipe going up and out through the roof. With clear air flow in and out, the chulhas burnt beautifully—one only has to conserve the wood! The temperature in Lahaul was so low that in the morning, Tara used to give me a bucket of hot water, which I quickly poured over myself before it cooled. A mug of water thrown on the floor would immediately solidify. The roof had three-foot-long icicles in the morning, made by the snow drops trickling over from the sloping roof.

The farmers stored supplies of grass on the housetops for feeding animals in winter. For themselves, they buried cauliflower and other vegetables in the fields. Buried vegetables become slightly flat, but retain most of their nutritive value. They are a boon in the winter when fresh vegetables and fruits are not available. The preparations for winter reminded me of people getting ready for a long siege. And just as well it might be one. With the closing of the pass, all contact with the outside world was lost. The valley then became like a vast prison with three gates: the Baralacha pass to the north, the Kunzam pass to the east, and the Rohtang pass to the south, each impossible to cross. For six months or more, the people had to live on their own resources. The government officials posted in the valley found it even more difficult, as during this period, they lost all contact with their kith and kin in the plains. The radio was their only source of amusement and news. With little work and limited contact with the state government in Chandigarh via a poor wireless link, they had long winter days of idleness to pass. Little office jealousies emerged. Some others fell prey to regular drinking, a habit they found difficult to give up in later years. The Indian army too faces this problem on remote mountain pickets. Twice during the long winter, a group of Lahaulas made a daring walk to Manali over the dangerous Rohtang, and came back with letters and newspapers.

At Kyelang, Goswamy was the sub-divisional magistrate and Dewan was the superintendent of police. Lahaul-Spiti had no crime worth the name, and really did not need police stations or a superintendent-level officer. But once the structure of a district is created, each department fills its slots. (Sometimes, having little work, junior police officers created problems.) Seeking company, the three of us, all young men, spent our time together. After an evening walk, we were tempted to sit either in my Moravian mission-built house, or across the road, in their one-room flats. To pass the long winter evenings, it was easy, as I found out, to start taking a casual drink or two every evening. Though only twenty-six and a bachelor, I was the deputy commissioner and *mai-baap* of all. I realized soon that we, three young men with high responsibilities, could slip down the slope. One day, I therefore decreed that we would take our next drink only on Republic day, six weeks away! We all held honestly to the ban. This fixing of future dates for a drink gave us a *Laxmanrekha* of self restraint, which stood us in good stead.

At the end of November, we again had heavy snowfall. Bad weather continued for four days and we ended up with about five feet of snow in Kyelang. Finally, the clouds disappeared, and the sun shone out of a clear blue sky. With a million snow crystals glinting in the sun, the glare was tremendous. Yard-long icicle spears hung from my sloping tin roof. There was not much to do, so Dorje and I decided to visit Karding monastery. Perched on the ridge below the fifteen-thousand-feet-high Dilburi peak, the monastery had always fascinated and beckoned me. It was right opposite my house, across the river. I had often seen smoke rising from its chimneys and after the recent heavy snowfall, had watched the lamas clearing snow from the roofs through my binoculars. At night, I heard the booming bark of their Tibetan mastiffs. I had already sent word to the abbot and they were expecting us. The sky was clear and we could finally go. I was excited.

We left at about 11.30 a.m. Dorje carried the bag with my cameras and an ice axe to make steps on slippery slopes. The valley is so placed that Kyelang gets the maximum sunshine in winter while Karding gets the minimum. Lying at the base of the precipitous Dilburi peak, Karding sees the sun only when it rises above the left shoulder of the mountain. After a short period, the sun sinks behind the right shoulder. Thus even when the snow has melted in Kyelang, it lies thick in the Karding area. The Moravian mission, which started in Karding, later shifted to Kyelang because of its sunny location.

We walked down the fields in front of the office, and came to a point where the road went zigzag down a sharp slope to a bridge over the river. At this corner was a beautiful chorten, about twenty-five feet high. One corner was falling apart and no one seemed bothered by it. Religion disappears when the so-called civilization steps in. We went down the path to the wooden bridge. The Bhaga river passes Karding through a deep gorge, and the bridge here was only about forty feet across. The water flowed at least seventy feet below. By this time, the water level had fallen and the silt no longer muddied the water, which had an icy green colour. Already, there were chunks of ice on the rocks, which didn't seem to melt. Icicles hung from the rock ledges. Soon, the river would freeze over, and flow below the thick ice crust. I thought of Coleridge's *Kubla Khan* where Alph the sacred river ran down to a sunless sea through caverns measureless to man.

Across the bridge, the path wound up a sharp slope. There was plenty of snow, but the villagers had cut steps in the bad portions. The snow had actually been beaten down, and was not too slippery. We toiled up the slope breathing heavily, but I liked the exercise after the long period of inactivity in Kyelang. Soon, we reached the fields and were walking down a poplar-lined avenue to the village of Karding. The twenty-odd houses of Karding stood on the edge, looking up and down the valley, towards Puikar in the north and to Tandi in the south. Across the valley, it faces Kyelang, which has displaced it as the capital. Outside the village was the usual collection of morose looking yaks and churus, floundering about in the snow. These animals do not move out of the way even if they are beaten, so listless are they! In the winter, the animals are almost starved. There is nothing on the ground. A little grass is stored on the roof of the house, but it is so meagre that the animal is given just enough daily to keep it alive. In Lahaul, no one can keep too many animals due to the lack of fodder. Looking into one of the rooms for animals, I noticed a stone stair going to the roof. I found most of the sheep sunning themselves there! The poor animals do not get exercise during the long winters for the ground is covered with snow, and at best, they can stand about, the sheep on the roof and the yaks out in the snow.

The village sarpanch Rigzin met us and took us to his house for tea, through lanes heavily piled with snow. The Lahaul valley gets considerable snow in the winter. A heavy snowfall leaves a foot or more on the flat roofs in the village. As soon as the sun comes out, the snow must be cleared, else it will soak and destroy the roof. For this, Lahaulas keep flat wooden spades. Immediately after a heavy snowfall, the women go to the roof and cut the soft snow into rectangular pieces with the wooden spatula, and lift and throw them like large pieces of burfi into the lanes below. The gullies are therefore packed with hard snow all through the winter. When the sun shines after a two-day snowfall, it is a sight to see all the village folk on their roofs, busy clearing the snow and chatting with each other. On sunny days, all families are found on the roof, warming themselves and catching up with their neighbours in happy conversations. The music of children's voices is heard across the villages.

We went up the stairs to the covered lobby and then into a room on the left. Kalimpong rugs had been spread and in the centre was a fireplace with four cooking points on it. The steel fireplace with a chimney is the gift of the Moravian mission to Lahaul. The room was clean and there were windows opening out on to the street. One of the cupboards held the community radio set, given to the village by the government. A loudspeaker on a high mast on the roof competed with the one in Kyelang as it was audible not only in the village, but even across the valley in Kyelang. There were also some cheap prints of Nehru and Gandhi on the wall.

Over some butter tea, I talked to the sarpanch. He was one of seven brothers and had about three acres of land, including *daang* grassland. One brother was a tailor in Kyelang, another was employed with a mule owner on about a hundred rupees per annum, and a third worked in Dharamsala. The father and a younger brother were lamas, while the youngest two were studying in Manali and Kyelang respectively. Only the sarpanch was married, but according to the customs of the country, the other brothers could also treat her as wife.

After a little while, a bright-faced youngster of about thirteen came into the room and was introduced to me as Tashi, the lama brother. I liked him straightaway and began to question him.

'When did you join the monastery?'

'A short time back.'

'Did you also study in a school?'

'Yes, I studied up to the sixth class.'

'Do you like it in the monastery?'

'Yes.'

'What do you do there?'

'I learn Bhoti and can read a little.' The boy then recited some verses to me.

I asked him, 'Do you like the monastery or the school?'

'I like both.' A diplomat!

'What does one learn in a school?'

'One becomes *aqalmand* [wise].'

He said he would be able to do simple *tana mana* prayers in a year's time, and would go out with the lamas. I jokingly told him that I would call him for a *dambargya* ceremony. The boy was so intelligent that I felt sad at such a waste of talent. I tried to reason with the brother, but did not find him receptive. I was determined to try arguing my case with the father.

We walked up through gently sloping fields covered with snow—a perfect site for skiing. The monastery is situated on a subsidiary ridge, at about twelve thousand feet, immediately below the Dilburi peak. From Kyelang, the frontal view is telescoped into a single steep slope from the river to the Dilburi peak and it looks like the avalanches will sweep the monastery away. I always wondered about the foolishness of the builders. Now I found that the monastery ridge is separated from the main Dilburi massif by a gully, and the avalanches go thundering down the side nullah to the river, merely rattling the monastery windows, and now and then breaking a few panes. The Dilburi peak, about 16,000 feet high, so prominently visible in the Kyelang valley, has a story of its own. It is said that long ago, Lama Ghantapa did a period of samadhi and *tapasya* at this peak. Now, there is a small Buddhist shrine in his memory.

In his *Kulu and Lahoul*, General Bruce records that in August there is a harvest festival in Kyelang where the village folk, all dressed up, climb to Rangcha Galli, the pass by the side of the Dilburi, go down to Gondhla, join in the festival there, and walk back to Kyelang in the evening. They thus do a complete *parikrama* of this holy mountain. Bruce also relates an amusing story of his own recklessness that I have referred to earlier. When they crossed into Lahaul in July, they first camped at Khoksar and made a determined attempt to climb the Gephan peak. Since Bruce himself had a shoulder injury, he sent Fuhrer, his Swiss guide companion, and Lal Bahadur, one of his group of Gorkha soldiers, to try and climb Gephan. The climb was a hard one, over sharp ridges, broken ground and steep ice ascents. Finally, 'They reached the last ridge–2,000 feet of really fine climbing; for the last part of the Gephan has a most sensational appearance. The face and ridge are at the steepest angle, and the western face goes sheer down on to the Sissu glacier, an immense rock face.' The weather turned worse, but Fuhrer kept going. He reported it to have been extremely hard work, but very fine climbing in ice and snow. However, 'When they had passed all difficulties, and when not more than twenty minutes from the top, they were suddenly caught in a regular *ourmente*, which nearly took them off the mountain, and without stopping a moment, they fled.'

Gephan is an angry devta, as Bruce had been told, and it was dangerous to cross his path. It is interesting that Fuhrer made no claim to a successful climb when he had overcome all difficulties and but for the fierce wind, could have easily got to the top. I say this because in my experience as the president of the Indian Mountaineering Foundation, odd cases kept coming up of doubtful claims. Later in August, Fuhrer and Lal Bahadur climbed Gephan III, a very difficult peak of 19,600 feet.

But to go back to the Dilburi circuit and Bruce's ways, after the Gephan adventure, Bruce marched his wife and camp straight on to Kyelang, while he and Todd followed at a leisurely pace. They had lunch at 6 p.m. at Gondhla, and suddenly, took it into their heads to climb straight up to Rangcha Galli, and go down on the other side, past Karding monastery, across the Bagha, straight into Kyelang. Bruce describes his experience thus: 'Why two ordinarily more or less sane people should think they could climb to this pass, and descend the other side, starting at 6 p.m., is beyond me, especially as the bigger idiot of the two had his arm in a sling.' Bruce and companion struggled up to Rangcha by 9 p.m. They were carrying a lantern to light the way! As they walked down towards Karding monastery, it began to rain in torrents and Bruce says, 'All we could see were certain twinkles of lights, two thousand feet below us in Kyelang. I thought the night was never going to end. I had to go with the greatest care, as a slip would probably have damaged my shoulder badly.' Struggling down the mountain, in darkness and rain, at about two in the morning, they stumbled into Karding village; a sleepy man took them down the steep track to the wooden bridge over the Bagha gorge. Three o' clock in the morning saw 'a most bedraggled crew, absolutely wringing wet, and covered with mud, in the dak bungalow.' The Rangcha Galli pass is about 14,600 feet high. Later in the season, on his return from Patseo, Bruce again climbed up the Rancha Galli in order to try and climb Lambuchoks, the high peak along the ridge, so prominently visible from Kyelang when looking north.

The site of the Karding monastery is beautiful. It seemed to nestle in the coils of the Dilburi, which rises above the valley like a giant cobra standing on its tail with hood outspread, ready to strike. From its safe position, the monastery watches over the mundane activities of the mortals up and down the valley, like a benign presiding deity.

This monastery is not a very old one. It was founded in about 1920 by Lama Norbu. Now it is the biggest monastery in the Bhaga valley and has about thirty lamas and nuns. Belonging to the red-hat sect, its practices are not so rigid. Nuns are allowed in the monastery on equal terms with lamas. Lamas can marry and they stay in summer in their homes working in the fields, and when winter comes, settle down in the monastery for a few months of meditation. Lama Paljor, the abbot, lived in Kyelang with his family, but in the winter went up to Sha-shur gompa, situated on the ridge above Kyelang, to spend a month or two in isolation and meditation, contemplating the mysteries of the universe. As of now, in 2009, Lama Paljor is ninety-two and frail, but very much alive. He leads the prayers when I need the Almighty's help.

The presence of women sometimes leads to amorous interludes. I was told that year two nuns of Puikar monastery were pregnant. In such cases, efforts are made to hush up the scandal, and the couple gets married and leaves the monastery. In Spiti, the stricter yellow-hat sect predominates, and I did not see women at Kye monastery or elsewhere.

In Kyelang, there were two lamas with families that I knew of— Lama Paljor and Lama Kalzan, the Kyelang sarpanch, or as we all liked to call him, the Mayor of Kyelang. Kalzan was a small man with a perpetual smile. He dressed like the rest of the people, but joined the Sha-shur lamas, as he belonged to that monastery, at dambargya and other ceremonies.

Each monastery has its sphere of influence. Its monks perform all the birth, death, marriage and other lucrative ceremonies in certain villages. The monks are also generally from these villages, thus establishing a link. The Karding monastery has under its wing the villages of Karding and Guazing.

As we struggled up the last steep bit, lamas with gyadungs and *gelings* began to play a welcome song, high up on the monastery roof. Fascinated, I stopped and threw back my head to watch. In their maroon robes, and with the sun glinting on their polished brass instruments, they looked perfect against a background of multicoloured prayer flags, the clear blue sky and snow-covered peaks. They reminded me of the 'Visit India' posters I had seen as a child at railway stations: red-robed lamas playing on gyadungs against a background of snowy mountains. Only, this scene was more beautiful than any that the poster painter could have ever imagined.

On turning a corner, I was suddenly face to face with the monastery mastiff, a shaggy, malevolent-looking Cerberus. His spirit had been apparently so broken by his perpetual chains that he did not even growl, but gave us only a bored look and continued to sit on the snow. These Tibetan mastiffs, with their deep-throated bark, are heard right across the silent valley at night. They all wear four-inch wide metal spiked collars as protection against snow leopards.

We were met by the master of ceremonies, a man of about forty-five with a thick Victorian moustache. No white scarves were offered as they were at Kye monastery in Spiti, nor was the head lama present to greet us. The chamberlain came only to show us the way. We walked down a lane with the main monastery building on the right and individual cells built in a cluster on the slope on the left. Entering through a small door, we passed down a dim gallery, lined with the dark figures of lamas and giggling nuns. Taking off our shoes, we entered a room lit by a number of windows on the opposite side. In front of these windows sat two dignitaries on raised seats padded with Kalimpong rugs. On the higher seat was a splendidly robed man of about forty-five, with Mongol features, smooth yellowish skin and a well-fed, portly appearance. The collar of his costly maroon gown was laced with gold. Around his shoulders, he had a lovely green Chinese silk cape, lined inside with the softest of lamb skin. On his left, at a slightly lower level, sat an old man with a white beard and a prodigious, warty nose. His dress was shabby compared to that of his neighbour. I recognized him immediately as Kungaji, the lama of Khosla's *Himalayan Circuit*.*

The room was plain with a fire-place in the centre, on which stood a number of tea kettles and pots. A plain wooden almirah in a corner contained cups and other odds and ends. On the ceiling, over the dignitaries, were hung two hand sheets printed in a maroon and white pattern. I recognized them as typical prints from Punjab.

I sat down to the right of this portly gentleman, who reminded me of Parson Adams. When Dorje entered, he went up to Parson Adams, and kneeling, paid obeisance. Adams touched him lightly on the head. Incidentally, his hands were soft and smooth like a woman's and he had a beautiful ring on his podgy third finger. The other lamas then came in and offered similar greetings. They sat down along the walls. Then an old lama

---

*'The head lama was a bearded old scoundrel, with a pimply nose, a knowing look in his lecherous eyes. His face at the moment was in quiet repose, but the lines round his mouth and a glint in his eyes spoke of fervent activities, and orgies of self-indulgence, in which his wicked body must frequently have taken a prominent part. There were several chomos (nuns) living in the monastery, and some of the younger ones were not unattractive. Indeed, one of them, who giggled and frisked about provocatively, quite unlike a nun, had a great deal of physical charm, and I am extremely doubtful, if the saying of prayers was her sole occupation in the monastery.' (G.D. Khosla, *Himalayan Circuit*, London: Macmillan and Co. Ltd, 1956, p. 208)

This unfair charge only bespeaks Khosla's own vivid sensual, imagination. It was resented in Lahaul where Kungaji is deeply revered. He died in 1965 and his remains are in a chorten in the monastery. In 1967, on a request from the lamas, I presented a photograph of Lama Kungaji and Hishe Rangdol to the monastery where they have been given a place of honour in the main chapel.

entered—a small wizened man. Everyone, except the two senior wranglers and the guests, stood up out of respect. The old man stood for some time at the far end of the room, muttering prayers. He then advanced holding the end of his wrap in his left hand, and knelt, bowing low in obeisance. He was given a two-handed benediction and seated next to Jimmy Durrant! Benedictions are of three grades: with a mere nod of the head, with one hand and lastly, with two hands. If two senior wranglers meet, they touch foreheads!

When everyone was seated, tea was served in Gwalior porcelain cups. The two seniors were served tea in painted Chinese cups on silver stands covered with silver lids. These cups had no handles and they drank their tea by picking up the stand with the cup.

Butter tea was served to us. The method of making this tea is fascinating. Water is boiled with tea. This is poured into a long slim bamboo or wooden barrel; butter and salt are added and the liquid is then thoroughly mixed. This is then put in a brass kettle, which is kept hot at the fireplace. Before serving, the kettle is shaken to mix the tea and salt that might have settled. If the butter is clear and the tea is properly made, it is pleasant to taste. It is most refreshing and has considerable food value. In the high Himalayas, salted tea is considered a good restorative. As soon as you take a sip, the cup is refilled. The Lahaulas can consume prodigious quantities of this beverage. In order to escape the host, one should quickly finish the cup and hide it. Now, of course, the people are learning our ways and customs.

The tea served at the monastery was of three grades—one kettle for us, another for the two senior lamas, and a big brass vessel for the monks, which contained almost nothing but hot water! Over tea, I started a conversation with Dorje acting as interpreter. I was anxious to know something about Parson Adams. He was a Tibetan named Hishe Rangdol and had been head of the monastery at a place called Kifug, south-east of

Lhasa. Due to Chinese persecution, he came to India through the North East Frontier Agency (Arunachal Pradesh) and Assam. He lived near Gangtok for some time and came to Karding in August 1961. He had been brought there to take over the stewardship of Karding from Lama Kungaji who was too old. As the seating showed, he was already the abbot. Kungaji lived most of the time at a small monastery at Gauzing, a little distance beyond Karding.

Kungaji seemed to know Rangdol well, for his grandfather had been Kungaji's guru. The guru, named Togdan Shakya Shri, lived at Dugug Tsete Khang in Kham, and later at Kifug. Lama Kungaji went twice to eastern Tibet, the first time in about 1910 and later, in 1925. He stayed seven years the first time and about four years on the second visit. He travelled the first time through Arunachal Pradesh, and on the second, through Bhutan.

The Lahaulas seem to have a fairly strong link with Sikkim and Bhutan.* Many of them travelled to Tibet through this area, perhaps the route to east Tibet was easier, rail and road being available up to Gangtok. Even now, they have brought a number of émigré Tibetan lamas from Sikkim and Bhutan to run their monasteries. Tibet is no longer available for the training of lamas and Lahaul provides no facilities. Most lamas here can read the scriptures, but few know the meaning. The literary Bhoti is to them what Latin is to the average Westerner.

I then questioned Hishe Rangdol and Kungaji about the famous Lama Mifan Dorje who lived in the time of the thirteenth Dalai Lama. Lama Rangdol told me his correct name was Rimpoche Mifan Namgyal Gyatso and that he was truly a great seer. Lama Kungaji agreed. I questioned them about some of the

---

*'A tribute of the value of rupees thirty is sent every year by the Abbot of Guru Ghantal monastery in Lahaul, to the Abbot of the Togna monastery in Ladakh, whence it goes in the same way, to the monastery of Pangtang Dechinling in Bhutan, of which the Abbot bears the title of Nawang Namgyal.' (*Kangra District Gazetteer*, 1897)

reported miracles of the lama. Hishe Rangdol told me this story about the venerable lama: the lama lived in a cave by the river bank on the road to China. The Chinese attacked Tibet and the thirteenth Dalai Lama had to flee. When the forces were passing by on their way to Lhasa, one of the Chinese generals who was a Buddhist went to pay his homage to the seer.

When he inquired about the guru's health, the guru queried, 'Why do you inquire about my health when your mission is to destroy Tibet?' The general then asked for a drink of water. The guru offered him tea. He asked one of the soldiers to fill a kettle with water. He then sprinkled a little of that water on some ashes, and at once, flames sprang up. The guru put the kettle to boil and put ashes a number of times into it, saying each time, 'This is salt, this is butter, this is tea.' When the tea was ready, the guru said it would have eight different flavours. It did!

The wonderstruck general went and told this to his superior who happened to be a Christian. The latter appeared the next morning before the lama and ordered him to be shot. Many volleys were fired, but the bullets only bounced off the noble man's chest! At this, the angry general ordered him to be cut down with a sabre. The lama was slashed across the chest and shoulder, and left bleeding on the ground. Great was the general's surprise the next day when the lama was found perfectly fit, except for some scars. To say that the general was astonished would be an understatement. He retreated.

Rangdol then told me about another occasion when some Christian missionaries came from China and settled on a field across the river from the saint's cave. They converted the people and soon a flourishing village sprang up. The people got worried and went to the great one, requesting a miracle to save the faith. At first, he refused. But they persuaded him. The next morning, he took a stick and carefully aimed it like a gun at the Christian settlement. Then he threw some ashes towards it, each time shouting, 'Boom!' in the manner of a cannon. Nothing happened.

But the next day, there was an earthquake, which swallowed up all the fields of the Christians. The people were spared. The mission immediately returned to China.

Lama Kungaji added some more information: once Mifam Rimpoche was praying at the foot of a hill, when a rakshasani rolled down a stone as big as a house. The venerable lama merely pointed his *phurpa* at the stone and it rolled back up the hill! This reminds me of the story of the Panja Sahib gurdwara in present-day Pakistan where Guru Nanak merely lifted his palm to send a stone rolled off a hill by Wali Kandhari rolling back upwards. At another time, there was a great forest fire in Kham, which the lama stopped by his mere presence. I asked Kungaji if he had seen any of these miracles. He said no, but related that when he was in Kifug, a fire threatened the monastery. When Lama Mifam moved a cloth at the fire, it was stilled. Kungaji told me that he had seen this happening. The lama was also reportedly a great expert in the Tibetan system of medicine. He could blow on a vessel full of water and give it to the sick as a guaranteed cure. He was also an expert in making charms called *shringa*, which means 'to save'.

It was evident that Mifam Rimpoche was famous all over Tibet as a great healer and seer. When Lama Kungaji talked of him, he leant forward slightly; there was a light in his eyes and he talked in slow passionate tones. Everyone listened with rapt attention. Their facial expressions showed complete belief and there seemed to be no doubt in their minds about the powers of the rimpoche. These grave-faced people, listening to the slow cadences of a cadaverous-looking white haired man, seemed like a Catholic ecclesiastical council in session.

I then asked Lama Rangdol about a matter which always intrigued me. Tibetans visit the Golden Temple in Amritsar in large numbers, and what is more, they treat it with great reverence. While Sikhs walk around the sacred tank, Tibetans circumambulate it, that is, they will stand, mutter a prayer, then lie full length, stand up and again say the prayer. Considering that the walk around is almost half a mile, the feat calls for considerable faith and devotion. Lama Rangdol said that Tibetans considered Guru Nanak to be an incarnation of Guru Padma Sambhava. There is no mention of Guru Nanak in Tibetan writings, but somehow, this fact was widely known in Tibet. Though Tibetans did not come to India for a special pilgrimage to Amritsar, they invariably visited it after Bodh Gaya. Strangely, they do not care about other gurdwaras, not even Nankana Sahib, the birth place of Guru Nanak. Perhaps they have associated Guru Nanak entirely with the Golden Temple. Lama Kungaji said that Lahaulas did not know of this legend and so did not visit the Golden Temple.

Dorje told me another theory later. At first, the Tibetans felt that the Sikhs were just another sect initiated by Guru Padma Sambhava. Then Gedun Chomphel, a great Tibetan scholar, who spent some time with Nicholas Roerich at Kulu, and later visited Oxford, showed by historical research that Padma Sambhava could not have founded the Sikh faith and that Guru Nanak was really an incarnation of Guru Padma Sambhava. Whatever the fact, the Tibetans revere Guru Nanak. There is a large portrait of Guru Nanak in the main shrine at Riwalsar in Himachal Pradesh, which is an important Buddhist pilgrimage centre.

While we were talking, the young Lama Tashi came in. I immediately turned the conversation on him. Why would they not let him study? Why should they force him into lamahood when he was too young to decide for himself? They seemed embarrassed and the master of ceremonies tried a weak reply. The boy was very bright. His father, also a lama, wanted him in this line. I replied that precisely because the boy was bright, he should study and that it was wrong for the father to settle the boy's future. The chamberlain then confessed that there was a lack of good initiates. No one wanted to become a lama, he wailed. I replied that no faith could be kept alive by the press gang method. There must be a spontaneous love amongst the flock for the shepherd. He then played his last card: a very wise lama had died in a neighbouring village some time back. From the boy's early actions and behaviour, they were convinced that he was the incarnation of the good lama! They wanted to make a great lama out of him. To this I had no reply! I also felt that it may not be correct for me to press them beyond a point. I dropped the subject, though I felt sorry for this bright young lad. The faith was already disappearing. With a few more years of roads, jeeps, community development and contact with the plains, it would lose whatever little power it had. The boys of the Kyelang High School were going out to a world of vast opportunities. Tashi could have been with those boys. Years later, I met Tashi again, now a young lama, and a fine painter of thankas.

As we were getting up to leave, the lamas pushed Tashi forward to request for powdered milk. It was amusing to find that lamas in a remote Himalayan monastery were addicted to such milk. Indeed, the twentieth-century Romans conquer with powdered milk!

We then went to have a look at the monastery. There were only three rooms worth any interest. Two were at opposite ends of the gallery, and another one was down a dark flight of stairs.

As we entered the first room, we saw a silver mounted chorten about four feet high in the left corner. This contained the skull and ashes of Lama Norbu, the founder. He died in about 1952 and was a colleague of Lama Kungaji. Together, they had built the Karding monastery. On the right of the chorten were two statues of Padma Sambhava and Tara Devi. At the far end of the room, near the window, was a statue of Tagdun Shakya Shri, the guru of Lama Kungaji, and grandfather of Hishe Rangdol. All the statues had the usual seven cups of water in front of them. None of them was of any great beauty. Behind the statues, in pigeon holes along the wall, were the one hundred and three books of the *Tangyur*. No monastery in Lahaul has all the two hundred and twenty-six volumes of the *Tangyur*. In the centre of the room, in wooden pigeon holes, were the sixty-four books of the *Tantras*. These contained instructions on samadhis, healing formulas and other occult practices.

The walls were lined with paintings on big sheets of mounted paper. They were obviously the work of Darjeeling artists and were not very good. They were draped with thin cloth, which was so dirty that it had lost all colour, and was literally rotting through the action of accumulated grime. There were, however, three or four thankas of the wheel of Avalokiteshvara and Guru Padma Sambhava, which were good. The colours were bright and the lines of the figures masterly.

The second room was the main prayer room. The main statue there was of Avalokiteshvara. It had eleven faces, one above the other. The practice is to have one, eleven, or a thousand faces. On the right was a raised seat with the cloak and other possessions of Lama Norbu, the founder of the monastery. This seat is not occupied by anyone. In a box in front of this seat was a *thotpa*, a human skull bowl. It had three lines and a hole in the middle. The bone was worn smooth, though the inside was rough and blackish. The lamas were acutely embarrassed by my interest in it.*

---

*Thotpas are nothing but hollowed-out skulls. People generally declare their intention of donating their skulls during life. After death, the skull is sawed in such a manner that it has a bit of the nose bone, the eye sockets, and the ear bones. After cutting, it is buried in moist ground and taken out after about six months. By this time, the flesh disappears, and only the firm bone remains. It is then cleaned. A senior lama performs a special puja for three days and eats the first offering of food out of it. The thotpa is then ready for use.

Thotpas are usually made in Tibet, where it is easier to get a skull as the dead body is broken and fed to the vultures. In Lahaul, cremation

We then went to the third room, the lamas visibly relieved at my departure from the second room. The way there was down a dark staircase. At the start of the railing was a mounted prayer wheel. I gave it a clockwise push and it spun noiselessly like a top, saying my prayers for me. Down below was a gallery with a room on the left. Outside the door were more mounted prayer wheels. The room was dimly lit by a window and the light from the door. In the left hand corner was a huge prayer wheel, the wooden drum was over six feet high. It was perfectly mounted and balanced, and began to rotate on a single push. On the top was a brass bell. Every time it passed a certain point on the

---

is the custom and it is not easy to get anyone to donate their skull. I could not find any recent example of the making of a thotpa.

Thotpas are said to be of eighteen kinds. Some have a crack or line running down from the forehead to the neck, and another one from ear to ear. A thotpa with only one of these two lines is known as *dambu-chigpa*, and is preferred. If a thotpa has a small hole at the bottom, it is liked very much, for then the bowl has only to be held over the cupped hands of the devotee and the chhaang will drip into them. I saw a thotpa in Sonam Ram's house. Of all places, it was placed casually on a sewing machine! Dorje pointed it out quietly and while pretending to admire the dumbargyee kilkhur, I had a good look at it. It had two lines and was of a muddy colour, with a smooth highly polished outer surface. (I did not make my interest obvious as it might have embarrassed my host.) The thotpa is highly valued by the lamas as it is an essential part of all pujas. When Lama Norbu, the founder of Karding monastery died, he left behind considerable wealth and a big dambu-chigpa thotpa. His disciples, numbering about fifty, quarrelled for a long time over its ownership and the matter was settled with great difficulty. No one bothered about the rest of Lama Norbu's property.

All lamas cannot eat out of a thotpa. Only those qualified and allowed by their guru can do so. But once permitted, they do so normally and without any fuss. For them, there is no excitement in it. The cup which provided romance and high drama for the poet Byron and his friends is an article of convenience only for many in Lahaul.

circle, it knocked against an iron point and rang. The walls had some more paintings on paper. In front was a statue of Arya Devi with faded thankas on the wall behind.

I was glad to get out of the dungeon and went to see a lama's cell. The one we went into was of two nuns. It had two small and clean rooms. One room had an iron fireplace and cooking utensils. The other contained the clothes and other knick-knacks. There was a small latrine of the local type.*

Finally, we went up to the roof to take some photos. The sun was sinking fast behind Dilburi and I wanted to hurry. When I asked Hishe Rangdol to pose, he immediately gave an order to his factotum in Tibetan. The man soon returned with the most magnificent hat I have ever seen. It was of heavy red Chinese silk and shaped like a Catholic bishop's mitre. Hishe also put a golden silk mantle around his shoulders. In full regalia, he looked like a cardinal from Rome. I have always wondered at the great similarity between the robes of the Catholic and Tibetan clergy. The robes are so alike that but for the features and the setting, the Tibetan dignitaries can be mistaken for high Roman church fathers. Dorje says that the Tibetan dresses are copied from the dresses of the Russian Orthodox church. I am inclined

---

*The waste system in Lahaul is a hole in a small room on the first storey. The waste falls into an enclosure on the ground, away from the entrance to the house. Cow dung and mud is thrown in the hole to encourage decomposition after every use. The collected manure is cleared twice a year, in May and October. It is carried in baskets by the women of the house and deposited in the fields. There is no taboo about carrying it.

These latrines are ideal for Lahaul. The waste makes fine manure and there is no filth in the fields around the village as there is in the villages of the Punjab plains. Besides, in winter, one cannot use the snow-covered fields to relieve oneself. Necessity in this case happens to be a virtue. This practice is also known to other hill people in the country. The Apa Tanis of Arunachal Pradesh, who live on the upper storey of bamboo houses, use a similar system.

to agree. The influence may even have come from Constantinople along the old silk routes.*

I left Lahaul in 1963. In 1966, the Punjab was unfortunately divided up. Haryana was created east of Chandigarh, and the entire God-given Kangra valley, including Lahaul-Spiti, joined Himachal Pradesh. Punjab gave away all the hill areas above 3000 feet, including Simla and many other places. I was deputy commissioner at Ambala at the time of this division, and then went to Jalandhar as deputy commissioner in the new Punjab. The loss of the mountain areas only made my passion for Lahaul even greater. In 1967, before I went to Cambridge, my newly married wife, Vinnie, and I went to Lahaul for a visit. I wanted to show her this lost Shangrila. We stayed in Manali at Nehru's forest rest house. The next day, we hoped to get a lift in a PWD engineer's jeep to Rahla, and then walk straight up to the pass and beyond. I was now a stranger to Himachal, an outsider. The engineer never turned up till the middle of the day. Mountain walks are best taken with an early start. But we had no choice and we started late in the day from Rahla, climbing straight up to Marhi. I still had the foolish pride of my past fitness, but as we climbed those thousands and thousands of rocky steps, my

---

*'The third grand lama of Tibet visited Lahaul while I was there in 1867, inspecting the monasteries, and giving his benediction to the people at places where he halted. He travelled in quaintly shaped, bright coloured tents carried on yaks, with a considerable retinue of monks. I saw him seated on a throne or platform, built up in the open air, dressed in a mitre and silk canonicals, extraordinarily like those worn by Roman Catholic prelates.' (Sir James Lyall, quoted in *Kangra District Gazetteer*, 1897)

stamina began to give way. Vinnie and my Jalandhar peon, Karamchand, felt just fine. Karamchand, in fact, had never seen these high mountains, but like Kipling's Hurree Babu, umbrella in hand, he went up like a mountain goat. Vinnie too traipsed along, making fun of the great Tenzing-trained mountaineer's woes!

As we went above about eleven thousand feet, past Marhi, every step became a torture for me. I knew we had to get to the top as there was no turning back, and Khoksar on the other side was a long long way away. I struggled on. Finally, we made it to the top. I had a splitting headache and there was no way we could make the long walk down to Khoksar rest house in the late evening. The top had a single typical Tibetan teashop. The front of the shabby tent was the shop and the back, the sleeping place with a hillman's blankets and yak-skins. I asked if we could stay. The man welcomed us. Over tea, we watched the evening fade into darkness from the top of the pass. The slow changing of the cloud-shot sky's colours from gold to russet to maroon to dark grey remains painted in my memory. I slept surprisingly well in the Khampa's modest bedroom and woke up fresh in the morning. We had the experience of a lifetime, watching the sun come up over the Kulu and Lahaul valleys. After parathas, we walked gaily down to Khoksar, picking daisies and buttercups on the way.

Once at Kyelang, we again went to Karding gompa, and surprisingly, met two young English girls there. They were pupils of Professor Snellgrove of the School of Oriental and African Studies, London, and had taken monastic orders from a high Tibetan lama in Dalhousie. Their guru had sent them to Lahaul to live in the monastery, learn of the faith, and practise austerities. They declared themselves completely content with the life at the monastery. The short bespectacled younger girl seemed more open to the world. When on the terrace of the monastery I wanted to take pictures, she was happy to stand with the older monks and look into the camera. The older girl, then in her early twenties, seemed much more focussed on her religious pursuits and kept her head down, refusing to look at the camera.

Later, we kept going back to Lahaul. In the 1980s, I went with Vinnie and my three girls. Since I always kept in touch with Lahaul people and Dorje, I had learned that one girl had gone back to England and a householder's life, but the other, named Diane Perry, had continued to practise her austerities with great determination. Dorje told me that she had ultimately moved to an isolated cave, high above Kyelang, barricaded it against winter visits by snow leopards, and spent years and years in isolated meditation. When we went to Kyelang in the 1980s, I expressed the hope of meeting her. Dorje said that she rarely came down for human contact. There must have been some telepathic communication between us because that afternoon, she came down and met us in the rest house. At the time, our second daughter Gauri used to have nightmares and was afraid of the dark. The English *chomo* talked to Gauri gently, held her with piercing eyes and gave her great comfort. I remember she assured Gauri, 'Think of me when you are frightened and I will be with you.' Gauri's worries of the darkness ended that day.

More years passed, and on later visits to the valley, I was told that the nun had left following harassment by the police. She had taken a Tibetan name, Tenzin Palmo, and had set up nunneries in Italy and Palampur. A couple of years back, she lectured at the India International Centre in Delhi, where I met her. She now goes around the world promoting Buddhism and the cause of women in the faith.

But to go back to my story of then, Dorje and I finally said goodbye to the lamas, and in the golden evening sunlight, started down to the emerald river and home. How many times have I since then been to Karding, often at different seasons of the summer! The walk from the Bhaga up the slopes, through bushes of wild roses, pink and yellow, with poplars standing tall against the Goshal snow peak above Tandi can never be erased from my memory. We would sit on the grassy slope, watching the rills of ice cold water gurgle past, while we sipped tea and looked down at the camel-coloured cube houses of Kyelang. The scene is fresh in my mind and its recollection always brings tranquillity to the soul. Photographs, after all, fade but the reel in the mind never does till the final stillness. I am reminded of a Wordsworth poem that I read during my school days:

> For oft, when on my couch I lie
> In vacant or in pensive mood,
> They flash upon that inward eye
> Which is the bliss of solitude;
> And then my heart with pleasure fills,
> And dances with the daffodils.

The Rising of the Dead

We are the Pilgrims, master: we shall go
Always a little further: it may be
Beyond that last blue mountain barred with snow,
Across that angry or that glimmering sea . . .

—James Elory Flecker

I was having a leisurely Sunday lunch in the sun when Dorje dropped in with the news that an old lama had died in Beeling. If we hurried, we could see the funeral. I rushed through my lunch and we were off. The rhythmic beating of drums could be heard clearly, and it appeared that the body was being taken out. We hurried through Beeling down to the village cremation ground in the fields.

The body was already fixed in stacks of wood and the lamas were saying the prayers. They had made a small altar under a willow tree. The usual *sattu* lumps decorated with butter had been put on it. The lamas were sitting on the ground. Every now and then, a bleary-eyed lama, still dizzy from last night's chhaang would yawn massively, but the prayers went on at a fast pace. Some men from the village who were to burn the corpse were standing around smoking and joking. They would also have been drinking chhaang, but my presence was perhaps a dampener. According to custom, the family of the dead provides chhaang to the pall bearers at the cremation ground.

The men waited casually for the lamas to finish. One of them went a few yards from the pyre and began to relieve himself there. The *lohaar** played the funeral dirge on his drums every now and then. The atmosphere was not at all heavy with sorrow. Having finished that particular prayer, the lamas lighted a piece of bhojpatra. This was handed to one of the men and he set fire to the pyre. Holy water was sprinkled on the pyre. Drums were beaten and conches blown. A couple of young boys got hold of one of the two conches and blew it in turns, thoroughly enjoying the fun. The lamas immediately started a *havan*. I was surprised to find this typically Hindu practice adopted by the Buddhists. Offerings of rice, barley, mustard, ghee, wheat, grass, cloth and food had been laid out on a red cloth. The lamas had a *havan kund* made of iron. It was about six inches square at the top and had a long handle. On the floor, it had a *dorje* symbol. The top of the handle was also fashioned into a dorje. The *sarua*–the little cup with which the offering was poured into the havan kund–was similarly fashioned, with a dorje at the end of the handle. There was thus an obvious mixing of Buddhist and Hindu religious practices in the shape of a havan kund with dorje symbols.

---

*'The lohaars consider themselves of a higher caste than the Shipis, but both are said by the other Lahaulis, to have no religion at all; still they have certain rites which are performed in cases of sickness and burials. For instance, I was present one day by the sick bed of a lohaar, and saw a Shipi profess to charm away the disease, by biting off the ears and tearing to pieces with his teeth a black kid, which had been previously shot with a gun.' (Reverend Hyde, quoted in the *Kangra District Gazetteer*, 1897)

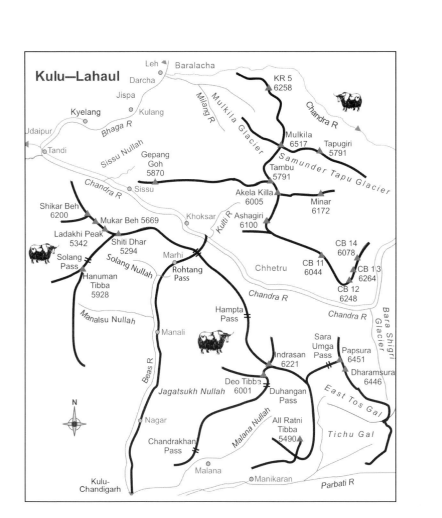

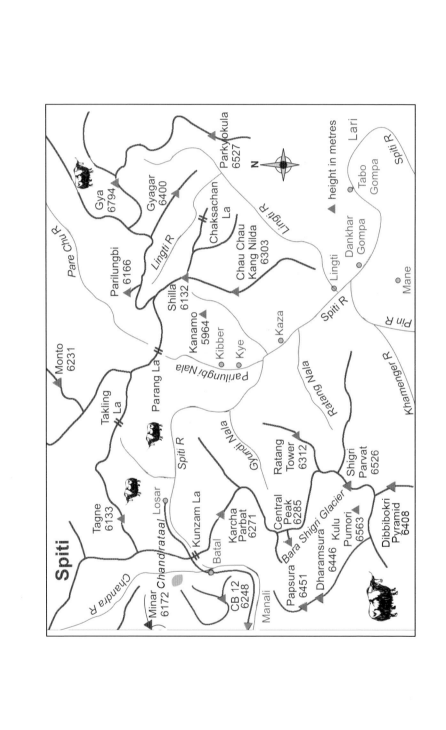

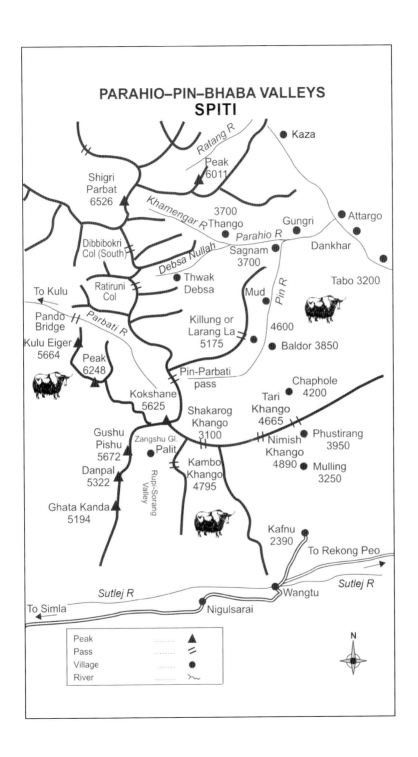

PARAHIO–PIN–BHABA VALLEYS
SPITI

Ratang R

● Kaza

Peak
6011

Shigri
Parbat
6526

Khamengar R

3700
Thango
Parahio R

Gungri ●

● Attargo

Dibbibokri
Col (South)

Debsa Nullah

Sagnam
3700

Dankhar

●

Tabo 3200

To Kulu

Ratiruni
Col

Thwak
Debsa

Mud ●

Pin R

Pando
Bridge

Parbati R

Killung or
Larang La
5175

4600

Kulu Eiger
5664

● Baldor 3850

Peak
6248

Pin-Parbati
pass

Chaphole
4200

Kokshane
5625

Shakarog
Khango
3100

Tari ●
Khango
4665

Gushu
Pishu
5672

Zangshu Gl.
● Palit

Nimish
Khango
4890

Phustirang
3950

Danpal
5322

Rupi-Sorang Valley

Kambo
Khango
4795

● Mulling
3250

Ghata Kanda
5194

Kafnu
2390

To Rekong Peo →

Sutlej R

Wangtu

Sutlej R

← To Simla

Nigulsarai

Peak	....	▲
Pass	....	∥
Village	....	●
River	....	〜

N

A Lahaul lama.

Kancha of Yoksum village,
Sikkim, *circa* 1960.

Gaddi beauty on her way to Lahaul pastures, *circa* 1960.

A Spiti lass harvesting barley, *circa* 1960.

The young Spiti lad in Gue village dressed up for a wedding, *circa* 1960.

Lahaul schoolgirls, *circa* 1960.

School children in Gue, Spiti, *circa* 1960.

My Kyelang neighbours
in winter.

The Gotsi mother.

Spiti beauties, *circa* 1961.

A Spiti family, *circa* 1961.

Time for a chat. The Goshal peak is in the background.

A Punjab Armed Police jawan at Kaurik, looking down at a Tibetan valley.

Fauja Singh.

Tenzing Norgay and me.

Vinnie with the two English nuns at Karding in 1967. Tenzin Palmo
is on Vinnie's right with her eyes downcast.

Dumbaji, the abbot of Sha-shur, started the havan ritual. One of his assistants gave him a cup of grain placed on the red cloth and he went through the motions of putting it in the kund, all the while chanting, 'We consign to thee his grain.' Then he poured the grain on a brass plate and the man went and flung it on the burning pyre. Next, ghee was offered and they chanted, 'We consign to thee his ghee,' and it was put on the pyre, and so on, all the while with the chanting, 'We consign to thee his cloth. We consign to thee his seeds. We consign to thee his riches . . .'

While the name of the material consigned was in Tibetan, the phrase 'Om swaha' was used each time. This is Sanskrit and it slowly became obvious that Buddhist and Hindu practices are mixed and used in the funeral ceremonies. As soon as the lamas had finished the havan ritual, they went back to the house of the deceased. The villagers stayed on till the pyre was completely burnt. Nowadays, they sometimes go home earlier if it gets too dark. The corpse is left to burn out during the night.

Before the pyre was lighted, I had a close look at the dead lama. The body was naked and in a sitting position; with me like Aristotle contemplating a bust of Homer, and the corpse like the famous nude of Bernard Shaw leaning forward, in a thinking pose, right elbow on the knee, the fist supporting the chin.

I shall now try to explain the Lahaula death rites in a chronological manner. As soon as a person dies, someone runs out and informs the village people. Immediately, one man from each family in the village arrives. The body is left lying as it is and is not touched. A sheet may be spread on it. A lamp is lit. The lamas are sent for, but even they may not do anything till the umzad has arrived. The umzad is the master of ceremonies at funerals and is none other than the head lama of the local monastery. He goes up to the corpse and whispers 'You are dead' thrice in its ear. The original custom in Tibet was to catch the ear and shout into it. Now the umzad leans forward and whispers. Till this is done, the ceremonies cannot start. The belief is that the soul is not convinced of the death of the mortal body till the umzad tells it so. Then, it begins to realize this fact and as it looks down on the mortal remains, it sees not a human body, but an animal one, depending on its year of birth. Thus, if the dead person was born in the year of the rat as stated in the Tibetan calendar, the soul sees a rat; and if he or she was born in the year of the monkey, the soul sees a dead monkey, and so on. The Tibetan calendar has a cycle of the following twelve years—rat, ox, tiger, rabbit, dragon, snake, horse, sheep, monkey, bird, dog and pig.

After this, the body can be touched. The lamas start praying while the *robdagpa* lift the body and place it in a sitting posture, if necessary, tying it in place. The body is screened off by a cloth curtain and is also wrapped in a white sheet. I must explain who the robdagpa are. Originally, they were men from four families of Gumrang who alone touched the body. They also brought the conches and the funeral flags. They carried the body out. For these services, they were given money, clothes and grain. The estates of Barbog and Karding had their own robdagpas. These families gave up this traditional work at least forty years back, maybe longer. Now each village has its own flags and conches. As for the bearers, any person who touches the body is considered to be the robdagpa. In other words, the body is now carried by the people of the village. The robdagpa are given some money on the last day along with the lamas, and they are also fed. If they do not come to the house on some day, food is sent to them.

Two funeral flags, about two by six feet, with red, yellow, white and blue checks in four horizontal and twelve vertical squares are carried with the bier. The flag sticks are burnt with the pyre, but the flags are brought back and are usually kept in the monastery along with the two conches.

The grieving family decides the number of days that the body is to be kept in the house. The maximum reported duration is three days. During these days, the lamas read the scriptures the whole day through. In the evening, after a bout of chhaang, they sleep there. At night, the village men, well-fortified with chhaang keep vigil by the body.

Dorje told me an amusing story about this practice. Once an old man died in his village of Guskiar, which had only six families. A couple of men went off to inform the relatives and lamas. Only Dorje and his cousin Nawang Tashi were left to guard the body at night. Reluctantly, they sat down by its side. Both were nervous and finally Tashi said, 'Dorje I am scared. Bring some chhaang.' With courage in the form of liquid fire inside him, he forgot his fears. After some time, the corpse passed wind and sounds were heard in its belly. There is a belief that after the soul has left the body an evil spirit can enter the body, which then gets up and begins to dance.*

Now, as the gases in the corpse grumbled, Tashi thought they were about to see a rolance. But the chhaang had done its work. Instead of getting scared, he gave the corpse a couple of sound cuffs, and then tied it with ropes. Both attendants then slept soundly till the morning!

---

*This phenomenon of the revival of corpses is known as *rolance*—*ro* means corpse and *lance* means to rise. As soon as it rises, the corpse-devil blows on the men in the room, and they turn into spirits, that is, they maintain their bodies, but have evil spirits in them. The whole party then goes out dancing, led by the rolance. On the way, they will blow on anyone who meets them and he too turns evil and follows. The devil keeps going straight on, and like the Gadarene swine, is often thrown off a precipice, along with the men. All are killed. Sometimes, they may run into a holy lama, who will then destroy the rolance, and restore the men to sanity. Therefore, if a dead body begins to move, the chances are, that it is about to become a rolance. To prevent this, the body should be cut immediately. The evil spirit enters a whole body only. The cut flesh should be burnt or fed to a dog. If it is thrown carelessly, it will come and rejoin the body, making it whole, and dangerously receptive to rolance.

The family of the dead person are kept separate and do not enter the room in which the body is kept. The lohaars sit on the roof if it is summer or in a room nearby and play a dirge on their drums. The body is usually bathed on the day of death or the next. This is done in a perfunctory manner and is not even considered essential. If the body is to be burnt on the day of death, the bath can be dispensed with.

The family then decides when the body is to be burnt. Once the decision is taken, the lamas look up the time of taking the body out. They ask for the year of birth, and then look up a book, which gives the appropriate time for persons born in each of the twelve years of the Tibetan cycle.

Meanwhile, the lohaars prepare a bier for carrying the body. The bier can be as simple as one with sticks lashed together, to which the body is tied in a sitting posture. These days, in places like Kyelang, they place a chair on a bed and tie the body on it. The custom was to burn the bier with the body, but now no one wants to lose valuable chairs and beds. They are left at the site of the cremation for the night and brought back the next day. This is enough to cleanse them. The carriage poles are cut to make steps—the idea being to provide a symbolic ladder to heaven.

The robdagpa carry the body out at the appointed time and tie it to the seat. The body is tied in a white cloth. Jewels are put on females. These are brought back later and used normally. Around the chair, a cloth screen is fixed and the cloth can be of any colour.

While the body is inside the house, some jewellery is tied in a bundle and placed next to it. This is called *yangkhug puja*. The idea is that all the goodness of the person passes into the jewellery. When the body is brought out, the jewellery is also brought with it. The lamas then hold prayers, the last one being yangkhug. After this prayer, the jewellery is given to some member of the family who takes it inside the house, thus taking with them all the goodness and other qualities of the dead person. The person taking the jewellery in does not come out or look at the body till it is taken away.

All the relatives kneel and bow to the body and take leave of it. They then go back inside the house and do not accompany the funeral procession. The flag and conch bearers and the lohaars circle the body in a clockwise direction. After this, the body is carried out by the robdogpa. But if it is too heavy, as it generally is with the chair and what not, then others help. The funeral procession is led by a lama band. Every now and then, the bier is put down and the lohaars and flag bearers circle it to the beat of drums. The family decides on the number of circles to be taken on the way because they have to pay for each circle. Circling is considered good because all the money paid is charity in the name of the deceased.

At the funeral ground, the body is completely stripped; if it is a woman's body, this is done behind a screen. The clothes are given to the lohaars. If the cremation ground is new, then the lamas conduct a puja and mark a circle with a dorje and lotus drawn in it. In a funeral ground already in use, only the dorje and the lotus are marked on the ground where the pyre is to be set. If sand from Bodh Gaya is available, it is spread on the ground. The body is then fixed in wood in a sitting posture. The white coffin cloth is torn and tied to the four corners of the pyre, and one piece is placed on top of the centre.

The lamas then start the prayers and the pyre is lighted with bhojpatra. Once the pyre has been lighted, the havan that has been described earlier begins. The lohaars continue to beat a dirge on their drums and conches are blown. When the havan is completed, the lamas go back to the house, but the village men stay till the body is burnt. No relatives or women attend cremations.

Meanwhile, after the body is taken out of the house, the place where it had been kept is plastered with dung. Barley flour is sprinkled on the spot and the area is covered with a basket on which a carpenter's saw is placed. The next morning, when the basket is lifted, it is said that the footprint of the animal into which the soul of the deceased has been reincarnated shows on the barley flour.

This news is conveyed to the relatives of the dead by people from the village. At this point, they come crying and lamenting into the village, very much like the Punjabis. They also bring chhaang and sattu, the quantity depending on their customary dealings with the family. Sattu and chhaang ration is also collected from all the families in the village.

The family then decides on the type of prayers to be offered. It may be one or even two expensive dambargyas, or it may be a cheaper prayer ceremony, such as *tshogs* or *mithugpa*. The lamas return from the cremation ground, say some prayers and then settle down to chhaang! The next day, the prayers begin and go on for a number of days, depending on the type of ceremony being performed.

On the day following the cremation, the lohaar goes to the cremation ground and plays his drums. Then one lama goes and collects the bones. He puts these in a bag and the bones are taken to the house, and kept near the praying lamas. The lamas put a paper on the bag of bones, with the invocation, 'Om *aha hung*'. On the last day of the prayers, the bones are thrown at the confluence of the Chandra and Bhaga at Tandi. The lama carrying them is escorted a little way by the full lama band, and a little further by the lohaar drummers. He then proceeds alone. At the confluence, he takes out the bones one by one and throws them into the river, all the time reciting specific mantras. The bag, however, is brought back. Earlier, one bone from each cremation was kept by the lamas. The collected bones were then ground and made into slabs and placed in caves above the Guru Ghantal monastery. Guru Ghantal is situated on a high ridge overlooking the Tandi confluence. This custom has since disappeared, but some of these slabs may be seen even today.

Once the prayers are completed, the lamas are paid. Some money and utensils are given to the monastery, and some money is paid to the lamas. In its division, the umzad naturally gets a bigger share.

Before leaving, the lamas look up a book that indicates if good or bad luck will come from a particular death. The calculation is made considering the year of birth and the time of death. The lamas rarely predict good omens. The poor family then has to request a tana mana prayer immediately afterwards to ward off evil. Thus, these holy ones remain perpetually in business. Last year, on a death, they predicted ten more deaths in Kyelang. Eight people soon died, and the deputy commissioner remarked that it might be his turn soon!

The very next day after the Beeling lama's death, the mother of Kalzan, the Mayor of Kyelang, died. The lamas left the prayers for the poor Beeling lama and rushed to Kyelang, knowing that Kalzan would spend a lot of money and that chhaang would flow freely. The old lady was carried on a decorated chair covered with green cloth to sounds of the orchestra and the beating of drums. Later, three successive dambargya were performed and the prayers lasted eight days. Kalzan paid two hundred and fifty rupees along with some utensils for the monastery. This was considered lavish.

There is an alternate theory that the body should be kept in the house for seven days because the King of Death is considered to be so busy that he makes mistakes. There may be people of the same name in the village. It may happen that the mistake will be discovered, the clerks chastized, and the man restored to life! It is also believed that ideally, after the cremation, prayers should continue for forty-nine days. Yamraj, the lord of the other world, is always busy. It takes him a long time to weigh the person's good deeds against his bad ones and decide whether he is to go to heaven or hell. In this, Yamraj is assisted by two clerks, one with a monkey's face and the other with a bull's. When a man is born, two spirits, one evil and one good, come with him. All through life, these two are in constant conflict. When the soul appears before Yamraj, these spirits appear with it. The clerks then weigh the soul's good deeds against the bad and rewards or punishment are given. The prayers for the soul till the forty-ninth day after death are believed to count to its good deeds fund. Sometimes, these may tip the scale in favour of heaven and thus save the soul. Nowadays, of course, no one can afford the expense of such lengthy prayers. The body is kept at home for a maximum of three days, and prayers do not last more than ten days.

In the case of Kalzan's mother, the lamas pronounced evil omens for one of the family's women. They prescribed a tana mana, which was promptly requested! Now all is well.

Sometimes the supposed evil influence is believed to be so severe that it will last for years. The lamas perform a tana mana and go away. After a year, if a sheep dies, the family rushes to the lamas, who piously hold forth that the evil spirit is so powerful that it has come back. Reluctantly, they go back for another tana mana. This goes on and on and the family does not rid itself of these benefactors for years. All these rituals remind one of the doings of the pandits of the plains, who milk the people equally effectively. The lamas were still busy at Kalzan's house, when another old woman died in lower Kyelang. They were in luck and the prayers, the chhaang and money flowed all over again.

Every night, I could hear the deep-throated gyadung and the shrill geling. They sounded so ominous in the still, silent, moonlight-bathed valley with the ghostly peaks as sentinels. I could not take my thoughts off death. It seemed to stalk the village and I wondered who would be next. I began to hate this death music and prayed for the departure of these holy men.

Within one year following his mother's death, Kalzan

distributed sattu dumplings called *gewa* to the three villages of Gumrang, Karding and Barbog. Only those who come to his house on an appointed day will get these. Poor people do not generally give gewa as they cannot afford it. On his mother's first death anniversary, Kalzan gave food and chhaang to the entire village. This has to be done even by the poor. After this, the family can rest at last, or more likely, prepare for the next departure.

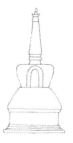

Tales of the Dead

Like one, that on a lonesome road
Doth walk in fear and dread,
And having once turned round walks on,
And turns no more his head;
Because he knows, a frightful fiend
Doth close behind him tread.

—Samuel Taylor Coleridge

Rolance, or the 'rising of corpses', is a widely believed phenomenon in Lahaul. In this chapter, I have related some cases of rolance, which reportedly occurred in the past.

The first case is from upper Kyelang and occurred about a hundred years back. There was a woman in the village who had a red mole above her right breast. From this and other signs, a lama had predicted that there was grave danger of her becoming a rolance after death. He advised people that her body was to be burnt on the very day she died. Even in life, there was something about her that scared people.

Now, it so happened that in the month of February, people were observing the Nye Nye Nyung Ne festival, similar to the

Christian retreat. For two days, people keep a vow of silence and fast, spending their time listening to religious discourses by lamas. The woman died during this retreat. Most of the men, bound by a vow of silence, were unable to help in the funeral and the woman's body had to be kept for the night. There was an agnostic couple in the village, who had not kept the retreat and they promised to keep vigil by the body along with some lohaars. They tied up the body with ropes, and after trussing it to a seat, also tied it to the ceiling beam. For any emergency, they kept an axe with them.

Sometime during the night, there was a rumbling in the body. The couple woke up and watched fascinated as soon, the body began to fill with gas. It expanded and burst all the ropes holding it like a circus strong man. Its tongue hung out until it was almost down to the navel. The eyes took on a fiery glow, became big and started bulging out of their sockets.

The rolance stood up and walked to the door. By this time, all the lohaars had run away. Now, the door happened to be a small one; before the Moravian missionaries came to Lahaul, the doors were small and windows, non-existent. It was well known that rolances cannot bend. While it was struggling with the door, the couple snapped out of their hypnotic trance. The woman was brave and she grabbed the rolance around its waist. The husband cut at it furiously with his axe, but the cuts healed instantly. Thus they continued attacking the rolance for a long time.

By now, it was dawn and the lamas, knowing of the prophecy, rushed to the house. Most people ran away on seeing the fierce appearance of the rolance, but Yeshe Meme, the head lama and umzad of Sha-shur monastery, stood his ground and stuck his phurpa into the rolance, which collapsed immediately. The villagers soon collected and the body was carried out for burning. When the bier was being taken to be cremated, a fox suddenly leapt out of it and ran to the cremation ground. As it reached the ground, a huge flame shot into the sky. The lamas alleged that the evil spirit had thus been driven out. This story is well known in Kyelang and the rolance woman was an ancestor of Angrup, who lives in upper Kyelang.

There is another story from Karding, across the river from Kyelang. This also is about a woman who, in this case, lived with a young female companion. It so happened that when the older woman died, most of the men were away. Only a few cowardly men and the woman were left in the village. The young woman ran out at night to inform the people that her older companion was dead. The men went to the house and found the body lying on the ground under a sheet. They were discussing the funeral arrangements when the sheet began to move slowly. The head came up first. The people sat glued to their seats as life seemed to flow out of their limbs. The corpse sat up, opened its eyes, and asked for food. Quickly, a bowl of thukpa was produced, which it ate greedily.

At this point, the young woman said that in the past, the old woman seemed to have died a number of times, but in each case, got up after some time. She had therefore not informed anyone. This time, being sure of the woman's death, she had told the people. Since the woman once again seemed alive, the other people went back home. Late at night, the girl spotted signs of a rolance in the old woman's body. Blood flowed out of its nostrils and was licked in by the tongue, which was beginning to hang out. Its eyes began to bulge. The young woman quickly got out of the house and locked it. She spent the night with friends. No one dared venture near the house to investigate. In the morning, when they opened the house, they found the body terribly bloated with the tongue hanging out. The people lost no time in burning the body.

This story was related by Dorje's maternal grandmother named Doma, who belonged to Karding and claimed to have seen this event. She was over eighty when she died about ten years back.

Another rolance tale is about the village of Khering in the lower Lahaul valley. The village is situated on the left bank of the Chandrabhaga in Pattan valley. It is reached by taking a rope-jhula bridge across the river from the Udaipur road. A village of about thirty families, it is approached by a beautiful path along a water kuhl that flows through a poplar and willow forest. It was the practice of the men of the village to go into Bara Banghal in the Chamba area before the winter properly set in. They spent the cold months there, working as timber loggers to earn some money. They returned in early spring for the Basant festival.

A young man named Namgyal lived in Khering with his wife and little son. He was a good farmer and cultivated barley and *kuth* in the summers. One winter, along with other men of the village, Namgyal crossed the Kaali-sho *jote* into Chamba to work in the forest. Months went by, and as the snow began to melt and the first buds of spring appeared on the trees, his wife Pangmo longed for his return so that they could enjoy the Basant festivities. Every day, she watched the road across the river and the rope-jhula for her man to appear. One dark night, she was sitting by the kitchen fire when she heard a big thud on the roof as if somebody had dropped a load. She rushed out to look and was overjoyed when she spied Namgyal on the roof. She greeted him with warmth and quickly brought him in.

Namgyal went and sat in a corner of the room. Pangmo was surprised that he did not look at her or ask of his family's welfare. This was strange. She invited him to come and sit by the fire for some warmth, but he made excuses. Pangmo became suspicious as it was well known that rolances do not come near fire and iron. She went out to the roof and checked the load. It was surprisingly heavy and was full of rounded river stones that were all dry!

She went back into the house and looked for his shoes. There were none. Her doubts increased and she asked Namgyal about his shoes. He answered, 'Shoes are for humans, not us.' Pangmo was fairly certain now that this was not her living husband but a rolance. Quickly, she tied her son on her back, kept the fire going, and took an iron ladle in her hand. She ran out and raised a cry for the villagers. People gathered and carrying lighted torches, they all marched back to her house. Pangmo set fire to the house and burnt the rolance inside.

After some weeks, other young men returned to the village, but not her husband. They told her that he had died when a cut tree had fallen on him. He was buried, but some days later, they found the grave open and the body missing.

The Miyar nullah, and the glacier above it, which are beyond an impressive gorge that is difficult to climb through, are well known to mountaineers. Foreign visitors keep coming every summer to force their way through the gorge on to the glacier and to climb the high peaks that stand around in a circle. Numerous articles in the *Himalayan Journal** testify to the popularity of the Miyar nullah glacier.

But to the Lahaul people, this area is known as the Patnam valley. The small village of Udgos is perched on a high flat above the gorge, near a deep forest. An eighty-year-old woman lived all by herself in the village. She had no family or relations. She was,

---

*The *Himalayan Journal* is published by the Himalayan Club founded in 1928 in Simla.

however, fit enough to collect wood from the forest and do her own cooking. She was popular in the village and loved to have children come and play on her roof. The village people liked her and always offered her help, which was generally declined.

One day, a bunch of children were playing on the old woman's house's roof. Normally, she sat with them and told them interesting stories while they picked lice from her hair. Not finding her, they looked through a sky window into her house. Great was their surprise when they found the old woman walking around in a stilted fashion. Her eyes were like two pieces of glowing charcoal, her tongue hung down to her naval like a snake, and blood dripped from her nose on to the tongue. The frightened children ran to the village to tell their parents about what they saw. Soon, a group of men and women holding lighted straw torches came to the house. They found that the rolance had come into the outer cattle room. It was trying to get out of the house, but a cow was pushing it back. It was well known that cows could check rolances. The frightened villagers lighted fires and collected all the village cows in a circle around her house. All night, the rolance was kept in check using this device. As the sun came up over the hills, golden light flooded the house and the rolance fell down in a comatose state. It is known that spirits cannot bear the sun. Taking courage, the villagers went inside in a group, carrying axes; they quickly chopped the body, took it well away from the village, and cremated the remains of the woman. People say that as the pyre burnt, a fox suddenly shot out of it and loped uphill into the deodar forest.

The most fascinating story I heard was from Kham in eastern Tibet. Dorje had heard it at Guge during his sojourn in western Tibet. There was a small monastery at a place called Umdog in Kham. It was really the subsidiary of a very large monastery, about fifteen miles away, and was used by old monks, who wished to meditate in quiet surroundings. One day, a monk died at Umdog. The abbot of the main monastery was immediately informed and soon, about one hundred monks arrived to perform the funeral rites. The body was washed, dressed and tied up in a sitting posture in the main room. A cloth screen was draped around it and an altar was prepared on a low wooden table—the kind found quite commonly in homes in Tibet, Lahaul and Ladakh. A butter lamp was lit. Prayers were started and it was decided to keep the body for the full seven days that are ordained. For three days, the lamas droned away at their prayers. On the third night, the lamas, tired with staying awake, fell asleep. Some were in the main room, while the rest were in an adjoining room.

There was a young novitiate lama, about twelve-years-old, in the room with the body. He could not sleep due to fear and lay awake watching the screen behind which the body was. At about midnight, things began to happen. The flame of the butter lamp began shooting up to the ceiling every now and then. Then the screen fell away. The corpse opened its eyes slowly and rolled them, as if testing them. They began to bulge and took on a fiery glow. The tongue came out slowly till it hung a foot down the chest. Blood began to drip from the nose on to the extended tongue.

The boy was terrified and watched speechless. He could not even scream. He crept under the altar table and continued to watch. The body began to fill with gas, and soon, the ropes which had bound it lay in pieces on the ground. It was free. It stood up and slowly rolled its head, taking things in. The lamas slept and the boy watched hypnotized. The rolance then walked to the butter lamp and dipped its finger in. In the dark, it marked itself on the forehead. Then going around the room, it marked all the sleeping lamas. Going to the next room—unfortunately, the door was big enough to allow it to pass through erect—it marked the remaining lamas. Coming back to the main room, it tried to mark the boy also. But it could not bend to get under the table. In vain, it tried to stretch and reach him. Once or twice the outstretched searching fingers came within inches of the boy's skin, but he fused into the wooden side at the far end and narrowly escaped being marked.

The rolance then gave up and began to dance. At once, the sleeping lamas came to life and took up the rhythm. They danced with a wild jerking motion and seemed in a state of trance. Their eyes had a fixed unrecognizing stare.

By now, the boy had collected some of his wits and had lost some of the initial paralyzing fear. He began to think of escape. There was an open chimney on one side of the room. Given a chance, he could pull himself up on to the roof. He watched carefully. As soon as the dancing rolance moved into the adjoining room, he made a dash and jumped for the chimney. Getting a hold, he began to pull up desperately. At that very moment, the rolance returned. It made a grab for the boy and caught his right foot. It was left holding a long Tibetan boot—the leg had slipped out and gone up through the chimney to safety.

Sitting on the roof, the boy watched the room through the opening. The effort of climbing up the chimney had drained all his energy and he lay panting. He watched as the rolance put a black mark on the boot and it also began to dance!

By now, the dawn was in the sky. The boy ran to the monastery fifteen miles away and told his story of horror to the lamas there. All listened, but no one could do anything. The rolance was too powerful. They waited for the senior abbot, an old man with great spiritual powers, to break his samadhi. In the meantime, fires were lit and fierce Tibetan watchdogs guarded the monastery with the rolance.

After three days, the old lama opened his samadhi and everyone fell at his feet with their tale of woe. After much thinking, he consented to face the rolance. Stripping himself completely naked, he rubbed red mud all over his body. Then with a *kangling* in his left hand and a little drum in his right, he went to the monastery.

Going up to the roof, he blew his kangling into the room through the chimney. The dancing stopped. He then went down and playing his kangling and drum, entered the monastery dancing. The other lamas and people watched from a respectable distance. As the lama danced inside, the rolance and the bewitched lamas began to dance with him. After some time, he came out, followed by the rolance and the others, all dancing. The pied piper of Kham! He walked for many days with this strange retinue till he came to a lake. The holy one waded in, followed by the strange retinue. They were all drowned; only the old lama returned.

In Tibet, people believe in the rolance stories completely and Dorje met many people who had seen one. There is another rolance story about a village in the Pattan valley of Lahaul. Pattan is Hindu, but the influence of its neighbour has permeated it, or perhaps they have retained their pre-conversion demon beliefs.

An old man died in Zangbar village, leaving behind a wife and child. At night, the body which was lying on the ground began to show rolance signs. The woman became afraid and left the house after placing a sacred book on her dead husband's chest. This is supposed to be a deterrent against rolance.

After some time, an old friend of the dead man, who was

travelling through, dropped in. He knocked for a long time, but only heard a moaning sound. Curious, he pushed his way in and found his friend on the ground. He sat down and began making small talk, but his friend seemed to be behaving in a queer manner. He groaned about a weight on his chest and asked the traveller to remove it. The traveller became suspicious and prevaricated. The body then asked him to make thukpa. The visitor asked for the butter. At this, the man on the ground stretched out his arm—it seemed elastic and became very long— and plucked the butter tin from the shelf. Now the traveller was sure that this was a rolance.

He quickly lighted a fire and while getting out, put it at the front door. As his luggage was inside, he could not go away. He hid in a nearby mustard field. Mustard is also a protection against rolance and spirits, and is carried by all lamas. The man could hear the rolance stamping about inside the house. After some time, the fire in the doorway died down and the rolance came out. It walked around the field to get at the man, but it dared not enter the field. It gave up and walked around the house looking for the wife and child. Not finding anything, it picked up the pole ladder and walked off down the road.

In the morning, the body was found lying on the road with the ladder by its side. The common belief is that the sun defeats the rolance. It is a general belief all over India that spirits do not walk forth in the day. Why, even Shakespeare thought the same!

I have heard,
The cock, that is the trumpet to the morn,
Doth with his lofty and shrill-sounding throat
Awake the god of day, and at his warning,
Whether in sea or fire, in earth or air,
The extravagant and erring spirit hies
To his confine . . .

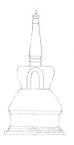

The Dark Ones

Sweet to ride forth at evening from the wells
When shadows pass gigantic on the sand,
And softly through the silence beat the bells
Along the Golden Road to Samarkand.

—James Elory Flecker

The people of Lahaul firmly believe in the existence of spirits and demons.* These spirits are found all over the area and may be met with in the many nullahs that cut their way down deep gorges to the Bhaga and Chandra rivers. The spirit may take the form of a donkey, a midget, or perhaps a giant. It may even roll along in the shape of a luminous ball. Sometimes, you may see a man coming down the gorge of a nullah not by the goat path, but gliding down effortlessly, like Christ on the Sea of Galilee. You may be sure that this is a spirit!

---

*'There are a great many spirits or demons, known as *Llhas* who are supposed to dwell in trees, rocks, or on the hill tops, and before whom the Buddhists sacrifice sheep and goats. In addition, they believe greatly in witches, sorcerers, and the evil eye, and have a host of other superstitions, in common with all the other Lahaulis.' (Reverend Hyde, quoted in the *Kangra District Gazetteer*, 1897)

A story is told of a villager who was returning after shopping at Kyelang. In the Shaks nullah, just beyond Kyelang, he came across a donkey. Feeling somewhat groggy after a bout of chhaang, he decided to steal a ride on the donkey because the owner seemed nowhere in sight. For some distance, the donkey went along quietly. But suddenly, it vanished and the man fell down with an uncomfortable thud. At first the man thought that he had dozed and fallen off. He cursed the chhaang. But soon he realized that the donkey was nowhere to be found. Inquiries made the next day revealed that it was none other than the well known Shaks nullah *bhoot*! Even today, villagers do not like to cross the nullah alone at night. If they occasionally have to do so, they carry a piece of iron or a glowing stick. The belief that fire and iron can keep spirits away exists even in the plains of Punjab.

There is a very powerful and well-known spirit at Darcha on the way to the Baralacha pass. Its name is Zimug Sringpo and it is a spirit of the type known as *dergot*. A dergot spirit is one which has vanquished one thousand other spirits and has acquired their strength. Naturally, it is powerful and greatly feared.

Many years ago, there was a village at Darcha. One day, God came to this village in the shape of a poor lama. The lama went from house to house begging for food. Most of the men were busy drinking chhaang and gossiping. They turned him out with rude remarks and coarse jests at his expense. Only one householder offered hospitality. The owner, seeing a lama, stood up and offered his own seat. He then treated his guest to food and tea.

That night, there was a fearful storm. At about midnight, a massive avalanche engulfed the village. Everything was destroyed. But God, in his mercy, spared the house of the hospitable villager. Miraculously, it was carried across the Bhaga and deposited on a safe site. The family exists even today, and is known as 'Lungpa Chanpa', meaning the family of the house that flew!

Since the whole village had perished, there was no one left to perform the funeral rites of the others and to offer prayers. The spirits of the dead, therefore, continued to haunt the area; they could not find peace. These spirits were constantly at war with each other. The stronger ones continued to vanquish and assimilate the weaker ones till there was only one spirit left—the great Zimug Sringpo.

Darcha lies on the route to Leh over the Baralacha pass, and during the summer months, there is considerable traffic on this route. This malignant spirit continuously harassed the locals and travellers. Once, four Kolong men were going to Patseo with their sheep laden with gram for the trade fair. They halted at Darcha for the night. For dinner, they prepared sattu in chhaang. Before eating, one of the men made a symbolic offering to some of the lesser spirits of the area—one in the Barsi nullah and some others. Unfortunately, the man did not make any offering to Zimug Sringpo.

While his companions fell asleep soon after dinner, this man lay tossing and turning. He felt restless and could not sleep. The sheep also seemed disturbed and the dogs were barking continuously, as if at something. It was well known that animals could sense the presence of a spirit. For example, dogs will sometimes tuck in their tails and whimper in fear. About midnight, the man dozed off, but by some prescience, woke up soon after. He found a man standing near his feet. The queer thing about the man was his head, which was ten times the size of a normal one. He guessed at once that it was none other than the irritated Zimug Sringpo. There was an axe lying near his feet, but he dared not get up and pick it up. Slowly, he began to slide it up with his right foot, all the while keeping his eyes on Zimug. As the axe reached his outstretched fingers, he jumped up and began to shout. His companions woke up and they searched all around, but found nothing. They lighted a big fire and spent the rest of the night keeping watch. In the morning, the man found one of his sheep dead. There was no wound or mark on the carcass.

There is another case of mischief by Zimug Sringpo, but in this case, as will be apparent, Zimug was clearly provoked. At Khangsar lived a lama. He was a powerful man in the prime of life. There was nothing of the lama about him, save his habit. He had not studied much and hardly knew any of the sacred mantras. But he was very proud. He earned his living by grazing the thakur's horses. The lama used to often go across the river to his village Sumdo. He always carried a big knife. In those days, there was no bridge at Darcha and he crossed the river on a horse. Each time he passed Darcha, the lama stopped, took out his knife and brandished it in the air, daring Zimug Sringpo to come out and face him. He would paint vivid pictures of what he would do to Zimug if he ever saw him. He would abuse Zimug loudly and cast aspersions on his ancestors. This went on for about twenty years, but Zimug did not appear to face this wrestler-like lama. People began to believe that the lama was more powerful than Zimug.

One day, the lama was going to his village and began crossing the river at about midday. It was a perfect sunny day. As was his habit, he stopped across the river and began to abuse Zimug loudly. Some people of his village who were in the fields stopped to watch. Suddenly, they saw a black mass issue from under the big rock where Zimug was reputed to live. It flew towards the gesticulating lama sitting on his dripping horse. There was a wild commotion and the lama's horse pawed the air. The villagers watched in horror. After a little while, the rider-less horse galloped up to the village. It was terribly nervous and its eyes were dilated. Immediately, people collected, and praying loudly, went to the Darcha *maidan*. There, they found the dead lama. There was no mark of violence on him, but his knife was bent double in the shape of a U.

The people of the Bhaga valley were quite worried by this obstacle on their main trade route. In about 1890, the abbot of Hemis monastery in Ladakh came to Lahaul to visit the monastery of Gimure, which is of their sect. The people of Kolong went to him and petitioned him to rid them of this evil. The abbot then went to Darcha and performed various prayers and recited mantras. On his return, he informed the people that he had tied Zimug Sringpo up thoroughly with powerful chains, and that henceforth, they would have no trouble from him. The people were happy and time passed. One day, a lama who was passing through stopped at Darcha and began to shout and gesticulate violently. After some time, he came to the village and told the people that over the years, Zimug's chains had become loose, but he had now riveted them tightly! The people thanked the lama and entertained him at Darcha for a number of days.

Now Zimug is quiet, but he still indulges in minor mischief. Recently, an amusing incident took place. A lama by the name of Nyima Namgyal happened to go up the Darcha nullah to visit a small village. The people were kind and hospitable. Though he wanted to get back early, it was fairly dark by the time he finished his last glass of chhaang. As he came down towards Darcha, he suddenly remembered Zimug Sringpo and got scared. Soon he began to see ominous shapes in the dark. The poor man began to mutter prayers feverishly. But he still saw old Zimug. Desperately, he began to throw stones to scare him.

Now, as it happened, he was quite close to the Darcha bridge by this time. The constable on guard heard the noise and thought, 'Surely it must be Zimug!' Quickly he called the rest of the guard. They chased the spirit with lanterns, sticks and rifles. The poor lama ran for his life and ultimately jumped down into the Darcha nullah and hid under a rock. The policemen were mystified. They had seen a human figure and then it had disappeared suddenly. Surely it must be Zimug Sringpo! The lama spent the night shivering in the open. He dared not approach the bridge in the dark. In the morning, as a dishevelled lama went past the bridge, the guard asked him solicitously where he had been. 'Oh, I had gone to the village yonder to pray, and got late,' he replied casually. I wonder if Zimug Sringpo was to blame!

When out on the road, the Lahaula has to be wary of various spirits and other evil beings that lurk by the way. But he is not altogether safe even in his village. An enemy, in the shape of his neighbour, may often bewitch him.

It is well known that a she-demon or *jogini* lives in the high hills. Women generally obtain her favours by performing puja in her honour. This is done by using the kitchen fire as a havan. The woman will throw in gram and food offerings while chanting a special mantra. It is easy to control a jogini and it can be done in a single night. Women often teach the art to their daughters and sometimes a girl is rejected in marriage because her family is reputed to control a jogini.

Having obtained this power to control a she-demon, a woman can send the jogini in the shape of an avenging fury to harass her enemies. The person so attacked will begin to cry and sigh loudly. One should then hold her ring finger tightly and slap her. If the patient becomes silent, it is established that she has the jogini in her. The people do not say that the patient has the jogini, but that such and such a woman, the suspected evil-doer, has entered her. This usually happens to women, though it may occasionally happen to a man. It does not happen in summer, for then the flowers bloom in the high alpine meadows and the joginis are fond of playing with them. In winter, joginis come down to the villages and most cases occur at that time.

On the first occurrence of a jogini attack, the patient is thoroughly beaten. The belief is that the demon inside suffers. She then names herself and says, 'I am so and so of the village.' She is then threatened that if she returns, she will be beaten more severely. In the belief that all actions hurt the evil person, strange things are done. In Tibet, the hand of the patient may be immersed in boiling oil. In Kyelang, once they cut the hair of a patient. In the morning, the patient's hair had reportedly regrown fully, but that of the evil woman had fallen off! On another occasion, a red mark was put on a patient's forehead. The next day, it had disappeared, but was seen on the forehead of the woman suspected of sending the jogini.

The jogini may go away after the beating, but can return later. In that case, the patient is beaten more severely and the jogini is driven out. If there is another relapse after some time, then the lamas are called and the *demo puja* is performed. A sattu effigy is prepared. This is blackened. If the hair of the woman suspected to have sent the jogini can be obtained, it is put on the effigy. Mantras are recited and the eyes of the effigy are knocked out with a vulture's beak; it is scratched on the body with the claws of an owl; the tongue is pulled out with an iron hook; it is cut with a knife and the arms are hacked off; the head is crushed with a hammer and beaten with a dorje, and finally, its heart is pierced with a phurpa. The prostrate effigy is then beaten with a leg of mutton. The remains of the effigy are tied in a piece of cloth and buried. The meat of the leg of the mutton is then eaten.

This procedure normally cures the patient. But, sometimes, the jogini is more powerful and returns. In that case, the lamas also return and perform a *tagpo jinsrang*. Tagpo means 'powerful' and jinsrang means havan. A havan kund is prepared in the middle of the room and wood is heaped on it in the shape of a triangle. A fire is started and offerings of grain are thrown in it. Then an iron frame used for cooking is put over the logs and a vessel full of oil is put on it. Offerings of chhaang, salt and the blood of a dog, donkey and camel are put in the vessel. The oil burns fiercely because of the alcohol. If possible, the hair or nails of the woman who sent the jogini are put in the havan. The blood of a dog or a donkey is obtained by making a slight cut on the animal's ear. As for camel blood, the lamas are said to carry around pills of such blood.

The prayers and havan of the lamas sometimes prove ineffective. In that case, after a few days, the patient again has an attack and shouts, screams and sighs. Drastic remedies are called for as it is clear by now that the jogini is very powerful. Simple prayers or a little blood will not do. A sacrifice must be offered. This, however, the Buddhist lamas will not do. Then a *bhatt* from the Pattan valley or a *goor* from the Chandra valley is called. Bhatts are counterparts of the lamas in the Pattan valley, which is predominantly Hindu. They may be bhatts as a family and Brahmins by caste, but this is not mandatory. A person of a caste other than Brahmin may become a bhatt by learning the trade from a guru. The bhatts preside at funerals and other ceremonies, and also perform mantras for the sick. The goor is the *chela* of a devta, that is, the devta is said to manifest himself through the goor. The goor goes into a trance and the devta then answers the people's queries through him. The goor is generally a lohaar and keeps long hair, like the Sikhs. He also wears a round cap. The priest of the devta is always another man.

On his arrival, the bhatt prepares a chapatti of wheat flour. On this, he places a small goat made of sattu. A few pieces of meat are put in this goat to give it the semblance of a real sacrificial animal. Four oil lamps are then lit and the patient is given a sword or knife to hold. The bhatt also has a sword and is always naked above the waist. Various offerings are thrown into the kitchen fire. The bhatt passes the sword over the fire, jumps about and pierces himself in the cheeks or the stomach with the sword. It is said that though he pierces himself, no blood oozes out of the wounds. Sometimes, he heats a sickle till it is red hot and then touches his tongue and the soles of his feet with it. After these antics, the bhatt takes the sattu goat out. This is accompanied by a lot of shouting and gesticulating, as if he is fighting some invisible enemy. The sattu goat is then burnt at some crossroad near a nullah or at the cremation ground. The bhatt dances about the fire, threatening the malevolent spirit. He tries to scare it by taking the names of other great spirits whom he has vanquished, shouting his victories like battle honours. He then draws a line with his sword and warns the cowed spirit that it is not to come beyond the line on pain of punishment. Sometimes, as an additional precaution, the bhatt will return to the house, and drive four wooden pegs at the four corners of the house after chanting certain mantras.

It is possible that the fake goat may not appease the spirit. In that case, the attack recurs with all the usual symptoms. The bhatt then returns and offers a real sheep or goat as sacrifice. The ceremony is the same except for the animal. The sheep often bleats and disturbs the proceedings, but when the bhatt recites a mantra and sprinkles water on the animal, the sacrificial sheep falls silent, lies still and watches the magic!

After the ceremony in the house, the animal is taken out to be sacrificed. It is held tightly while the bhatt makes an incision just below its ribs with his sword. He then reaches in and plucks out the animal's heart. I fancy the Roman soothsayers did something similar. The heart is burnt and the sheep eaten by everyone other than the patient's family. The bhatt is always given one leg of mutton. If all other remedies fail, this will surely succeed and the jogini leaves the patient.*

---

*'There is a small temple, with the image of a Llha near Yanample. Every third year, a yak is sacrificed there, the victim being supplied in turn by all the kothis of Lahaul. This custom dates from the time of the Kulu Rajas.' (*Kangra District Gazetteer*, 1897)

It is interesting that similar beliefs and practices existed in the Punjab in the twentieth century. Of and on, I lived in my village near Amritsar for short periods till I went to St George's College, Mussoorie, an Irish Catholic school. It was widely believed that ill-inclined neighbours, always women, could do *jadoo* on other women by secretly feeding them a magic potion or by conducting a tantrik rite. The afflicted women would start behaving in a strange hysterical manner. A group of men and women who claimed to deal with such evil spirits would be called to the house, like the Lahaul bhatts, to treat the sick person. I saw one case as a child. In the middle of June, all of us children went into a neighbour's compound. In the dark living room with no ventilation, a fire had been lit. On one side, under numerous quilts, lay a woman with open dishevelled hair. Opposite her sat three, maybe four people. They chanted mantras and made aggressive gestures, all the while talking to the bhoot that was supposed to be in the woman. The 'doctors' threatened the bhoot and directed it to go away. Every now and then, the woman sat up and started gyrating her upper body in a quickened circular motion, her wild hair flying. She had an unseeing glitter in her eyes that frightened us. One can imagine her condition, under quilts in a closed room in the June heat, with temperatures above 43°C. We ran away, having seen enough. The next day, the bhoot-expelling party would come out into the compound, shouting that they had vanquished the spirit, and saying, 'See there, it is flying away. It has broken the branch of that tree.' They left full of money given by her husband, the poor farmer. The patient, of course, was no better.

Some time in February or March, the joginis of Lahaul are said to hold their annual get-together at the Karga maidan above Tandi. This annual event is known as Ledtsog Kuns and lasts for three days. Each year, the Joling lama informs the people of the exact date of this get-together. About fifteen generations back, the thakurs of Barbog, located opposite Kyelang, settled a lama on some land in the village of Joling. This lama was to protect the thakur's house from the joginis' visit. The post is now hereditary in the family of the first lama. The lama goes into isolation in a room and meditates. For nine days, he will not leave this room and will receive only a few important visitors. People go to him with various questions to be answered about their future. A question may be sent to him, but should be accompanied by some personal article of the questioner. The lama also names various women of nearby villages, who are or have become joginis. The evil spirits of these women are thought to fly to Karga maidan for the annual meeting. They reportedly go flying on the wooden cross beams of houses. How similar to European witches! Each spirit is expected to bring something for the feast—a yak, a sheep, even sattu. It is believed that joginis come to Karga for this event from as far away as Tibet, Zanskar and Chamba, and many people are afraid to pass Karga during those days.

The following is a widely current story: Long ago, there lived a woman who was a jogini. She was, in fact, one of the most powerful she-devils of her time. One year, she was asked to bring two yaks for the annual Karga feast. She searched far and wide, but could not find any. Finally, in sheer desperation, she decided to take her own yaks for the promise had to be kept. When she was about to leave for Karga, by chance her son came back from the fields and found his mother in her jogini form, with her breasts hanging to the ground and long sharp teeth protruding out of her mouth. Hiding in the next room, he watched her take both the yaks, one under each arm, and get on to the cross beam of the roof. As she was flying off, the son quietly jumped on the beam behind her without her knowing. They flew along the valley till they reached Karga. The woman was welcomed with great warmth by the gathered spirits. Evidently, she was a well known jogini, greatly respected in her profession. The son watched all this from behind a rock. The yaks were cut and cooked, and there was a great feast with plenty of dancing and singing.

Another jogini had been asked to bring an ibex. She could not find one, so she borrowed one from a rakshasa who lived high up in the Muling forest. This was also cut and eaten. While they were eating, the jogini who had brought the ibex exclaimed that the rakshasa would be very angry if his animal was not returned. At this, one old jogini told her not to worry and to keep the bones after eating. In the evening the old jogini put together all the bones. One rib could not be found, so she substituted it with a stick. Then she chanted a mantra and the ibex became whole and went racing off to his beloved forest. It is well known that many years later, a hunter shot an ibex in the Muling forest and on cutting it open, found that it had a wooden rib!

After the feast, the woman returned to her village. The boy also quietly jumped on the beam and went home. The next morning, when he awoke, he found both his yaks dead. There was not a scratch on them. When the meat was cooked, it tasted like ash.

The son, however, did not say anything to his mother. He dressed the two yak skins and made two big grain bags out of them. In September, when the barley was cut and winnowed in the fields, the boy filled both the big bags with grain and asked his mother to carry them home. She exclaimed in surprise, 'How can you expect an old woman of my age to carry such heavy bags?' The boy replied casually, 'Since you could carry two full-grown yaks, I thought you might not find these heavy!' The woman got such a shock that she fell down in a fit and died.

It is but natural that living with the gods, always subordinate to the elemental forces of nature, people in these desolate valleys should have a strong belief in joginis, bhoots, and spirits of every kind. There are unlimited stories of the doings of the spirits. Every valley and gorge, and every mountain and pass in Lahaul-Spiti has its own tale of fear and mystery.

Beyond the Baralacha pass, which is more than 16,000 feet high, lie the Lingti plains. This vast high tableland is drained by the Yonum river, which goes northwards through Lingti and the Zanskar valley to join the Indus at Nimmo. The Lingti plain has the richest blue grass and is a favourite grazing ground for flocks of sheep and yak. The Kangra Gaddis bring their sheep here while the yaks come from Lahaul, Ladakh and Zanskar.

There once lived a very powerful merchant named Lingti Po, who grazed a thousand yaks and ten thousand sheep on the Lingti grasslands. He was the sardar of these vast plains of blue grass, the most nutritious in Lahaul. Lingti Po would travel about the grazing grounds to check and guard his flock. Once he came to a stream and camped by it, away from other yak herders. He liked being alone in this empty wilderness. Late at night, Po was cooking his thukpa when he heard the musical jingle of the shringaar of a horse, little bells ringing in the silence of the night. He wondered who could have come at this time of night! Stepping out, he saw a beautiful girl dressed in silk on a black mare, decorated with lovely trappings. Keeping to the hospitality of the road, he invited her in and offered her a meal, which she politely declined. Later, on seeing him put some meat in the thukpa, she asked if he had a round knee bone of a sheep. He did and offered it to her. She took it happily and left the tent to camp at some distance from him. Po went back to his cooking and meal.

After some time, Po went out of the tent to see if all was well. Great was his surprise when he saw that some distance away, the young lady had lighted a fire with yak dung and was heating the round sheep bone that glowed red hot. She held it in her hands, which did not seem to burn. Po could not understand the mystery, but suddenly everything became clear when the girl turned in his direction. Her eyes glowed with a blue light, her nails were long and sharp like a cat's claw and her feet were turned backward. Po knew this was none other than the Lingti rakshasani. She flew at him with the red hot ball in her hand. Quick as a flash, Lingti Po pulled out his sword and slashed at her, cutting the glowing bone in her hand into two. The rakshasani gave one terrible scream and flew away. She, of course, left her mare behind. Lingti Po was shaken, but he was used to such happenings in this lonely land.

Many years passed by, and every year, an old woman would approach Po's camp and ask, 'Where is Lingti Po?' His servants always replied that he was resting and the woman would go away. Fourteen years passed like this. Once more, the old woman came and asked for Po. The servants, knowing that Lingti Po had died many years back, thought it was time to tell the woman the truth. One of them answered, 'He is dead long since.' The old woman suddenly transformed into a young beautiful girl, went to her mare, which seemed to recognize her well, undid the rope, jumped on, and raced away.

During the three days of Ledtsog Kuns, the people of Lahaul have to be most careful. This is the time, when the joginis fly about and the chances of one entering the house are great. To avoid this, certain precautions are taken. Sharp wooden pegs are spread on the roofs and it is believed that any jogini coming down on these will cut her feet. No one sleeps under the roof beam, for everyone knows that the joginis are most fond of these. A little mustard, the sacred grain, is put into the hair of sleeping children. No jogini can then carry them away. Every evening, a fire is lighted in front of the house, and the village children collect and abuse the joginis, daring them to enter.

The year I was in Kyelang, during the three-day long Ledtsog Kuns, between 21 and 23 February, batches of young girls from the village came to my house every evening. They shouted out for me and when I went out, they lighted a fire on the veranda steps and loudly and vigorously abused the joginis. Very solemnly, they explained to me that sickness would come to the house if the joginis entered it. The children seemed to enjoy this fun of going from house to house, abusing the joginis.

Generally, wooden pegs and some iron nails are hammered in over the entrances to houses to prevent any jogini from entering. At night, during Ledtsog Kuns, men and women do not venture out. Even if they have to step out to relieve themselves, they go in twos and threes, chanting prayers and carrying wooden torches!

Beyond Thirot lies Chamba-Lahaul, which is Hindu. In fact, so is the Pattan valley. Interestingly, the people here also believe in joginis. At Udaipur village, six miles beyond the sacred Triloknath shrine, lives a Brahmin priest. Each year, he comes to Triloknath. There, he lives with the local thakur and goes into a nine-day-long meditation. He also informs the people about the feast of the joginis, though it is not known if the dates given by him coincide with those given by the Joling lama. At the temple of Udaipur are two wooden statues of *birs*, spirit heralds, in the manner of Mercury. The priest sends these out far and wide to invite the joginis. A huge brass vessel is left out at night to help the joginis cook their feast! People often hear the sound of the vessel being dragged about, but no one dares to venture out to investigate!

Though Guru Nanak fought mainly against superstitions and such foolish beliefs, the peasantry continues to believe in bhoots and spirits. Across from Bhakra dam in the new Himachal Pradesh is a Sikh shrine, controlled by one of the descendants of the Guru. Afflicted women, young and old, are taken by their fathers and brothers to the *dera* on Holi, the spring festival of colours. The women and girls are made to sit in rows and the dera keepers go around hitting them on the back with twisted and knotted cloth ropes. This ritual is said to cure them. The fact is that women in the Punjab and elsewhere are afflicted with psychological problems brought about by the multiple oppressions of a joint family. These hysteria attacks are sought to be cured through these charltan *jadoogars*.

Disease is a part of life. People in the best of health occasionally fall sick. Because of Lahaul's severe climate and poor nutritional levels, it happens more often here. In winter, many people go down with influenza, severe cold and pneumonia. The dirge sounds regularly for the dead. As soon as the disease appears, the lamas come and perform tana mana of various types such as *gyabje*, *chhogje*, *tsandoi*, *tyapo*, etc. There are approximately a hundred of these prayer ceremonies. The abbot of the local monastery finds out the year of birth of the patient to look up a book that lists the kind of tana mana that is to be performed. A sattu figure of a sheep, a rat, a deer, or even a man on a horse with a peculiar hat is made. Dorje told me that he had seen figures of almost all animals except the camel and the elephant. Prayers are then held, and the figures are taken out and thrown at a road crossing or in a stream.

Strangely enough, the patient does not always get better after this treatment. Indeed, he often gets worse and it sometimes becomes clear even to the faithful that he or she is on the point of death. But the Lahaula, aided by his lama and goor, will even try to cheat the angel of death. The *mitsab* ('in exchange for man') ceremony is then performed—*mi* means man and *tsab* means exchange. The point of this ceremony is to cheat death by substituting some animal for the sick man.

When Dorje's younger brother Sonam Angrup fell sick, the lamas tried various prayers and tana mana for a couple of months, but the young man's condition only got worse. Water seemed to have collected in his skin and his body had become soft and pulpy. It was evident that he did not have long to live. In desperation, Dorje's mother called the goor of Gondhla. The goor made a figure of a man out of sattu and dressed it in black. He also asked for a black sheep. A havan was performed, during which offerings of grain, oil, and country spirit were thrown into the fire. Finally the effigy was half burnt in the kund. All this time, the sheep lay still. It seemed hypnotized. The half burnt effigy was tied in a black cloth and put on the back of the sheep. The goor then led the sheep out with much jumping about and brandishing of weapons. A regular funeral pyre was prepared and the effigy was put on it. The sheep was made to lie down on top of this. It was not tied, but it seemed to understand and obey the goor! The goor sat on top of the pile and began to recite mantras as the logs were set on fire. When the fire got too close, the goor jumped off. Strangely enough, the sheep though free, made no effort to escape and was burnt. Dorje saw this himself. In order to mislead the angel of death, the men then shouted that Sonam had been dead for nine years—never more or less. Sonam recovered soon after!

The lamas perform mitsab in a slightly different way. This ceremony does not involve an animal sacrifice. Two sticks are tied together in the form of a cross. Over this frame, a sattu effigy is moulded. The effigy is clothed in white and if it is that of a woman, jewels are also put on it. A special puja is performed and the effigy is taken out at night with full ceremony, accompanied by the lama band. It is burnt, but not in the regular cremation ground. The clothes are given to the lamas. One man then shouts that so and so has been dead for the last nine years. The company then returns home, hoping for the best.

Tana mana may be performed, bhatts may be called, and the mitsab may be resorted to, yet sometimes, the patient will still die. Even in that case, all this is not meaningless. Friends and callers will then assure the family, 'You did your best. You spent so much money and performed all the pujas. Now it is God's will, and who can oppose it?' The calm acceptance of the ways of the gods is the only solace available to mankind.

In the event of a death, the lamas read up the omens for the family and the village and prepare to combat any signs that foretell ill luck. Once, after the deaths of two women in Kyelang, Lama Dumbaji, abbot of Sha-shur monastery, solemnly forecast that nine more people would die that season. In the face of such a potential calamity, the villagers requested a special puja to ward off the evil. The lamas prepared various sattu figures—man on a horse, bull, a man with three faces, etc.—and prayers were held. In the afternoon, all the sick and the old—likely candidates for death—came to the puja. The sattu figures were passed over the head of each individual in the congregation, three times to the right and three times to the left. These figures which seemed to have taken all the evil upon themselves were then taken out accompanied by the band and burnt. This ceremony is called *torma*.

Devtas and Mantras

Yet all experience is an arch wherethro'
Gleams that untravell'd world, whose margin fades
For ever and for ever when I move.

—Lord Alfred Tennyson

The long winters are hard to pass. Time stands still in the valley. Isolated from the rest of the world and with no scope for work or mobility in the snowbound valley, the people have to find amusement within their homes. Attuned to the environment, they do not fret. On the contrary, they find the silence of the winter ideal for prayer and introspection. Many villagers retire to the monasteries for a month or two of meditation and prayer. Even the most godless are driven to think of God by the magnificence of creation around them. The lamas from the monasteries are invited home to pray for the dead and the living, or just for one's peace of mind.

The government officials find it more difficult to organize the time that hangs on them like an unwanted load. Aliens in a harsh climate, many of them are unable to find new props in place of the letters, newspapers and government circulars, which cease to flow into the valley after the first heavy winter snowfall. The wireless remains their sole link with a familiar world and it is often not enough. There is no work in the office to provide useless but time-killing activity. Their condition then is similar to that of Charles Lamb after his retirement from the East India Company. As everyone knows, Lamb was a famous English essayist of the eighteenth century, living and working in London. Like all babus, he dreamt of retirement and freedom to do as he liked: sleep half the day or stroll in Hyde Park in the summer sunshine. The retirement came. Lamb went home. For a few days, he got up late and took the odd stroll in the park. But he soon grew tired of idleness and then a strange thing happened. Like a sleep walking man, his steps would invariably turn to Leaden Hall Street and the East India Company office! He was often found by former colleagues, standing and looking up longingly at his old clerical haunt.

On one such listless day, I was meditating on a point on the wall when Dorje came in. After I gave him a cup of tea from a kettle kept boiling all day on the fireplace, we began to chat about Lahaul superstitions. And then I heard the deep throated gutturals of the long trumpet called gyadung.

'What is going on at this time of day, Dorje?' I asked.

'Must be a puja in some house, Sir,' he replied.

'Look, why don't you find out about it, and we could go and attend it for a little while. There is nothing to do in the office,' I suggested. I recalled that the previous evening, a few lamas had come to a neighbouring house and sounded the trumpets as invitation to the devtas to descend to the house.

He was back after half an hour with the news that my neighbour Sonam Ram was holding the *dzeetha dambargya* prayers in his house. The expression means 'to banish enmity from amongst a hundred families'. The holding of this prayer is believed to ensure peace and amity between the supplicant and his relations even as far removed as a hundred degrees! This is the main puja ceremony in Lahaul. It is performed once or twice after a death, depending on the economic capacity of the relatives of the deceased. This is, however, not absolutely essential and the poor cannot generally afford this luxury.

All such ceremonies in Kyelang are performed by the lamas of the Sha-shur monastery. The sacred books are carried down to the village in advance. These books are printed on bhojpatra sheets, about two and a half feet by ten inches, and are bound between thick flat wooden boards. Each book weighs about five kilos. Since the monastery is situated a mile above Kyelang, at a height of about twelve thousand feet, the cartage of these books is quite laborious. But it is a labour of love. It is also a ritual. All the young boys and girls of the village dress in their best clothes and volunteer to go and bring the books. At the monastery, they are entertained with tea and chhaang. They come down in a gay procession, chatting, gossiping and joking with each other. Rest halts are frequently made on the way as each house that falls in their path must offer the traditional hospitality of chhaang to them.

Sonam Ram was delighted by my interest in the puja. He came himself to invite me to his house. We went up the stairs and past the animal sty. On the first floor, we found ourselves in a kind of enclosed and covered lobby. On either side were rooms. We went up another flight of stairs through a trap door and came out on to a terrace open on two sides. On the remaining side, there were more rooms. From one of these, a droning sound, like that of a large swarm of honey bees could be heard. Taking off our shoes, we entered, and found ourselves in a room, about twelve feet square and lit by the windows opening on the terrace. This morning, Dumbaji, the abbot of Sha-shur, had arrived with ten lamas to begin the puja. He sat on a raised rug-covered seat with his back to the windows. In front of him was a small altar; on a low table, were a butter lamp, a *delu* (bell), and a dorje. On either side of him, but at a lower elevation, sat two lamas. They were elderly gentlemen and one had a white beard cut in the Muslim fashion. The other had dark glasses on. Further along the walls, on either side, sat five junior lamas, some of them hardly in their teens. There were ten of them in all. The minimum necessary number of lamas for this dambargya is nine, as that many are needed to play the various instruments of the lama band, essential to the puja. The custom is for the house to invite the head lama to come and perform the puja. He may bring as many lamas as he likes with him; everyone needs to be looked after.

All the lamas had copies of the long bhojpatra prayer books on low tables in front of them. They were reading in a sing-song tone at a feverish speed, as if they were anxious to get it over with in the shortest possible time. I was reminded of the priests in Punjab villages, who when invited to houses to read the holy book, sometimes do so in such a mercenary fashion, anxious only for the end of the task and their monetary reward. Dumbaji paid no heed to our arrival, but the others all darted quick glances at us. The younger ones even smiled.

Across the room from the abbot was a *dambargyee kilkhur*. This is a wooden altar about four feet square, with four or five stairs running up to a flat top. Four butter lamps were burning at its four corners. The number of lamps vary, depending on the type of ceremony. The stairs of the altar were decorated with sattu sweets of two kinds. Along the lower stairs were coloured sattu balls, the size of dry coconuts. These are called *tshogs* and are made by mixing sattu in chhaang. On the higher stairs, and on the final platform, were more elaborate sattu decorations that looked like artificial flowers. These are called *chodpa* and are made by mixing sattu with water, and decorating the lumps with butter and ghee. As much as a quintal of sattu is needed for these decorations. After the ceremony, the tshogs are distributed in the village with one or two being given to each house. The chodpa, perhaps because of the butter, are eaten at home.

Two beautifully ornamented brass kettles, full of water, were also placed at the altar. The kettle is known as *bumpa* and the water it contains is called *bumchu*. This water is later distributed as *amrit* or holy water. One hundred and eight small lamps, called *gyam shhud kyonghu*, were lighted around the altar. Bowls of water (called *dontsar*) were placed on one stair. Donstars must always number seven or its multiples.

The seven cups of water are symbols representing offerings of incense, candle light, flowers, food, clothes, fruit and devotional music. At the base of the four corners of the altar were four carved daggers called phurpas. The phurpa is an important part of the equipment of a lama and is meant to symbolically destroy the enemies of the faith. Four silk handkerchiefs, green, blue, white and yellow, were hung from the top of the altar.

We sat down on brightly coloured Tibetan rugs. The lamas were hurriedly reciting some mantra, which they seemed to know by heart. They kept count by using rosaries with one hundred and eight beads. Having repeated the mantra for the required number of times, they began to read again from the scriptures. The lamas read fast, putting each leaf away as it finished. At a signal, all of them suddenly took up musical instruments and began to play them vigorously. Evidently, the prayers for one devta were over. They were now summoning the next one with music.

Dumbaji took the delu in his left hand and a small castanet in his right. Two lamas had gyadungs, long trumpets, two had gelings and two had kanglings, both pipe instruments. Flat drums called *nga*, were suspended from the ceiling in front of another two lamas. The last two had brass plates of two types called *rolmo* and *singnyal*, which they banged vigorously. All of them played with zest. Dorje said that there were different tunes for different occasions, but I could discern no rhythm or melody . . . but then, I have no ear for music. Dumbaji now and then put down the little castanet and took the dorje and made motions of sprinkling something in front of himself. After a little while, they put away the instruments. Presumably, the summoned devta had arrived! The reading was resumed. And thus it continued all day with musical interludes. The reading is invariably over by evening, well in time for the chhaang session. During the afternoon, the devotees are also given a kind of *prasad*, sattu balls and chhaang, out of a thotpa.

The Lahaula evidently attaches no special importance to such things. They are part of everyday life. The kangling of the lama band is also of two types: one made of brass and the other of the thigh bone of a woman! A bone is taken from a dead body and there is merit in giving it away, something like donating one's eyes on death these days. It is buried, cleaned and polished, and finally mounted in silver. The mouth piece of the kangling is at the top end of the bone and there are two openings at the knee joint. Molten wax is poured through the bone so as to make the pipe uniform. This improves the sound. When polished, it looks like yellowish old ivory and makes a beautiful pipe. These articles lie about in a Lahaul home like sewing machines and radios do in ours. They are hidden only from strangers.

The lamas are always honoured guests in any house. During the day, they are plied continuously with butter tea. Each lama in the house I visited had a beautiful silver or Chinese painted cup in front of him. In the centre of the room was a huge brass vessel on a fire place. The lady of the house moved about all the while, ladling out tea. For Dumbaji, there was a lovely ornamental brass kettle kept warm on coal in a vessel. This was special tea for the holy one with plenty of butter. I got a share out of it. I guess the junior lamas had to make do with more hot water and less butter! They all drank huge quantities of tea. I did not see a single one of them refuse extra helpings.

The real entertainment is in the evening after the reading of the scriptures is over. The relatives and friends of the family arrive. A chhaang party begins with the lamas leading. The next day, the session starts from breakfast and continues till the lamas depart! No wonder the expenses are considerable. Sonam Ram told me that he had used about a quintal of barley for the chhaang alone. His total expenses were close to six hundred rupees—a princely sum in those days.

And thus the winter passes pleasantly enough. The lamas keep busy, moving from one chhaang party to another. Most others want a dambargya. Who would not like such a happy meeting with the devtas? In a few days, I heard the sound of the deep throated gyadung from Karding and Barbog across the river too. The valley seemed to be busy making its peace with the gods.

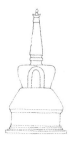

Festival of Lights

Think no more, lad; laugh, be jolly:
Why should men make haste to die?
Empty heads and tongues a-talking
Make the rough road easy walking,
And the feather pate of folly
Bears the falling sky.

—Alfred Edward Housman

On the eighth of January, we celebrated Halda. This festival has something in it both of the traditional new year and the Diwali celebrated in the plains of India. The exact date of the festival is calculated by Dumbaji, the abbot of Sha-shur. At one time, the local thakurs used to fix the date, but they have long since transferred their prerogative to the abbot of Sha-shur. On Halda night the moon enters a circle of five stars known as *birzi* for a little while. If the day happens to be a Tuesday, it is considered doubly auspicious, for *mangal* is the day of agni or fire and Halda is the festival of lights. In the past, the date was conveniently changed if it was in some way inauspicious for the thakur and his family! Not so anymore.

The word *halda* means a torch. The halda is made of dry willow and cedar fagots. The festival, which resembles Diwali in many ways, is not a Buddhist festival. The Shar-shur abbot fixes the date, but otherwise, the lamas have nothing to do with it. It is celebrated in all the three valleys, including Pattan, which is predominantly Hindu. Most likely, its origin goes back to the pre-Buddhist period in the valley, or perhaps, it is the result of the rule of the Hindu Rajas of Kulu over Lahaul for many years.

On the day of the festival haldas or torches are prepared with great care. One is made for each adult male in the family. These are put against the wall in the oldest room of the house. On the wall above these, a new coat of dung and mud is spread. A circle is drawn on the floor and divided into seven or nine parts, in each of which little cakes of flour and dried flowers are stuck. A nail is hammered into the centre of the circle. White wool is also pasted in it. This is the shrine of Shiskar-Apa. There are some variations in how this shrine is made from place to place. In some houses, the circle is drawn and decorated daily for as long as the festival lasts. The abbot fixes the length of the festival, which varies from seven to nine days. In most places, the circle is drawn only once and lasts for all the days. In Kolong village to the north of Kyelang, the people generally write two mottos below the circle—'*Losoma Tashi Shog*', which means 'New year greetings', and '*Lakhim Karpo Dzaldo*', which means 'The food of God, be in our mouths'.

During Halda, all other shrines and gods are ignored. The people worship the shrine of Shiskar-Apa each morning. The local image of Shiskar-Apa is that of an old woman with silver-white hair. She carries a golden stick and is out and about in the early hours of the morning. She may enter a house and bless it with all that the inmates wish for—goats, sheep, yaks and wool. So, people get up early to perform puja at her shrine to entice her. How similar to Santa Claus! But in Lahaul, this is not a child's belief. One can also catch glimpses of the Hindu goddess Lakshmi in the figure of Shiskar-Apa.

On Halda morning, the puja of Shiskar-Apa is performed and requests are made for various gifts. People are not extravagant in their demands on the poor lady. Chhaang is handed around and ceremoniously drunk. The Halda torches are first worshipped and then the men go visiting neighbours where chhaang is naturally offered again. They make it a point to visit houses in which a death has taken place in the course of the last year. Consolation is offered by saying, 'A new year is coming. Now you should put off this mantle of sorrow. You have mourned long enough. The dead will not return.' The relatives of those who have recently died are persuaded to put on flowers and jewellery, which they had discarded after the death, and thus the period of mourning traditionally ends at Halda.

In the evening, at an auspicious time fixed by the lamas, the torches are ceremonially lighted. Before lighting them, a short puja is held with chhaang, of which a cup is offered to each family member. One man carries two torches, while the rest of the family men carry one each. This is not a rigid rule and the number of torches carried by each family is fixed by tradition. Still in the house, the men chant, 'Om aha hum'. The torches are then taken out, handle first with the light facing into the house. Once outside the house, the torch is pointed to the west, and the men chant 'Halda Ho'. The extra torch is stuck outside the house. The men of the village then collect and march to the spot fixed by tradition for the burning of the torches, all the while chanting 'Halda Ho'. The women and children follow the men to watch the fire, while older people stay back in the house.

The torches are burnt at a considerable distance from the village. Thus the upper Kyelang people came to a place below my house in lower Kyelang. The lower Kyelang people went to the Beeling nullah, and the Beeling villagers went down towards Tandi. This is because of a belief that the torches carry all the evil of the old year with them. It is therefore best to burn them away from the village.

We were sitting in my veranda when the upper Kyelang procession came along. It was a lovely night with the moon almost full. The sky was clear with not a speck of cloud. The procession came in a blaze of burning fagots held high. The rhythmic chant of 'Halda Ho' preceded the procession of torches. Behind it came a crowd of women and children. We quickly joined them. Two lohaars were leading the way, beating a tattoo on their drums. The crowd went down the slope past my house and halted in a willow grove. The men threw their torches in a heap on the snow, where they began to burn with a fiery glow. In the light I noticed that the men and boys were wearing their best gowns. Each had a red sash around the waist and their green Kulu caps were adorned with dry marigold flowers. The men stood around the fire while the women and children stood watching from the slopes. All the participants then produced sticks, each about four feet long, with heads of sattu lumps. They gathered around the fire and balancing the sticks like javelins, with the heads turned towards the fire, began to chant 'Karding rana Bawala', this is, 'May it pierce the throat of the Karding rana', and 'Guspa rana Shosha', or 'May it pierce the heart of the Goshal rana'.

This ritual refers to another story. The ranas of Karding and Goshal were barons who ruled the area before the rule of the Kulu rajas. Obviously, they were tyrants. There is even a widely current legend, which depicts the cruel nature of the rana of Goshal. Many many years back, a drought hit the valley. All the springs and streams dried up. There was no water for crops and a time came when there was none even for men and animals. There was great suffering in the village.

One day, a sadhu named Udedu came from Chamba. All the people of Goshal, led by the rana, went to have his darshan and to request his intercession with the gods for water. The sadhu said, 'O rana, the gods are angry with your people and must be appeased with a sacrifice. A life from your house must be offered. Let it be your watch dog.'

'Holy one, if I sacrifice my faithful watch dog, who will guard my house?' asked the rana.

'Let it be your cat then,' replied the sadhu.

'If the cat dies, there will be no one to guard my hearth,' said the rana. 'I am, however, willing to offer my sister if she will do.'

'So let it be,' replied the sadhu.

Accordingly, the poor sister of the rana was dragged out to be sacrificed. She had two little children and she begged that she not be sacrificed for their sake. But the rana turned a deaf ear to all her cries. When she was about to be sacrificed, she begged for one last favour. 'Bury me half in the ground with my breasts out. While I live, I will be able to suckle my children,' she said. Her wish was granted and after two days, the poor woman died. Immediately, two springs gushed out near the village of Goshal. They flow even today. No wonder the people hate the memory of these ranas.

A last lusty shout of 'Guspa rana Shosha' and with a final flourish, the men hurled their javelins into the fire. A great shout went up from the watching crowd. The lohaars beat a farewell tattoo and the crowd faded away into the darkness.

Fires soon sprang up across the valley at Karding and Barbog, and down the river beyond Beeling. The scattered houses above Kyelang also signalled their presence. Shouts drifted across the valley as men hurled curses on tyrants long dead. It was a wonderful sight. The fires shone against the snowy background, like twinkling golden stars.

Before returning home, each man fills a brass vessel with snow from the place where the torches have been consigned. On reaching home, they find the doors barred. They knock for admission. The women inside first question them, 'What have you brought?' The men reply, 'We have brought goats and sheep, yaks and churus, woollen shawls of great price, gold and silver.' The reply is limited only by the imagination of each person! They are then admitted into the house. The bowl of snow is placed before the shrine of Shiskar-Apa in the house.

The next morning, the lohaar visits all the houses. No outsider can even be named in the house till after the lohaar's visit. For three days after this, no work is done as any noise is likely to disturb the old lady of the gifts whose entry into the house is vital. This appears suspiciously like Lakshmi puja in North India. However, after the second day, women may spin white wool. Wood cutting is taboo. People do not leave their houses. Now, government servants unfortunately need to go to office and the custom is breaking down. But earlier, people would not even go on to their roof. Fuel and water were stored beforehand for the retreat.

After four days, it is permissible to visit other people in the village. Entry to other villages, however, is forbidden till after the festival of Gotsi, which occurs fifteen to twenty days after Halda. Sometimes, one may be forced to visit another village because of pressing work. In that case, the visitor must carry an offering of sattu for propitiating Shiskar-Apa.

On the second day of Halda, each family makes sattu figures of goats, sheep, horses and other animals. These are roasted and kept on a shelf. On the third day of the new moon, these figures are taken to the roof. The moon is worshipped and pieces from each sattu figure are thrown in offering. The people bow down and touch their foreheads to worship the moon. Chhaang is offered and drunk. In Kolong and Sissu villages, a dried goat or sheep head is held up to the moon and is eaten the next day. The people pray to the moon, 'Ama dos tahe tshe', that is, 'Mother moon, may you have a long life'. The sattu figures are then given to the children and the next morning, they go from house to house with these. People give them sattu, and occasionally, money for their trouble. They then prepare thukpa and have a feast.

On the final day, people prepare lumps of sattu with butter and feed these to the crows and ravens early in the morning. The belief is that those who feed the crows early will finish their work on the crops early in summer. I was woken up at about 3.30 a.m. by shouts from the village. People were on their roofs shouting, 'Pos, Pos!' for that is how they called the crows. Of course, the crows took their time and came after sunrise!

A few days after Halda, we were coming back from a walk to Beeling bridge, when near the school, we were surrounded by a cheering group of youngsters. My friend Norbu Tshering was their leader. He had got hold of a pair of lohaar's drums, and had slung them around his neck. On these he was beating a lusty rhythm. A couple of boys had sattu figures in trays. They pressed these on us and demanded money. We gave them six rupees and they went away cheering wildly. My sattu figure was actually made with skill and had a yellow flower stuck in the entwined horns. The boys roamed the village extorting money and more sattu from householders.

The first month of the new year is most auspicious for prayers. One prayer made during this period is considered equal to one thousand at any other time. Therefore, the lamas spend this month in the monasteries in prayer and fasting.

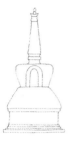

Thanksgiving

When once you have tasted flight,
You will forever walk the earth
with your eyes turned skyward,
for there you have been,
and there you will always long to return.

—Leonardo da Vinci

On 28 January, relatives began to arrive in Kyelang for Gotsi, in many ways the most important and colourful of all Lahaul festivals. It is celebrated as thanksgiving for the sons born in the village during the year. Prayers are also offered to the Kyelang devta for the birth of many more sons in the next year. This feast has nothing to do with the lamas or Buddhism. With their flair for worshipping diverse gods without any feeling of spiritual contradiction, on this date, the Lahaulas pray to the local Kyelang devta—a reminder of the times when human sacrifice was offered in this valley.*

---

*"Without doubt there existed a very low kind of religion in Lahaul before 'Buddhism' got hold of the people, and the latter has not been able to suppress it entirely. That early religion of Lahaul is still known under the name of Lung-pachhoi, that is, the religion of the valley.

The story goes that there was a powerful devta in Kyelang. Human sacrifice was offered to him, though it is not certain whether this sacrifice was made every twelve years or at some other interval. Each family and each village in the area had in turn to provide a man for the sacrifice. A person with any deformity such as lameness or blindness was not accepted for sacrifice. It is said that the chosen person was feasted for three days and then taken in procession to the devta's abode. He or she was then locked in the devta's room and thus died of starvation.

The people ultimately grew tired of the Kyelang devta and his voracious appetite for human flesh. One day, a famous lama came to the village. It was the day of the human sacrifice and the victim-to-be was the only son of a widow. The poor woman was lying prostrate with grief. On hearing of the great lama's visit, she went and fell at his feet, beseeching him to help. The holy man was moved by her state, and decided to take the place of the widow's son. When taken to the devta's abode, the lama challenged the god to eat him. Naturally, the devta could not oblige! The lama then broke the devta's image into pieces and threw it in the Bhaga river. These broken bits floated down the river, past Tandi, towards the Pattan valley. At the village of

When it was flourishing, many bloody and even human sacrifices seem to have been regularly offered up to a certain 'Llha', that is, gods or evil spirits residing in or near old pencil cedars trees, rocks, caves, etc. This cruel custom disappeared gradually after the doctrine of the Buddhists had influenced for a time the minds of the people. At present near not a few villages, sheep and goats are yearly killed and offered up to evil-disposed 'Llhas', and it may be that animals have now taken the place of men.' (Reverend Hyde, quoted in the *Kangra District Gazetteer*, 1897)

Jobrang, about ten miles below the Tandi confluence, the head of the devta came to rest on the river bank. Some Gaddi shepherds of Kangra, who were passing that way, recognized the god and offered to rescue him, provided he gave up human sacrifice and agreed to accept animals instead. The devta was in a sad plight and in no position to bargain, and readily accepted their offer. The head of the god was then carried across the Kugti pass and installed near Kugti village. Shepherds of the area hold a great festival in the summer at this spot and sacrifice numerous goats and sheep. The god here is still known as the Kyelang devta. Besides, though the people at Kyelang threw out their devta, they continue to have great affection for him.

A very ancient cedar tree near the house I stayed at in lower Kyelang symbolizes the abode of the devta, and the annual Gotsi festival is held below this tree.* In upper Kyelang, his abode is a small field in the centre of the village. On Gotsi day, the Kyelang devta is supreme. After the festival, the people calmly forget him and go back to their lamas till the next year.

The devta also has a separate priest called *labdagpa*. The priesthood is hereditary in a family of the Lonchhenpa sub-caste. Since the devta has two separate abodes in upper and lower Kyelang, the family has also split up and there are separate priests at each of the two abodes. The priests are dug up once a year on Gotsi; for the rest of the year, they are forgotten.

---

*'Near the village of Kyelang, a large dry pencil cedar was standing till last year, when we felled it for fire-wood; the story goes that before this tree, in ancient times, a child of eight years old was annually sacrificed to make the spirit who resided in it well disposed towards the inhabitants of Kyelang,' wrote Mr Hyde in 1868. Evidently, the Lahaulas did not give up the devta as Mr Hyde perhaps hoped. In 1962, I saw another 'large dry pencil cedar' at the same spot!

Early in the morning of 28 January that year, the lohaars went to the house of the priest. He gave them chhaang and sattu. They then began to beat a special tune called *rolma lulchi* to announce the start of Gotsi. I was awakened by the rhythmic throb of the drums. They no longer had the dull slow beat of the death march, but had a pleasant pulsating movement.

At about ten in the morning, a puja was performed before the devta. All families in the village sent one man to the puja with butter and sattu. Families with a son (I shall henceforth call them Gotsi families) brought sattu, butter, chhaang and the green twigs and branches of the cedar tree. The priest also brought along the same items. The puja was performed and offerings were made to the devta. Customarily, the puja had to be finished before noon.

At this puja, the priest moulds all the sattu that villagers bring along into a single mound called *dange*. The butter is then moulded into the form of a sheep and put on this mound. The priest murmurs some prayers and offers the sattu mound and the chhaang to the devta. The cedar branches are burnt as incense and drums are played continuously during this ceremony. It should be noted that no function is complete without the lohaar and his drums.

After the devta puja, by noon, everyone went home. In the afternoon, the Gotsi families sent men from the house with gifts of chhaang to the priest to invite him to visit them. The priest graciously accepted each invitation. After bathing with water that contains cow's urine—another Hindu practice—the priest wore his best gown and put on his cap. This cap was not taken off till the ceremonies were completed. To accompany him on his round of visits, he chose a friend as aide-de-camp, locally called *laupa*. (This is a coveted job for it promises many jars of chhaang in each house.) The priest then started his visits.

In each house, he was welcomed with great courtesy. Chhaang was drunk and dried flowers were tied to the caps of the priest and the laupa. The priest also sang traditional ballads in honour of the devta. (In view of the priest's tight programme, he is not expected to sing all the traditional nine ballads. For this, professional singers from other villages are hired by each family to do so. They sit the whole night, drinking chhaang and singing, and complete singing all the ballads by morning. One or two members of the house sit with them to ply them with chhaang, and to prevent them from dozing off. It is considered an ill omen if any of these tipsy gentlemen drops his cap.) After each visit, the priest is supposed to return to his house and bathe. If this condition was rigidly followed, it would have killed him! In January, a bath is no joke for a tipsy man. In practice, therefore, the priest only washes his face, or even ignores that. Besides, the priest has to finish all visits by next morning! If there are a good number of houses to visit—eleven in upper Kyelang to visit this year—the priest staggers from house to house in a losing race against time and sobriety! He is accompanied by the village men who also knock down plenty of chhaang. Men hold the priest as he staggers around for it would be terrible if he fell and dropped his cap. The belief is that the Gotsi child will die if that happens. This bacchanalian revelry ends in the early hours of the morning when the priest retires to his house to pray (!) and prepare for the next morning's ceremonies. The lohaars also visit the Gotsi families. They carry little arrows and arches made of brass and are rewarded with chhaang. Echoes of Cupid?

Early in the morning, each Gotsi family prepares a big mound of sattu and places it on a wooden tray. The mound can be as much as twenty kilograms or more. One or two torches of cedar twigs are also prepared. Generally, these are made and kept at the time of Halda, and a ceremonial butter mark is put on each torch. The professional singers sing another song at this time. Meanwhile, the priest also staggers home. Alone, he communes with the devta and performs puja nine times.

The ceremonies of the next morning are best described in terms of my own experience of the day. It was a brilliant day, clear blue sky and lovely warm sunshine. I was up and ready by ten in the morning. I did not want to miss any of the fun. Shortly after, Tshering Dorje arrived with the news that the ceremony would be first held in upper Kyelang. We could watch it and then come back in time for the lower Kyelang ceremony. At about eleven in the morning, we walked to upper Kyelang, loaded with cameras. Below the road, there is a small field surrounded by houses. This was to be the scene of the festival. We jumped over a hedge of piled wood. In the middle was a small fire and sitting near it was the laupa. His cap was bedecked with dried flowers and within reach of his right hand was a kettle full of chhaang and a cup. Under the conditions, I could guarantee that the reason for the lustre in his eyes was an innocent one! Against the fence were piled the *khultsi*. These are lambskins filled with straw and sewn up. Each khultsi was tied at both ends to sticks to facilitate carriage. Each Gotsi family brings one of these. In lower Kyelang, these are brought to the abode of the devta in the morning with the main procession. Upper Kyelang has a different custom. These are placed in the field on the night preceding the ceremony. The poor laupa, fortified by chhaang and with a fire to keep him warm, is expected to guard them against stray dogs. The temperature at this time of the year is -10°C or lower! The upper Kyelang laupa was, however, none the worse for his vigil. We joked about his ordeal and I pressed the chhaang on him for he was shy of drinking in my presence. I could see that he needed it!

Normally on Gotsi day, the ground is piled thick with snow—there may be three to five feet of it. The sky is often cloudy with portent of more snow to come. This hampers the festivities to some extent, though it facilitates the snow fights later in the day. That year, the snowfall had been very light. Long before Gotsi, the ground was clear. Snow remained only on the flat fields and the surrounding mountains. The slopes of Kyelang were dry. The sky was a deep blue and the sun shone bright and warm.

Soon, people began to gather around the field. The roofs were used as convenient stands, windows were thrown open and children began to press into the little field. Everyone was dressed in their best clothes. The women had washed, oiled, combed and plaited their hair into many glossy pigtails. These were bunched below the waist, and held by massive silver clips. On their nape, they wore heavy silver flowers, gold plated into the central core. On the edges of their foreheads, they wore yellow plastic bulbs, held in place by silver chains. Silver necklaces with heavy brooches were visible in abundance. The dresses were a uniform chocolate colour, which is the only colour worn by women. The girls had evidently spent a lot of time on their toilette. Some looked startlingly beautiful. Mothers carried their babies tied in woollen shawls on the back. Soon the surrounding roofs were packed. It was a magnificent sight: the mass of chocolate-robed, bejewelled beauties outlined against the snowy peaks and a clear blue sky. I climbed on to a roof to get a better view. There, the peaks towards Jispa came into sight. Kyelang lay in a series of terraces, along a gentle slope. Opposite us, the Dilburi peak glistened in the sun. Could anyone in Chandigarh even visualize this sight?

At about 1 p.m., the Gotsi processions suddenly emerged out of a number of houses and began to converge on the field. From the roof, I could look into almost all the streets and had a perfect view. Each procession was led by men carrying lighted cedar torches. Behind the torch bearers came four young men carrying the sattu mound on a wooden tray. They were brilliantly dressed and some wore gowns of heavy Chinese silk, obviously relics of the days when Lahaul men traded extensively with Tibet. These carriers are called *karipa*. Each procession was accompanied by a *kalchorpa*—a girl, married or unmarried, whose parents are alive. The kalchorpa is a most essential part of the ceremony and is certainly responsible for a great deal of the colour in the festival. Girls are picked for their beauty and are dressed beautifully, with a lovely yellow silk shawl around the shoulders. But what caught the eye was their magnificent jewellery. Entwined into the pigtails on both sides of their heads were a mass of silver rings, about three inches diameter, heaped one upon the other. These covered their ears and hung over their foreheads and cheeks. The face and the eyes could not be seen from the sides. In their noses, the girls wore large rings, and on their heads they wore crowns of turquoise. Necklaces completed the set. The total weight of the jewellery must have been almost a kilo, yet the general effect was not oppressive. Each girl carried a beautifully carved silver goblet, full of chhaang. Led by the drummers, each procession made for the field.

The proud father was lost in the medley of drunken men by now, some of whom stumbled every few steps. The mother, decked in her finery, and loaded with ornaments came last. She carried the son, the cause of all the celebrations, tied securely on her back. Before leaving the house, each procession would have had a little ceremonial chhaang—cynics might call it one for the road! Everyone wore flowers on their caps. During the summer, wild rose and marigold flowers are dried, pressed and sewn between round slips of coloured paper. These are then put by for the winter festivals. The men wear flowers on their caps at all festivals. These processionists chanted 'Hai siwara ke ree ho' in a dull monotone. The words mean, 'Hail mountains of the East'. This was originally a long ballad of invocation to all the mountains. Now the people remember and sing only this single line.

The priest came with the processions that came down the central street. His cap was loaded with flowers. He had a large shawl thrown around his shoulders and hidden beneath its ample folds, he carried his sacred bow and arrows. The spread of the long flowing shawl gave him the look of a monarch in ceremonial robes. It reminded me of the cheap prints of British kings that were so abundant in India before independence. The priest walked with a slow regal gait, with vigilant attendants, ready to hold him if he tottered. His bloodshot eyes proclaimed the night's revels.

Soon, the processions reached the field; the sattu mounds were placed in a group. The girls, who reminded me of the vestal virgins, sat down in a row and began to pray. The priest also started a separate prayer. The men began to distribute the sattu. Shares are given to each family of the village. Bunches of giggling girls stood about, perhaps envious of the kalchorpas. The roofs seemed to be crowded with bent heads. The priest bowed thrice and made offerings of sattu and chhaang to the devta. He then sprinkled a little chhaang on the ground. By now, the girls had also finished their prayers. They came to the priest one by one and poured chhaang from their silver kettles into his cupped right hand. They also marked the left side of his palm with a little butter. The priest drank chhaang from each kalchorpa. On being thanked, each girl replied by slightly cupping her hand and touching her forehead, very much like the greetings of Muslim ladies.

After the priest had drunk chhaang, the village elders insisted that I too have the drink. I was only too glad to do so! The chhaang had a pleasant taste of butter milk. The girls then went around offering chhaang to all those present. The proud mothers also took a sip. It was a perfect picture: the bejewelled mother with the papoose on her back, taking chhaang in her cupped hand from a silver goblet held by a beautiful girl. Who can gauge the feeling of fulfilment in the mother, and perhaps, of yearning in the girl!

I was busy taking photographs of this lovely setting when I was suddenly pounced upon by a young man, no doubt properly primed with chhaang. He proceeded to rub a fistful of snow into my beard, much to everyone's amusement. He declared it to be devta prasad! I thought good humour was the better part of valour and took the rubbing without resistance. The elders of the village full of chhaang and courage, came up to me again and again to shake my hand and declare what an honour my presence was to them. I had a few digs at them in return.

The priest and the kalchorpas soon returned to a nearby house, no doubt to refresh themselves with a few cups of pick-me-up. They were to rest for some time before the archery. I suppose the priest badly needed some rest. I decided not to wait, but rather to go to lower Kyelang for their ceremony. After all, I was a resident of that hamlet. We strolled down the road, followed by all the young boys and girls of the village. It is the custom for the upper Kyelang folk to witness the lower Kyelang Gotsi and then go back for their archery. The snowball fight takes place at lower Kyelang.

As I have said, the lower Kyelang devta resides in an ancient cedar tree by the side of the main road. We waited near it. Soon the youngsters began to arrive in little groups. They began to pelt each other with snowballs, but stopped after a little while as there was not much snow on the road as in former years. To give an impetus to the game, I sneaked into a field with a few others and we began to pelt the boys. They retaliated vigorously. Soon there were little fights going on all over the hill side. Boys and girls played freely. Some youngsters played on the roofs of the houses, chasing each other around the hay-ricks. A bunch of girls filled tins with snow and poured them on any unfortunate who happened to pass down the street! We officials were left alone . . . I suppose the boys were a little scared of the magistracy! But the girls were not. Some of them sneaked up and suddenly let fly a fearful barrage. The schoolboys joined in. A few junior officials with old scores to settle also lobbed a shell now and then. We tried to counter attack, but were outnumbered and out-manoeuvred. Soon the bureaucracy was in full flight!

The timely arrival of the Gotsi processions saved us from a total rout. That year, there were only two families with boys in lower Kyelang and hence only two processions. But the lower Kyelang men, perhaps a little ashamed of their performance, made up for it by boisterousness. They were more tipsy and more rowdy. Drums were played with greater vigour. Mayor Kalzan led the processions. As soon as he spied me, his face lit up with a broad Cheshire cat grin, and he prepared to give me devta prasad! I took another rubbing of snow without resistance. Another old man put a mud mark on my forehead. Lama Norbu Dorje, in a state of perfect inebriation, thanked me again and again saying, 'We are poor. This is all we can show. We are honoured.' Every time he swayed forward in grateful thanks, we all laughed. Lama Dorje was a vigorous dancer, and I was told that he was the star attraction of the annual Sha-shur monastery festival, when a morality play is enacted through dance mime.

The lower Kyelang priest is more impressive. A tall man with a florid, puffy face, and a luxuriant moustache, he has a commanding presence. Standing on the road with bowed head, he prayed to the devta. The kalchorpa then offered him chhaang. Of course, I too had my share. The lamb skins were placed at the roots of the tree, about twenty-five feet away, and we prepared for the most vital ceremony of the day. The priest shoots at these skins. On his skill and steadiness depends the harvest of sons in the next year. If he hits the stuffed skins with difficulty, then there will be no sons in the village in the next year, and the people will have a dry or *Kam* Gotsi. If he strikes easily, there will be plenty of sons. The point where the skin is hit indicates the part of the village in which sons will be born. Thus, if the skin is struck on the top, sons will be born in the northern part of the village. If the bottom is hit, then in the south.

As the priest prepared, we waited nervously. Last year, lower Kyelang had done badly—only two sons against eleven in upper Kyelang. What did the devta have in store for us this year? But whatever the cause of last year's failure, the priest was determined to do better this year. He took an arrow and facing towards the

Dilburi peak, opposite the devta tree, he prayed silently, passing the arrow around his arms, back and legs every now and then. Then fixing the arrow to his bow he shot one off towards Dilburi. He now turned and faced the lamb skins. We held our breath. With a steady aim he put the very first arrow through the centre of the skin. A great shout went up. The devta had obviously relented. Again and again, he hit the skins, now in the north now in the south, till the straw stuffing was beginning to fall out. We shouted ourselves hoarse in acclaim. Next year we would show upper Kyelang!

The cedar torches were now piled in a bonfire in the centre of the road and the men formed a circle around it. They danced in a slow movement, a languorous shuffling step. It would not be altogether incorrect to say that they stumbled around!

The party soon broke up and everyone went home. The relatives who had come for the festival stayed for another day or two. At night, I heard the pulsating drum. No doubt, the last of the chhaang was being polished off. A day or two after the celebrations, the priest starts on another round of feasts. Each Gotsi family invites him for a quiet dinner. The reasoning is that in the rush of the festival, the house has not been able to entertain the priest properly!

Expenses? Tshering Dorje celebrated the Gotsi of his first son this year. He spent about five hundred rupees. Many large jars of chhaang were prepared for the feast. But who cares about the expenditure? After all, a man is not blessed with a son every day.

Women dancing at the
Tabo monastery.

The Kyelang flagpole that
replaced the cedar stump.

Kyelang schoolboys playing
in winter, *circa* 1960.

Clearing the roof of snow after
a heavy snowfall in Kyelang.

Ploughing at Kibber village in Spiti.

Khoksar women beating straw from which winter
shoes are made.

Karding monastery.

My first welcome party
at Kyelang.

Karding monks welcoming me on my first visit there.

The Gotsi procession–girls in Kyelang.

The archer ready to shoot for sons near the Kyelang
pencil cedar tree during Gotsi, *circa* 1961.

Bringing the sacred books down from Sha-shur for a
dambargya in Kyelang.

A failed attempt at skiing–but I look the part!

Climbing up to the Rohtang in the early morning
with me leading.

Dorje leading us over the Rohtang.

Kaza village, *circa* 1960.

Early twentieth century postcard showing the Moravian Mission in the Kyelang valley in 1854.

The Tandi confluence–Bhagha to the right, Chandra to the left, and the Chandrabhagha going down the Pattan valley.

Kye gompa, *circa* 1961.

The Gondhla castle.

The Blue Pines of Sha-shur

I cannot rest from travel; I will drink
Life to the lees.

—Lord Alfred Tennyson

January was exceptionally dry. There was no snowfall in the second half of the month and the sun shone bright and clear. Soon the slopes were dry and the roads were turning slushy.

I was getting tired of the enforced inactivity and on the first Sunday in February, I decided to walk up to Sha-shur monastery with Tshering Dorje. Sha-shur means 'in the blue pines'. Sha-shur is the church for Kyelang and lies about 1,500 feet above Kyelang on the same slope. About two hundred years back, Dewa Gyatso, a missionary sent by Nwang Namgyal, the king of Bhutan, came to Lahaul via Tibet and introduced the Drugpa, red-hat sect, in this area. Namgyal was the founder of this sect and the name originates from 'Dug' the Bhoti name for Bhutan. This perhaps explains the intimate connections between Lahaul and Bhutan. Namgyal was later deposed by the founder of the present dynasty in Bhutan.

There was a small monastery at Sha-shur at that time. Dewa

Gyatso built the present imposing structure and stayed at Sha-shur till his death. It is said that when he was cremated, his heart did not burn. It was enclosed in a black image of Gyatso, which is in the main shrine of the monastery today. A statue of Nwang Namgyal, the founder of the sect, is also in the monastery along with numerous statues of the Buddha. There is also an interesting *dechhog* group in the shrine. This shows a four-faced god with eight arms in standing union with a female. It is made of mud plastered over rags, and seems to have been later painted in bright colours. It symbolizes the union of the soul with shakti or God.

We started at about 10.30 a.m. in perfect sunshine and climbed straight up a goat track from the village water spring. Girls were standing about, waiting to fill their jerry cans with water from the newly-installed tap. Fetching water, particularly in winter, used to be a taxing job. Girls had to walk considerable distances, often through deep snow, to reach a spring. Now, in most villages, we have installed water supply systems by building small tanks at the springs and bringing the water through alkathene pipes to the villages. In the early days, water was carried home in small wooden barrels, very much like beer barrels. Now everyone uses empty kerosene oil tins. These are slung on a wooden frame made to fit the back.

After a long period of virtual hibernation, I revelled in the exercise of climbing to Sha-shur. We halted now and then, panting for breath in the rarefied atmosphere. Soon we got on to the main ridge, and could look directly down at Beeling. The height and perspective made it look like a few overlapping brown squares on a white sheet, draped just above the Beeling nullah escarpment. The slope was now easier and there was snow on the ground. There were a number of animal pug marks here— some of which we recognized as those of dogs, but there were others which were bigger and longer. These Dorje attributed to a snow leopard. These lovely animals are found in this area and perhaps one had come down looking for a dog. Across the nullah, there was a sheer drop from the blue pine-dotted snow slope to the village. Tangrols or ibex (*Capra sibirica*) often come down to these ledges for safety during heavy snowfalls. We carefully scanned the chocolate-coloured face with binoculars, but saw nothing. Last year one of my assistants shot an ibex here. He fired across the void and the animal tumbled down into the Beeling nullah. Its beautiful horns, almost forty inches long, were broken.

The sky was clear and all the peaks seemed to draw nearer as we climbed higher. The magnificent peaks opposite Gondhla, normally hidden by the Dilburi ridge, rose into view. With their razor sharp pinnacles and sleek flanks, dropping sheer for many thousands of feet, they would be deadly adversaries for a mountaineer. Now they floated pure and ethereal in the distant blue. My neighbour, the Goshal cone, looked even better. The glaciers on both ends seemed more blue and the triangular lingam, with its beautifully fluted sides, seemed to rear its head defiantly.

The snow lay in patches here. Sometimes we crunched through pure white granulated sugar, and at other times, we squelched and slithered through chocolate-coloured mud. But it was good to see the bare muddy slopes with water trickling down in gentle furrows. The earth seemed warm and held promises of a renewal, of rebirth. We were now among the blue pines and junipers of the Kyelang forest. The trees were widely dispersed over the slope. In this cruel climate, forests do not come up easily. Wood is a valuable commodity. The slopes above Kyelang had many more trees before 1940, mostly planted by the Moravian mission. When the mission left, it sold them, and they were promptly cut down. Now the re-entrant above Kyelang is bare. The nullah that flows down its slopes brings a mass of eroded material every spring and dumps it on the high school ground. The forest department is making intensive efforts to plant more trees. New cold-resistant varieties of plants have been imported from Russia and other European countries and are being tried here. Alfa is a particular success.

In the pine and juniper forest, we came across a lovely house standing in lonely splendour; it commanded a beautiful view of the snow peaks all around. Here, I thought, is a place to rest the weary mind. A big black sheep dog was already barking fiercely and soon, a man appeared. We introduced ourselves; the dog was chased away with snow balls. The man was from Tandi. His father had bought the house and land from the mission. General Bruce, in his book *Kulu and Lahoul*, wrote about living in a lovely house belonging to the mission, high above Kyelang. He writes that Tingtse Cottage, as it was called, was admirably situated, '. . . commanding the whole extent of the view, up and the down Bhaga river; a really remarkable situation, and a perfect climate, for its height was considerably over 11,000 feet, and the air extremely fresh, and invigorating. . . . The Sha-shur monastery, which was on our hill side, and not more than 300 yards from our cottage, and divided from it by fields of peas, and some little rough ground and juniper trees. The monastery is quite an imposing building, white washed as usual, and flat roof, and some three storeys high. The situation is perfect, commanding the finest of all the views of the Bhaga Valley, and especially of the tremendous savage peaks south of the junction, the great Goshal Peak, and its neighbours.' I was sure this was the house,* and for a little while I mused on its tenant of fifty years ago. I complimented the owner, but he complained of the distance

---

*'It was like an Italian cottage. A strip of veranda led into a cheerful parlour, where my supper-table was neatly spread. A hot bath was ready, and I fell asleep to the music of a water-course, which gurgled past my bedroom window.

My waking eyes fell on glaciers and mountains, for my bed was close to the open window, and the most perfect air in the world soon drew me out on the mountain-side.' (Lady Bruce in C.G. Bruce, *Kulu and Lahoul*)

from Kyelang, the lack of drinking water and the height. The beauty of the place had hardly any effect on him for he was too oppressed by his problems.

The monastery was only a few hundred yards farther up. There was the usual cluster of buildings on the slope. The shrine itself is in a nondescript building of no particular beauty. It looked like any of the big Lahaul houses. A portion of the building was still unfinished. The inner shrine had a walk around it with polished brass prayer wheels mounted in niches. The faithful circumambulate it clockwise, giving the prayer wheels a swing as they go by. The wooden balcony above the main door was attractively carved and painted.

Lama Dumbaji, the abbot, and Lama Paljor of upper Kyelang showed me around. (Lama Paljor, in 2009, a sprightly ninety-two-year-old and a family man living in Kyelang, had retired to a cell to meditate for a month. In Lahaul, people manage to keep a perfect balance between the ascetic and the material world. During the summer, the lamas live in the householder's world, coping with all the trials, tribulations and joys of family life. In the winter, they retire to a monastery to meditate. What a boon it would be if all people had the time to retire and meditate on their past actions. Perhaps there would be less madness in the world.) There were not many thankas. Some were undoubtedly very old, but they had faded badly and were in tatters. However, there were two big ones that were superb, the colours fresh and bright. They are displayed only during the annual dance festival.

Outside the monastery were three huge chortens, the biggest of which was about twenty feet high. These are conical pillars of mud and stone surmounted by a moon and star. On top of this emblem, generally, there is a lotus. Chortens are built to house the bones of famous lamas and sometimes those of the thakurs and other rich people. The bones are put in an earthen jar, and with it are placed small quantities of grain of every variety, an oil lamp, seven *dun tsar* cups full of water or salt; bits of gold, silver, semi-precious stones, and bhojpatra leaves with prayers written on them. Old *pothis*, prayer books, are also consigned in chortens. The common people may build chortens in memory of the dead, but may not keep the bones in them. These chortens can be seen all over Lahaul, generally outside villages and near the monasteries. Sometimes a small chorten is built inside the main shrine of the monastery to house the bones of a rimpoche. These chortens are generally covered with silver leaf. The chorten of Lama Norbu, the founder of Karding monastery, is in the main shrine and contains his skull.

Chortens are of eight designs. There are slight variations from one to the other. It is said that Lord Buddha's bones were taken away and put in chortens of different designs by eight kings. Hence the eight designs. The Tomba monastery, near the house of Thakur Prem Chand in Gumrang contains all eight types of chortens. Generally, three out of the eight types are found in Lahaul. The most common is the '*jang chhub chorten*' known as the '*bodhi chaitya*' in Hindi. The difference in designs is slight and only an expert can recognize the different kinds.

To get back to Sha-shur, on either side of the chorten were two giant poplar trees. They were local varieties and not the Lombardy poplar introduced by the missionaries. Between the poplars hung strings of brightly coloured prayer flags, which showed all the brighter against the snow.

Below the chorten, in a hollow, lay the open-air theatre. This was a flat rectangular ground with a pole with bright prayer flags in the centre. The ground was walled in by cutting the slopes. On the northern side there was a covered dais along the wall. The abbot of the monastery sits here on a special seat along with the lama band. The dressing room was next to the monastery to the south. Steps led from it to the enclosure below. The audience sits on the slopes above the hollow, set in a forest of blue pines against a backdrop of the most magnificent snow peaks anywhere. This is the loveliest open-air theatre I have ever seen. There is something of the Greek theatres in its pristine simplicity and dignity. In later life, long after I left Lahaul, I had the good luck to see many historic Greek theatres in Greece and Jordan. The little Sha-shur theatre reminds me very much of those Greek gems with a semi-circle of stone terrace seats going up a hillside, all facing a dramatic stage with two or three stories of dressing rooms at the back. The Greeks, of course, do not have giant Himalayan snow peaks for a backdrop.

In June, when the weather is perfect, and the skies are clear, the people of Lahaul flock to Sha-shur for the annual Chham or dance festival. By that time, the crops have been sown and the people are relatively free. Chhaang flows liberally and the lamas put on a spirited performance of devil dances, as they are generally known to the ignorant. In fact, these are morality plays, as in old Europe, telling elaborate tales of good and evil. The Jataka stories from the Buddha's life performed in the summer festival are a source of learning and entertainment for people.

There is an interesting story attached to the origin of these dances. In AD ninth century, about two hundred years after Buddhism came to the country, Tibet had a very religious king by the name of Gyapo Ralpacham. As was the custom, he kept his hair long. Only monks cut their hair short. He was so full of piety that he would spread his long hair for his guru to sit on, and would spend his time listening to religious discourses. His brother Langdarma, whose thoughts rested on more mundane matters, came one day and chopped off his head while he was lost in the other world. The people, particularly the monks, resented this act of sacrilege, but all the same, Langdarma became king.

King Langdarma also kept long hair, but for a different reason. He had a pair of horns on his head to hide. Every day, a young girl was called to the palace to dress the royal hair in an elaborate coiffure, so as to effectively camouflage the horns. To keep the secret, the girl was killed in the evening and a new one was called the next day. No one knew the reason for the girls' murders. But this action was not likely to endear the king to his subjects. To add to his troubles, the king began to relapse into the ancient Bon faith, which had been supplanted by Buddhism. The severe persecution of monks began.

One day, a girl went to the palace as usual to dress the king's hair. Knowing her fate she began to cry silently. A tear fell on the royal ear. The king looked up and asked her about the reason for her grief. When she told him what pained her, pity overcame his discretion and he spared her life after extracting a solemn oath from her to keep the secret. After some time, the secret began to oppress the girl. She longed to share it, but her oath stood in the way. In desperation, she dug a deep hole in the ground and whispered the secret into it. She then covered the hole with mud. After some time, long green grass known as *tsadam* sprang up on the spot. As it swayed in the wind, it sang, 'The king has horns.' The secret was out.

This was literally the last straw. The lamas who were against the king because of his attempts to restore the Bon faith decided to kill him. For a Buddhist to take life was a great crime, but to kill a king was an even greater one. After much painful deliberation, the lamas decided on a toss. The choice fell on one Lhaling Palgyi Dorje. To strengthen his resolve for this terrible crime, he went into seclusion and prayed. He also learnt to throw the spear and wield a bow. After he mastered these weapons, he threw the spear with such force that it split a rock. This rock can be seen at the famous Sera monastery in Tibet to this day.

It was necessary to entice the suspicious king to a place suitable for the murder. It was then that the lamas decided to give a dance performance for the first time. A gown-like costume with long loose sleeves was designed to enable the assassin to hide his bow and arrows. The dance went on for many days and the people came in great numbers to see it. On the final day, the king presided over the ceremony. The dancers started with a slow rhythmic movement. Slowly, they worked themselves up to a pitch till they gyrated like spinning tops. Suddenly, the assassin stood out of the circle and shot the king.

The lamas had prepared an elaborate escape plan. The murderer ran down to the Kichhoo river. A white horse painted black with charcoal was waiting there. As the horse swam across, it changed colour. The monk also threw his outer robes into the river. Racing to a cave, he sat down in a meditation pose, pretending to be a hermit. It is said, that some birds dusted him with mud to give the impression that he had been in samadhi for a long time.

The king's men were close behind. Soon they came to the cave and saw the hermit in the lotus pose with his eyes closed. One of them felt his heart and found it beating fast. They knew that this was the killer. They said among themselves, 'His beating heart betrays him as the murderer. But the king was a tyrant and is dead. What gain in catching the culprit?' So they went away and Lhaling Palgyi Dorje lived.

The dance then became a regular institution. The people celebrated the death of the tyrant king. Soon, it began to symbolize the death of all tyrants and the fight of good against evil. Animal masks were invented to portray the rakshasas, who were always defeated by the devtas. Intricate steps were invented, music was composed and stories written. The morality ballet had arrived.

At the annual dance at Sha-shur, a sattu image of a rakshasa is made. This is called *dahho*, literally, enemy. It is placed in a triangular box and is carried to the dancing arena in a square sheet held at the four corners by men wearing death masks. It is placed in the centre under the prayer flagpole. The dance is held around it. Great battles take place in pantomime between the rakshasas and the devtas. Finally, the leader kills the sattu rakshasa with his phurpa and dorje. At the end of the dance, the image is thrown away.

At Sha-shur, the dance lasts about three hours, with intervals to allow the dancers to pep up their flagging spirits with liberal helpings of chhaang. At Lhasa, it used to last as many as nine days. At Hemis in Ladakh and Tashigong in Tibet, the dance lasts two days.

I have since seen the Hemis festival in Ladakh in summer. Hemis is the greatest monastery in Ladakh, and the dance is held in a stone paved enclosure, below the four-storey-high gompa building. A huge thanka—about thirty feet long and fifty feet broad—is hung from the top of the monastery building. The head lama, accompanied by his retinue, comes down the monastery steps, walks across the dance courtyard and sits on a rug-decorated throne facing the monastery and the giant thanka. To his left and right are galleries for dignitaries. Large groups of lamas dressed in masks and dazzling silk ropes dance around the pole the whole day. People from the Leh valley and tourists from across the world come to see these morality plays performed in the most impressive amphitheatre known to the world.

After having a look around the monastery, we retired to the cell of Lama Paljor. It was a small room hardly eight feet square. There was a fireplace in one corner and a few rugs in the other. The shelves were full of books, pictures of the Dalai Lama and other knick-knacks of a religious nature. Lama Paljor had prepared some delicious sweets and tea. Over these we discussed various matters. He is an extremely cultured man and I felt as if I was with a Cambridge Don!

After tea, I asked him about the weather. He is well known in the area for his accurate predictions in this matter. He took out various books and made his calculations. Then, in a most matter-of-fact manner, he told me that there would be light snowfall in the second week of February and a very heavy one from about the fourth of March to about the eleventh. There was no doubt in his voice; even meteorologists are more cautious.

The worth of the prediction may be judged by its result. On fourteenth, fifteenth and sixteenth February there was moderate snowfall. From the third to the tenth of March, we had six and a half feet of snow, including three and a quarter feet on the ninth, which was the highest ever recorded for a single day. After tea, we said our goodbyes and strolled down through the terraced fields to the village.

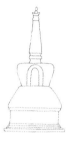

Marriage and Polyandry

The untented Kosmos my abode,
I pass, a willful stranger;
My mistress still the open road
And the bright eyes of danger.

—Robert Louis Stevenson

In February, I witnessed a marriage in lower Kyelang. Sharab, the son of Norbu Dzangpo, our local tailor, literally kidnapped a girl named Palmo from upper Kyelang. The girl's parents quickly accepted it as fait accompli, and for many days, lower Kyelang heard the drums, while the guests soaked themselves in chhaang.

Kidnapping is the most popular method of marriage prevalent in northern Lahaul. Since there are no rigid social taboos, boys and girls meet freely on equal terms. Love cannot be kept out and young people often choose their life partners without the knowledge of the parents. When matters have progressed sufficiently, the boy offers the girl a ring or some other personal possession as a token of engagement. If she accepts it, the matter is settled. This understanding is known as *nya*, which means 'to tie'. The couple then fix a time and rendezvous for the elopement. Generally, the girl proposes to spend the night with some girl friend or goes out to the fields on some pretext. The boy comes with a few young friends and takes her away. The girl may not walk; she must be carried on the boy's back all the way. Though the young bucks come well fortified with chhaang, this can be quite a test of stamina, particularly if their village is some distance away!

Last year, Tshering Dorje was going home in the afternoon after attending office, when he ran into a party of his village boys, struggling home after lifting a girl from near my house. All of them were drunk. They immediately pressed Dorje into service and put the girl on his back. The upper Kyelang folk watched in amusement and shouted, 'Marriage, marriage!' Dorje was terribly embarrassed, and literally ran all the way to his village. After all, it would not do to have the deputy commissioner know that Dorje took part in kidnapping in his spare time!

The boy's parents never refuse the girl, though they may not always agree with the choice. For all practical purposes, the marriage is complete with the elopement and society accepts it. But an effort must be made to placate the girl's parents. An uncle of the boy, known for his smooth diplomacy, is sent the next day to talk things over with the offended parents. To help the conversation along, he carries some chhaang. His appeal is something like this, 'It is a pity that the young people have taken things into their own hands. Your girl is so beautiful and accomplished that we would have liked to ask for her ourselves. However, now that it has happened, please give your consent.' The girl's parents generally spurn the olive branch on the first occasion. Two or three visits have to be made by the emissary before they finally agree. When they do, the girl is brought back and a proper marriage is performed with all ceremony. This form of marriage is known as *baglog*. Occasionally, the parents are more stubborn. In that case, for a year or two, there is no contact. Then the girl, with a child or two comes home for a visit and all ill-will is washed away in the emotional flood of reconciliation. This form of marriage is becoming more and more popular as it is simple and inexpensive.

Marriage according to old customs is still prevalent and is a very elaborate affair. In this case, the parents select the girl. Marriage with a brother's daughter or within the sub-caste is forbidden. All other relations are allowed. When a girl has been chosen, the boy's uncle goes to her house with a pot of chhaang. After exchanging pleasantries with the parents, he stands up and formally asks for the girl. He says, 'Your girl is pretty, accomplished and smart. I have come to ask for her hand for my nephew.' The parents hold a quick consultation. Much is said through the eyes. If the match is found unsuitable, the mother makes a great show of consulting the daughter and the father replies, 'Our daughter is grown up. She knows best. Persuade her and we will have no objection.' Thus, the offer is politely rejected. The emissary understands, and goes back, leaving the chhaang undrunk.

If the proposal is acceptable, the parents ask a few more questions: 'The boy no doubt is well behaved. But are his younger brothers also so? Do they obey him in all matters? Will any of them insist on marrying separately?' The uncle assures the parents that the younger boys are the very paragons of virtue. They are completely obedient to their eldest brother and would never dream of doing such a disgraceful thing. He points to the noble traditions of the family. As far as he can remember, he says, the family has always insisted on one wife for all the brothers in a generation. This assurance is the most important one.

Polyandry is the general practice in Lahaul. The eldest brother gets married and the younger ones take the same wife as they grow up. If the age difference is considerable, the younger brother might find an old woman as wife when he comes of age. This can lead to interesting situations. Tanzin of Gumrang had a much older brother who got married. As a child, Tanzin was suckled by his brother's wife. When he grew up, he took her as wife and fathered children by her.

Polyandry is a rigid social custom.* The people here have practised it since time immemorial and find it normal to share a wife. The custom has an economic raison d'etre. There is very little agricultural land in Lahaul, only about 4,500 acres in an area of almost 2,200 square miles. Due to the severe climate and the height of the valleys, over 9,000 feet at the lowest point, only one crop can be grown in the year during the short summer season. Thus, Lahaul, like many other hill areas, cannot support a large population. Polyandry has acted as a suitable social method of population control. The population of the area was 5,970 in 1868. In 1951, it was 10,147 and in 1961, it was 15,154. This includes a lot of labourers who were working in the valley at the time of the Census. The small land holdings are prevented from fragmentation by the custom of polyandry.

The Lahaulas, therefore, consider this custom most useful and try to adhere to it as much as possible. Now education has come to this area and many young people are finding employment with the government. When they see the customs of the plains, they tend to feel ashamed of their social set-up. Many of them

---

*'Polyandry or the taking as wife of one woman by several brothers is a recognized institution, and is very general; the object is to prevent the division of estates. When asked to defend this repulsive custom, they say that their holdings are too small to divide, and that experience shows them that it is impossible for two sisters-in-law, with separate husbands and families, to live together, whereas two or more brothers, with a common wife can agree.' (Kangra District Gazetteer, 1897)

now desire to have a wife to themselves. This often leads to conflict in the family with the fathers insisting on the old customs.

Rigzin Shewang of Yurnath near Kyelang passed his high school and found employment with the Forest Department. He has four fathers and two brothers. When the time came for him to marry, he informed his fathers that he would not share his wife with his brothers. There was a tremendous row. One of his fathers exclaimed, 'We are four brothers, and have managed with your mother. You are only three, and yet you dare to say, that you must have a wife for yourself. You should be ashamed of your selfishness. You will ruin the family.' The boy tried to resist, but the family pressure was too much. He gave way. After marriage, he never went home from his posting in Kangra. The wife now lives with the next brother.*

It must be remembered that this is a perfectly natural situation. The elders will always stand up for the old customs. The young will always break them. It is as if a young man in the plains should decide to marry outside his caste. In Lahaul, polyandry is the honourable, sacrosanct custom, sanctioned by long usage. In the plains, it is monogamy. One need not laugh derisively at either.

While polyandry is a partial solution to the economic problems of the area, it is also the cause of considerable human suffering. Because of the system, a large number of girls remain unmarried. Their lot is a hard one. Many join the monasteries and become nuns. They live there in small cells. Their families give them some grain for subsistence. For the rest, they work and beg at

---

*'Sir James Lyall mentions a case which came before him in which one of two brothers, living in polyandry much wished to separately marry a girl, by whom he had had an illegitimate child, but the wife of the family objected strongly, claiming both brothers as husbands, and refusing to admit another woman into the household, and she eventually prevailed.' (*Kangra District Gazetteer*, 1897)

harvest time. Twice a year, they go out begging—in September after the buckwheat crop is harvested, and in October after the barley crop. They are also given a little money for a suit of clothes by the monastery every year. Some of them knit and sell socks. (Incidentally, knitting was introduced to Lahaul by Mrs Hyde, the kindly wife of the first Moravian missionary.) By and large, the life of these nuns is miserable. Who can gauge the emptiness and frustration of their lives?

Everyone cannot get married.* Those who do not become nuns remain at home. The unlucky ones wither slowly over the years, like vines that are denied water. While the parents are alive, their lives are tolerable. On their death, the brother's wife takes over. Then the unmarried sister is just a house servant. She does all the work. She fetches water, cuts wood, cooks and cleans. For this, she gets food and a yearly suit of clothes. She also has to put up with abuse and ill treatment by the mistress of the house. The brothers are of no help. In a polyandrous household, the wife rules and the men obey.† If one of the brothers has a soft corner for the sister, the wife works up the other brothers against him. Thus the poor girls lead a miserable existence. They are often turned out of the house and have to work as servants in the village. It is common to see girls of one family as servants in the next, and vice versa.

To illustrate, one of Rigzin Shewang's fathers is named Koolu. He is rather plain looking and is not much in favour with the

---

*'The women outnumber men in the proportion of 108 to 100—a peculiarity, which was observed both at the census of 1881 and at that of 1891.' (*Kangra District Gazetteer*, 1897)

†'"Thy Gods useless, heh? Try mine. I am the woman of Shamlegh." She hailed hoarsely, and there came out of a cow-pen her two husbands, and three others with a *dooli*, the rude native litter of the Hills, that they use, for carrying the sick and for visits of state. "These cattles"—she did not condescend to look at them—"are thine for so long as thou shalt need".' (*Kim* by Rudyard Kipling)

wife. His sister Tshering Dolma is a nun at the Bokar monastery. She lives in the monastery in winter and comes home to help in the summer. Like most unmarried girls she is ill treated. Koolu was fed up with his wife on both counts. One day, he came home drunk, and knocked out two of the wife's front teeth!

Such is the condition of the girls of Lahaul. One can only hope that with the spread of education, polyandry will disappear and every Jill will have her Jack.

To get back to the marriage customs, once the girl's parents are satisfied on all points, they accept the proposal. The chhaang is drunk and the boy's uncle puts a mark on the forehead of each of the girl's family members with butter. The boy's uncle visits the girl's house two or three times more with chhaang. This is probably to get acquainted with the family. On the last occasion, he informs the parents of the date of the marriage. This is decided by the lamas after seeing the years of birth of the boy and girl. The uncle also gives a silver rupee to the mother of the girl. Occasionally, a few silver ornaments are also given for the girl.

On the appointed day, all the relatives collect at the boy's house. In the evening, a marriage party of about fifteen people leaves for the girl's house. People wear their best gowns and marigold flowers on their caps. The bridegroom does not go. He is represented by a person known as the *bagthidpa*—a kind of substitute. He wears special clothes, including silver bangles. He also carries an arrow with a white piece of cloth tied to the tip. Generally, a cousin of the groom acts as the bagthidpa. A woman in the party carries a pot of chhaang and a boy carries a load of sattu and butter. The party is well plied with chhaang before it leaves. All villages along the way must also entertain the party with chhaang.

At the bride's house, the party finds the door closed. A clump of grass hangs over the door. A knock produces a rude answer: 'Go away. We are lions and elephants. You are jackals and donkeys. We will not give you our daughter.' The marriage party replies, 'You are the donkeys and jackals. We are the lions and elephants. Open, and we will take your daughter.' This sort of exchange of compliments goes on till the party decides to buy its entrance. The bride's people demand fabulous sums while the groom's party demurs. Finally, five to ten rupees are paid. The door is opened and the grass over the door is cut.

Before entering the house, the party is cleaned of any evil spirits that might have come with them during the journey: a lama carries a tray with three oil lamps and three lumps of barley on it. This he passes over the head of each one of the party while chanting mantras. The barley lumps are then thrown away. Drums are beaten and the lama cries, 'Sarva bhoota preta gaccha' ('Go away, all evil spirits'). The marriage party then enters the house. Sometimes, they are put to a final test before entry. A buried sheep's heart has to be located. Hints are given through a song as to its exact position. Unscrupulous members of the party even try to buy the secret from the bride's people!

In the main room of the house, special seats are prepared for the guests. Plenty of Tibetan and Kalimpong rugs are spread out. Eight auspicious figures—umbrella, circle, fish, conch, pitcher, a Sanskrit sign called watsa, flag and lotus—called the tashi tagyad are outlined in barley, the sacred grain. The party sits down with the bagthidpa on the first seat to the right. A small table with a wooden bowl full of barley is placed in front of the bagthidpa. He places his arrow on top of the bowl and must guard this arrow. If it is stolen, the party needs to pay more money to retrieve it. The girl's relatives sit opposite the groom's party while the girl waits in another room with her friends.

Chhaang is served to all. In Lahaul, special flat bronze bowls of various sizes called *pagsgormo* are used for serving chhaang on all occasions. An average one can take about two bottles of the liquid. The biggest, the well-known Saji and Ludub of Beeling village can carry about four bottles. Chhaang is always measured out in a pagsgormo, like a peg measure. In every round, a pagsgormo is handed to each guest, who drinks it from a cup. Thus the rounds go on and a man may finish anything like fourteen to fifteen bottles in a sitting.

While everyone is drinking, the girl's relatives quiz the marriage party. These are in the form of songs. Questions and answers flow back and forth in song. An example is: 'Name a bird which suckles its young.' The answer: 'Bats.' The questioner demands that if the party does not know the answer, they should bow thrice before him if they wish to know the answer. If an answer is missed, the party pays money to avoid the humiliation of bowing. In Kolong, the hosts actually beat their guests with sticks and leather thongs saying, 'You are such stupid people. Why have you come for our daughter?' After the questions, the marriage party dances. The girl's relatives may join in if they wish. After the dance, every one eats. Having eaten, they all sit down. The marriage party offers the chhaang and barley cake that they have brought to the girl's relatives. Sometimes, they bring dried meat and this too is distributed.*

This is the time when the marriage party formally claims the bride. The bagthidpa and two or three other members of the party go to the girl's room. At the door, they sing another song and are offered chhaang. The girl is also given some chhaang by her parents and a butter mark is put on her forehead. The

---

*'Five or six sheep are killed in each house at the beginning of the winter; the flesh dries, and will then keep good for any number of years; the older the meat, the greater the delicacy of the taste to a Lahauli.' (*Kangra District Gazetteer*, 1897)

bagthidpa then ties the arrow to the girl's back and the party returns to the main room after this ceremony.

The girl's dowry is laid out in another room and the guests are then taken to see it. This generally consists of fifteen to twenty-five suits of clothes for the bride, pots and pans for cooking and some jewellery made of silver and semi-precious stones. People in Lahaul do not attach as much importance to the size of the dowry as the plains folk do. They look to the girl, who should be smart and healthy, so that she may be able to do all the work. This is important since almost all the field work, except ploughing, is done by women. It is also useful if the girl has a large number of relatives because they can be called for help whenever there is a lot of work to be done.

By now, it is generally early morning and time for the bride's departure. The bagthidpa and two or three of his companions have to lift the girl. The bagthidpa lifts and carries her to the main room, where all the relatives of the girl, from the grandfather to the youngest brother, sit in a line. Each has a cup of chhaang in front, as it is considered auspicious. The girl goes to the grandfather, touches his feet and sits before him crying. The old man blesses her and gives her a few words of advice, 'Give up the manners of this house and learn those of your new home. Forget your girl friends. You should pay no attention to the gossip at the water spring. Treat all your husbands equally, without favour or prejudice. Respect your mother and fathers-in-law. You should work in the fields from the time the morning star disappears to the time the night star appears. My daughter, leave this house happily and enter the new house with joy. Be its foundation. May your children flourish like the branches of the sacred Bodhi tree. May you live till you acquire a new set of teeth as white as the conch shell.' (In Lahaul, it is believed that after a hundred years, a person gets a new set of teeth.) The old man then gives her a gift of money. The bride touches the feet of each relative, even the youngest. The elders always offer her advice and money. Thus, she takes leave of them.

The bride then moves to the hearth. She rubs her hand in a plate of flour, and puts the marks of her outspread hands with palms downward on the hearth. Crying, she makes an obeisance to the hearth, which has fed her for so long, and which she is leaving forever. A woman standing near her expresses her thoughts for her, 'O hearth, fed by you on the most dainty dishes, I have grown to womanhood. Today I take leave of you.'

The bagthidpa then lifts the bride and carries her to the outer door. The girl is so carried that at the door, she faces the house. Again, she dips her hands in flour and marks the door. The women of the house sing for the crying girl, 'There was a time when I was too small to cross your threshold. Now I can touch your top. Today I bid you farewell forever.'

The members of the marriage party take turns in carrying the girl as she should not walk. All villages along the route greet the party and offer chhaang. These halts are welcome since all brides are not as light as feathers!

On reaching their own village, the marriage party is welcomed by the village folk with chhaang. At the bridegroom's house, a lama gets rid of any evil spirits that might have followed the party by saying prayers, and passing a tray with three oil lamps and three sattu mounds over their heads. Sometimes, a live sheep is thrown down from the house on to the waiting wedding party. This is immediately killed and its heart and liver are eaten raw.

Inside the house, the bridegroom and all his younger brothers are seated on a long padded seat in order of age. The bride is seated next to the youngest brother. A sattu mound is placed in front of them and prayers are held. After offerings to the devta, a piece of the sattu is given to the bride and another is given to one of the brothers. They share it. The girl is then taken to another room, while the marriage party and relatives give themselves up to merry making. The eldest brother spends the first night with the bride. The younger ones can only claim their rights much later as they become familiar with her.

Divorce is not frequent. When needed, it is accomplished with a simple ceremony. The couple sit in the presence of relatives with a common thread tied to their little fingers. Both proclaim that henceforth they will have nothing to do with each other and snap the thread! The wife takes away her dowry on divorce. The individual seeking it also pays a fine to the other.

Winter Vignettes

White in the moon the long road lies,
The moon stands back above;
White in the moon the long road lies
That leads me from my love.

—Alfred Edward Housman

In winter, the snow lies two to three feet deep on the ground. The fields being somewhat flat are completely covered. Here and there, the willows stand out stubbornly with their skinny bare brown arms stretched out in defiance. The ridge above Beeling is completely covered with snow, except for the grey-brown perpendicular rocks, where the snow cannot hold. To the south, the Goshal massif is all white, with a snow plume blowing gently off the main peak. Far behind Karding, the Nilghar peaks, with their beautifully fluted flanks, are outlined sharply against a deep blue sky. The Dilburi ridge opposite my house has given way completely to the white tyranny. On its lower reaches, the contours are soft, white and rounded like lovely breasts. Higher up, the main ridge still retains some of its harshness, but even there, the snow has wrapped its more ugly scars in a soft muslin mantle.

Houses look like giant cubes of light brown on a pure white sheet. Patches of snow lie on the roofs. The hay ricks on the roof, from which the snow has not been cleared, look like cakes with sugar icing dripping from the sides.

The Lombardy poplars have turned an ashen grey, but they still stand stiff, with ramrod backs, like retired military colonels. The yaks and churus pushed out of their damp underground enclosures during the day, stand about disconsolately in the snow. Here and there a more enterprising one nibbles at the dry, brittle branches of a willow. There is no crop or green grass to eat and the animals live on a strict ration, just enough to keep them alive till the summer. Occasionally, a dog ploughs through the soft snow, looking quite miserable. The birds are still about. I have seen some chocolate-coloured tits hopping about in my bare wild rose bushes. Crows and choughs sail about the village looking for food. The blue rock pigeons, however, have disappeared.

On clear sunny days, the village throbs with life. Men and women are out on the roofs, drying grain and clothes, and doing other odd jobs. The children play with snowballs. Little ones toddle about near the edge of the roof, but never fall. Sounds drift across—the deep-throated hoarse call of a crow; the shrill voices of women in conversation; girlish laughter like the tinkle of silver bells; a youngster bawling lustily for his lost snow slide; the high pitched kangling, and the deep gyadung from some prayer for the living or the dead; the clanking of metal sheets as the carpenter fashions another oven; and the village radio blaring music. Occasionally, a plane drones across high above the valley leaving a thin vapour trail, probably on its way to Leh to supply rations to the army. At once, the whole village is out on the roof with the children cheering wildly. The plane is a fleeting, howsoever tenuous link with the outer world. The noise made by the children is like that at a football game.

At night, the stars drip out of a cloudless sky. The sky seems like the silver filigree drape of some young Punjabi bride. The stars seem so near that one is inclined to believe the childhood story of how a mother reached out and plucked a star to wipe her child's bottom. The stars are said to have receded at this sacrilege, perhaps so in the plains, but not here in the high Himalayan valleys. The fact is that the air is so clean and the atmosphere so free of dust that the brightness of the stars is unbelievable.

One big star hangs over the Goshal peak, and as the night progresses, it sinks lower and lower till it seems like the flickering light in some mountaineer's camp on the ridge flank. I think then of the lonely men waiting for the dawn in their little wind-buffeted tent, and preparing for their final desperate effort. What lies in store for them, triumph or tragedy? Soon the star disappears behind the ridge, the tent is no more, and I am shocked back to reality.

The moon drifts across from the north, bathing the whole scene in her soft beams. At first it catches only the peaks and they float about like icebergs in a dark sea. As it rises, the darkness in the valley disappears; the square houses come forward, putting their shadows behind them; the Lombardy poplars stand stiff and still, like sentries sensing an officer on his round. A dog howls in the distance. Surely it is not baying at the moon, for who could dislike such beauty?

The moon has begun to fill out and grow round in the middle, like a young woman with child. It even has a similar, soft transparent glow, and seems to shine on the valley with a Mona Lisa smile of self satisfaction. The nights are wonderful. I often stand out on the balcony, in the bitter sub-zero cold and watch the snow-covered ranges bathed in the soft light. All is silent, save the occasional gruff barking of the watch dog across the valley at Karding. No light shines in the village below. The murmur of the river drifts across now and then. The roaring torrent of the summer is gone. Now a small greenish-blue stream

gurgles through numerous icy caverns, reminding me of
Coleridge's poem.

In Xanadu did Kubla Khan
A stately pleasure-dome decree:
Where Alph, the sacred river, ran
Through caverns measureless to man
    Down to a sunless sea.

All is peaceful, silent. The valley sleeps while the white clad
giants keep watch. I think then of what Keats wrote:

And haply Queen-Moon is on her throne,
Cluster'd around by all her starry Fays . . .

But what of the dark days? Clouds rise behind the Goshal massif
and drift up the valley from Tandi, blotting out the scene, little
by little. Sometimes they are dark brown and menacing, often
they are a light dusty colour. They billow about in the cauldron
formed at Tandi by the meeting of the three valleys of the
Chandra, the Bhaga and the Chandrabaga, then creep up the
Goshal range veiling its base. The peaks float about in a murky
sea of clouds, sometimes looming suddenly into view, and then
disappearing as quickly, like in a Turner painting. The blue
dome disappears and is replaced by a dirty white sheet. Sometimes,
the blue appears through tears in the sheet, but these are
patched quickly by some unseen hand. Occasionally, the sun,
which has not appeared the whole day, manages before sinking
below the hills in the west to trap the cloud-encircled peaks in
its rays. The scene is then superb. The unseen sun lights up the
snowy peaks and the clouds in scintillating colours. All the
shades of the rainbow are present. As the rays get weaker, the
yellow changes to gold and the pink to red and maroon. The
dark valley is already filling with night shadows and the golden
peaks framed in coloured cloud bands—a scene never to be

forgotten. But the glory is transient, and fades fast. Soon, all is dark. The vision seems a dream.

Tired of spending all my time indoors and fretting at inactivity, I was determined to visit the Pattan valley. The weather was peculiar, cloudy in the mornings and generally clear at night. There was no new snowfall. I thought if we made a dash for Thirot, thirty miles away, our luck would hold. Early one morning, Dorje and I set out. Two coolies carried our luggage. We planned to halt for the night at Lote, eight miles away. Due to the clouds, the sun was kept at bay and walking was pleasant. We went down quickly past Beeling to the Tandi confluence of the Chandra and Bhaga, and reached the beginning of the Chandrabhaga. The confluence is a beautiful sangam. The green waters of the Bhaga join the somewhat muddy Chandra river and there is a beautiful white chorten at the confluence. Up in front is the great Goshal peak with the village below it on the flats above the river. This confluence is my favourite place. Summer or winter, I love to go down the road embankment, walk on the sand or snow to the exact point of the merging of the two rivers, and just stand in contemplative silence. Padma Sambhava went past this way and set up the Guru Ghantal monastery on the cliffs above the river. I tried to imagine him sitting here in samadhi. We stopped a while to drink tea and take photographs.

Just short of the Tandi bridge, we turned up the Pattan road, which goes along the right bank of the Chandrabhaga. We passed the Karga maidan, a series of gentle slopes, the well known haunt of the joginis in winter. At Tandi, we were met by Lalchand, the schoolmaster, and other village dignitaries. We chatted about local legends and customs over cups of tea in the schoolmaster's house. Reluctantly, we left the warmth of the fire and pushed forward to Lote in murky weather. The Pattan valley begins to open out here and the slope on our right was gentle and easy, going up to high ridges. Dorje pointed at Tholang village, where the schoolmaster Sukhdas was a fine painter who spent the long winters doing water colours of the Himalayan scenes around him. I wanted to walk up to his village, but the weather would not allow it and we left it for another day.

Long after my 1961–62 stay in the valley, when towards the end of the twentieth century, I was the Chief Election Commissioner of India, Dorje, with whom I have kept in touch all my life, and still do, turned up in Delhi and wanted me to inaugurate and support a painting exhibition by Sukhdas. I did, and what is more, I bought some of his paintings for the Election Commission and encouraged others to do so.

At Lote, we were received by the sarpanch and the villagers. The girls at the water tap stared in unashamed curiosity. An old man with a gown lined with soft lambskin came forward and led us to his house. He was our host. The house was huge, three storeys high with over thirty rooms. Massive glass-paned windows and doors studded the front. Lahaul homes are truly impressive, camel-coloured cubes, generally three storeys high, beautifully-built, with windows at all levels. The ground floor is for animals as they need the warmth and the shelter during the long winter. An internal notched log-wood ladder takes one to the upper floors, which are used for family living. Our host led us to a small room on the top floor. I slept on the floor on Tibetan and Kalimpong rugs. The dinner was a fine thukpa and cauliflower.

In the morning, in uncertain cloudy weather, we left for Shansha. This is a large village and deserves a future visit. We were keen to get to Jhalma as early as possible. Since the weather remained murky and also because we were fully acclimatized we could keep up a fast pace. At Jhalma, we repeated the stay of the earlier night in the sarpanch's house and left early in the morning for Thirot, the last village of my district. I wanted to get there and go beyond, to Udaipur in Chamba district, to visit the Devi Manikula temple there. It was a long day's walk, but we finally made it to Udaipur in the afternoon.

The Devi temple was worth all the trouble I went through to get there. It was a very ancient temple of wood, but the insides surprised and amazed me. All the wooden walls have the finest carved panels with scenes from the Mahabharata and the Ramayana. I photographed each panel. It is a treasure of our Himalayan heritage, which needs care and protection. In the compound, on a circle of sand, was placed a very large round stone. I was told that if seven men stood around it, put one finger each to the stone, and shouted '*Jai Devi Mata ki*', they could lift the stone above their heads! I asked to see this being done. The men with me did so as I watched. I then joined the effort and my group was successful too. I still cannot explain this phenomenon.

Having seen and photographed the temple, I was keen to return to Kyelang. We had some tea and started a brisk walk back. We managed to get to Lote the next day in tolerable weather, and stayed with the same farmer. In the morning, I had a leisurely breakfast and left somewhat late, at about 11.00 a.m., thinking the last stage would not be too much trouble. But soon, snow started falling and a wind came on. Already, the beaten track had been obliterated by the snowfall in the night. The wind coming down the valley drove the snow flakes into our faces with a stinging velocity. My face seemed to burn with a cold fire. Visibility was down to twenty yards. Bent forward and leaning into the wind, we continued to plod on. The snow got into my beard and froze my hair. At last, Tandi loomed out of the mist and we made straight for Lalchand's cosy house. While tea was being prepared, I examined the school children. School was being held in a room in the master's house with the children seated around the fire. The family women sat knitting nearby. Knitting socks is almost a cottage industry. All Lahaul women, young and old, are always found knitting away, the socks patterns being the same multicoloured, mathematical ones, which Mrs Hyde and Mrs Schnabel, the missionary wives, had taught their elders in 1868.

The school children were nervous and inspection by an outsider is a big bogey. The master fidgeted at their ineptitude and made matters worse. Slowly, I won them over. They were good kids. There were six girls in the class, a big number in this area. I then began chatting with the children. Had they seen a train? No. A plane? Yes, yes! Many pass over every day. Electricity? They had no idea what that was, but they had read that it gives light. Later, we were able to start a micro hydel unit on the Beeling nullah at Kyelang. Today, of course, both valleys have power in almost all the villages. None of the children had been to Kulu, which seemed to symbolize the civilized world to them. Would they like to go? Yes, of course. What would the girls like to become? Doctors? Teachers? Giggles!

We left Tandi at about 3 p.m. The sky was clearing up and patches of blue began to appear. We entered Kyelang in bright sunlight and cursed the fickle weather gods!

The weather is lovely; clear nights with the stars almost within reach, the days a mass of intense white light due to the snow. The snow is beautifully crystalline, like the best white sugar. It is intensely cold at night. Along the paths, the water freezes into a transparent glass-like surface, and woe betide any man who steps on it! Plastic articles such as purses and diaries have gone stiff and crack at the slightest pressure.

At about half past four, Dorje and I went for a walk towards Beeling. We do so everyday and this is my sole exercise. A reasonable path has been worn down and it is not too slippery. We caught up with two road gang men who turned out to be Zanskaris from a village near Padam in Ladakh. They had been in the road gang for the last two years. Many Zanskaris apparently come to Lahaul and Kulu to work on development projects. Zanskar is a poor region, cut off by high mountains and narrow river gorges from Kargil in the west, Leh in the north, and Lahaul in the east. The Zanskar river flows through the valley to ultimately join the Indus near Leh.*

Both men knew Hindi well and told me that one could reach Padam in seven days via the Shingu La. I asked them if they knew of the British women who had made an overland expedition in 1956. They seemed delighted and amused, and said they did remember three white women who had visited their village with Namgyal Ladakhi. Two of them were young women, but the third one, they told me, was old with light hair; obviously, in Padam, gentlemen do not prefer blondes! In 1956, a British Army Expedition came to Lahaul for climbing. While the men went around the valley climbing various peaks, their wives decided to attempt a rarely done trek over the Shingu La pass to Padam in the Zanskar valley of Kashmir. One of them wrote a delightful book titled *No Purdah in Padam*.

Lahaul is a climbers' paradise. The British knew this and General G.C. Bruce of the Gorkha regiment is the most famous

---

*I have in later years, photographed that dramatic confluence: the muddy Zanskar river with the icy blue Indus. In recent years, mountaineers have done a dramatic trek in the winter, walking on the frozen river through narrow gorges, all the way to Leh. The Kashmir government has also built a road from Kargil to Padam, and this is being extended to Leh, through the Zanskar river gorge. Trekking parties frequently go from Kyelang, over the 16,000-feet-high Shingu La pass, to the Zanskar valley.

climber to have come to the valley. He climbed these valleys in the early part of the twentieth century, taking a seven-month leave from the army. He came to the Kulu valley and climbed the mountains there in the summer up to the monsoons; he then crossed over into Lahaul, where the rains did not reach because of the Rohtang barrier, and left his wife in Kyelang with her dogs to climb the Lahaul peaks. He crossed back to Kulu at the end of the rains in September and finished with another flourish of climbing in Kulu in the autumn. He left excellent accounts of his Lahaul experiences in a number of books, the most famous being *Kulu and Lahoul*.

I believe that Lahaul is ideal for mountaineers from the west. People in Europe generally get short leaves only. It is possible to fly from London to Delhi, rush to Kulu by taxi and across the Rohtang to Kyelang, walk down to the Thirot and Miyar nullahs in Pattan, go up to the glaciers, and start climbing, all in about five to six days. A short two-week climbing holiday in Lahaul valley is therefore quite possible. Numerous articles in the *Himalayan Journal* testify to this possibility, and now I find, as a past president of the Himalayan Club, that young western mountaineers visit the Thirot and Miyar glaciers regularly.

We left the Zanskari men just beyond Beeling. They both smelt strongly of chhaang and admitted to having had two glasses each! I noticed that these days, no one moves out without chhaang inside; apparently, the Lahaula equates chhaang with socks and sweaters as a cold resistant!

The women have to walk considerable distances to fetch water—a terrible job in this cold. The Beeling women come to a spring near the Beeling nullah bridge, a walk of a furlong at least. They carry water in wooden barrels or kerosene tins slung on their backs, with the strap over their forehead. At the spring, I saw an old lady having her hair dressed; she seemed to have washed it, quite a surprise considering the temperature. I am told the ladies have wide foreheads because their hair falls out due to the weight of the silver ornaments on their pigtails. Now that this jewellery is being discarded, this will disappear. There is no doubt, however, that a wide forehead is considered auspicious. One of the important development efforts of the Punjab government here has been to lay polythene pipes to bring water from springs at heights above the village down to the streets. Every village is being provided with water taps and this has considerably eased the burden of women and girls.

At dusk, wrapped in my great coat, I went for a walk to the Beeling bridge. Some girls were returning from the fields. One of them stood in my way and pretended not to give way, and then they all laughed enjoying their little joke!

On the way back, I noticed a great noise being made on pieces of tin, accompanied by singing. I was keen to see the sort of games children play here. In the bazaar, I found a bunch of them, aged from nine to twelve, making a great commotion. I followed them for a while and then took them home. They were not in the least shy. They straightaway gave a recitation of various poems in Hindi, which they had learnt at school. Strangely, they knew none of their own folklore! Unfortunately, this is how local folklore and culture begins to disappear. A stronger culture comes into the area and the school text books all refer to stories from some other region and subplant the local folklore.

The children were thrilled by the pictures in my room. They recognized photographs of local scenes. But strangest of all, on going over a Russian calendar, all the children insisted that the boy with the deer was one of them and that the kids in a classroom included their brothers and class fellows! They knew about cycles and cars, and claimed pictures of power houses were actually pictures of Kulu. They danced for me while singing snatches of film songs from Hindi films. No one knew the meanings of the words, however.

Walking back from Beeling bridge, I found two boys lying on their stomachs on a donkey, their legs hanging on one side. A third boy was leading the donkey along. A fine game!

The Goshal peak and the other mountains look superb in the liquid light of the moon these days. Late at night, looking out of my window, I could see the lovely Goshal massif with a huge star above it. The sky is so clear these days that the stars seem like giant Diwali balloon lights. The eerie atmosphere is heightened on some evenings by the sounds of pipes and trumpets coming from the monastery high above Kyelang. First the thick gutturals of the long trumpets, and then the shrill sound of the pipes come haunting down the hillside in the stillness of the moonlight. What could a Coleridge have made of this?

From the seventeenth to the twenty-first of January, it snowed almost all of the time. The sky was a dull grey and the snow flakes drifting down seemed like a locust invasion. Soon, everything was white. The trees groaned under their load of snow. When the sun came out, the valley seemed like a giant mirror.

As soon as the snowing stopped, people, mostly old men, and women and children, came out of their houses, and in the morning sun, began to clear the snow off their flat roofed houses. All of Kyelang were on their roofs—working, resting, shouting and gossiping after the isolation of the last few days.

The flat-roofed houses are so close and interconnected that it is possible to run about from one roof to the other. The women worked with vigour, sweeping up the snow and throwing it down on the streets with flat wooden spades. The children fooled about on the roofs, getting in the way of their elders and sometimes throwing snowballs about. The men and women cut the snow, which was about one and a half feet deep, into cubes of one foot each, and threw it off their flat spades into the street below. The cubes of snow looked like giant pastries with plenty of cream.

The sun that came after the snow seemed to have brought an air of happy warmth. The animals also came out, and the yaks and churus wallowed about in the deep soft snow. The crows came out and sat about on the poplars, watching the scene. As if at a signal, thousands of ravens came flying over from the north, almost darkening the sky with their numbers as they flew on down the valley. There were giant icicles hanging down from my sloping tin roof. Some of them were almost seven feet long, while others were twisted like grappling hooks.

There is one old pine tree that still has green leaves. All the other trees have shed their leaves except this one; it looks so beautiful against the backdrop of white and blue.

Paths have been beaten down in the snow—but what paths! They are like glass, smooth and slippery. The kids go tobogganing down these sloping paths on wooden seats. They do not mind the cold and carry on till late in the evening, shouting and jostling for turns on the run. Sometimes they race, three or four on a single big sledge. The Moravian missionaries, familiar with skiing in Europe, tried to make skis here in Kyelang. They fashioned two logs of weeping willow wood into a pair of rough skis. They used to try skiing in this fashion. When Thakur Pratap Chand bought their house from them in 1940, they left him these skis. Dorje brought these to me, and one day, we went for a grand skiing expedition to the sloping upper Kyelang fields.

I tied the skis on and slowly went sliding down the slope. We had no wax and I was no champion, but we did take a few dramatic skiing shots with the Goshal peak in the background. Dorje had also brought a pair of tennis racquet-like contraptions with gut webbing and a place in the centre to fit the foot in. We could not understand what its use could be. Later, I learnt that these were snow shoes, which helped a person walk in soft snow without sinking.

The village kids with their slide games have worn the street paths so smooth that there is an ever present danger of slipping and falling. As it happens, the deputy commissioner's office is at a lower level in the village. Even during the winter, the routine is kept up of getting ready, going on time to the office, and spending the day there, waiting for the odd wireless message from Chandigarh. Frequent cups of tea and lunch are had on the missionary-designed tandoor that keeps the office room warm. These glass-smooth street slopes were an ever present danger to the ponderous dignity of the administration in the shape of the deputy commissioner. Every morning, I stepped gingerly along, being careful not to slip. Still, the foot shoots out occasionally and I had to grab a fistful of snow for support. On such occasions, the school kids line my way, nudging each other mischievously, and hoping for the worst. I am at my best, however, when on trial. This story is told of my predecessor who was making his way with great difficulty one morning to his office. He was wished on the way by a citizen. As he joined hands to greet him, he lost his balance, his legs shot out and he went down in the best Pickwick manner! The next day, he was negotiating the same place when he ran into one of his subordinates, who wished him. At this, all his pent-up sorrows burst forth and he shouted, 'What sort of place is this for wishing me? Can't you do it elsewhere?' As he said so, he went down again!

Even during the winter, if it does not snow for a while, it is possible to travel about in the valley. On one such occasion, Dorje and I went up the valley towards the Baralacha pass to visit Khangsar, the ancestral seat of Thakur Pratap Chand. We crossed Shaks nullah, his village Guskiar and walked towards Jispa. The valley broadens out here and one gets very dramatic views and perspectives of the central Mulkila massif peaks. At about ten miles distance from Kyelang, the path goes leftwards, cutting up the scree slope to a ridge promontory. The village of Khangsar is dramatically situated at this point. Pratap Chand's house on a flat ledge has a most dramatic view all the way down to Kyelang, and up towards the Baralacha pass. Sitting on fine carpets in the upper balcony of his ancient typically Lahaul house, and sipping arrack of excellent quality, we looked at a giant glacier pouring down a steep nullah from a high mountain. Elisa Hyde, the missionary wife who lived in these parts in 1868, named the peak 'the Lady of Kyelang'. The Thakur family was represented by Tsomo Dolma, a dignified elderly lady and Sher Singh, who had been a junior officer in the Indian Army. Thakur Pratap Chand had also been a captain in the army during the Second World War. I have never had a more pleasant hour in my life; the superb mountain scene, the fine arrack and two good people to talk to in the winter afternoon sun. It is a scene that is etched in my mind and I summon it whenever I want a calm peacefulness. We looked around the house and went to the family prayer room down some stairs; as at Tabo, here too, the murals of the Buddha's life were of a very high quality. They had been painted long ago and were obviously of value. It is necessary to preserve these murals as examples of Himalayan art.

After the early snow crisis in September on the Rohtang pass, those of us left in the valley settled down for the long winter. Early in the new year, we began to prepare for Republic Day celebrations on the 26th of January. Diwan, the superintendent of police, was determined to put up a parade, better than the Delhi show. There were many rehearsals and the drawing up of a programme as precise as that for the president of India. Diwan also gave me precise instructions for the flag hoisting ceremony.

My office was in a single-storey school building and the little playground of the school was to be used for the flag hoisting function. When the new district was formed, Vaishnav, the first DC, had made a thin pencil cedar log the flag post. Vaishnav cannot be accused of knowing the niceties of the military style of doing things. A Gujarati economist from the Delhi School of Economics, he revelled in long arguments over tea about the state of the economy. He was quite satisfied with the flag post on which our flag hung . . . at a barely acceptable height.

On a cold, crisp winter day, I put on my best suit and black shoes, and gingerly walked down the lanes to the playground. I was scared of slipping on the frozen glassy ground. Having been a part of the National Cadet Corps, I took my position on the platform in soldierly style. The police's guard of honour came to slope arms and a constable handed me the string. The Indian style requires flowers to be tied into the knotted flag at the top of the mast. When the flag's string is tugged, the knot opens and petals shower as the flag begins to unfurl. I have always worried about the knot and what happens if it fails to open. Luck was against me that day. I pulled gently and nothing happened. I pulled harder, still nothing. On the third tug, the string broke and the flag fell at my feet as the guard of honour came to a smart salute. For a moment, I stood frozen. Then I bent down, gently picked up the flag, and held it in my hand till the salute was over. We managed the rest of the show and quickly re-tied the flag to the pine mast. The superstitious might have read many omens, but fortunately, I reject all superstitions. Later, on a visit to the Rohtang pass, I picked up PWD water pipes lying there, brought them back home, made a proper circular cement base and put up a really tall flag mast, like the best in an army establishment. It was visible up and down the entire valley.

On 1 November 1966, Lahaul-Spiti left the Punjab, and became a part of Himachal Pradesh. I served long years in the Punjab secretariat in Chandigarh. The emotional link with Lahaul was never weakened or broken. Due to Kairon's policy of pushing education in those remote valleys, more and more Lahaul-Spiti boys started coming to Punjab University in Chandigarh for their graduate education. I became godfather to all of them. Tshering Dorje would ring me often, and I would take care of their problems. With the reservation for tribal people in the IAS and other services, many joined the civil services and have had distinguished careers. Thakur Pratap Chand's nephew, Ashok Thakur, currently additional secretary in the Ministry of Education in New Delhi, has been in life-long touch with me. Be he in Simla or elsewhere in the field, I continue to ring him and other officers to push them for giving better service and comfort to the people of these remote valleys. I still remind him of the necessity of preserving the murals in his ancestral home in Jispa.

At Gephan's Mercy

A broad and ample road, whose dust is gold, and pavement stars.

—Milton

Winters in Lahaul are fairly long. Freak September snowfalls notwithstanding, serious winter weather starts only with the mid-December snowfalls. In the weather pattern of North India, we generally get the first winter rains in the second half of December, around Christmas. Rain in the Punjab plains is accompanied by heavy snowfall in the mountains to the north, like the Lahaul valley. It sometimes snows in Simla, and even Kasauli. The second winter rain in Punjab normally comes in February, again accompanied by snow in the hills. In March, there is a false hint of summer, but towards the end of the month, and right up to mid-April, hailstorms, rain and strong winds are felt in Punjab and all along the northern plains, causing damage to standing wheat crop. At this time too, snowfalls, sometimes very heavy ones, can be expected on the Rohtang and in the valley. The December and February snows are brought about by a northern front that comes into the subcontinent from Siberia. The April hailstorms and snow are due to the clash of the northern cold winds with the southern hot drafts coming from the subcontinent's western coast. After April, the southern hot winds prevail and we go into a long summer.

As February came around during my time in Kyelang, I toyed with the idea of a winter crossing of the Rohtang pass. Lahaulas do occasionally cross the pass in the dead of winter by taking a chance with the weather. As the staff of the new district do not have access to any mail during the long winter, in the past few years, a group of Lahaulas are sent on the arduous walk through the snow-filled valley and over the Rohtang, all the way to Manali. They bring back the *dak* or letter bags so that letters and some newspapers can put the valley staff in touch with the plains. I had often heard about the fascinating experience of walking through the valley and Rohtang in the dead of winter. I knew that this was a dangerous venture. The Rohtang is unpredictable even in autumn, as the September heavy snowfall showed. The pass is like a wind tunnel between the Lahaul valley and the Kulu valley. The fierce winds are dangerous, even in better times, and in the nineteenth century, more than seventy men froze to death on the pass in late autumn.

I discussed the idea of crossing the Rohtang in winter many times with Tshering Dorje. Taking such an unnecessary risk seems foolish, but youth and the excitement of danger prevailed. Finally, I decided that I had to go.

We were a party of eight—Tshering Dorje, Rana, my Kangra Gaddi office assistant, two peons, three dak-runners, and I. On the first day, we expected to do the five miles to the Tandi confluence and then another four up the Chandra river to the village of Gondhla. During the night, there had been a light snowfall and the sky was overcast. In the last ten days, we had recorded ten and a half feet of snow at Kyelang. But I was determined to go. All through winter, I had lain dormant. Now I felt my blood tingling with expectation. I wanted to toil in the sun and snow, to sweat, and to feel the drowsiness of fatigue. Besides, Lama Paljor had predicted clear weather. Knowing the startling accuracy of his previous forecasts, I thought him as good a meteorological guide as any.

Leave taking delayed our start and we left Kyelang at 8 a.m. Earlier, some men from Gondhla had come to the district headquarters to collect development grants. They returned with us and I was glad for their company. We walked swiftly downhill along the jeep track, which was buried deep in snow. On our right were sharp cliffs, their loose soggy flanks crumbling under the weight of ice and snow. The Lahaul mountains are composed of stones buried in mud, a sure indication that they rose out of a sea or river bed in some cataclysmic upheaval. These rolling stones constitute the greatest danger once the sun is up, and minor and major snow slips start down the hillsides.

Boulders hung precariously over our path and water was oozing out of the soft mud that held them in place. Below us, the slope was littered with stones that may have come hurtling down yesterday or maybe even a few moments ago. We picked our way gingerly over the bad portions, hoping for the best.

Sometimes, we walked along the edge looking down at the Bhaga river, a couple of hundred feet below us. Gone was the brash, mountain torrent of the summer. Avalanches sweeping down from both sides of the narrow valley had choked it completely. Giant snow bridges had formed at places. Snow and ice had piled up along the banks, then cracked under the pressure of new avalanches, the blocks leaning crazily, like the cement ones lying around river bridges in the Punjab after the monsoon floods. Here and there, a patch of emerald green water appeared with pieces of ice circling slowly in eddies.

We reached Tandi after about two hours. The flat ground at the confluence was one vast snowfield; in the background, the giant Goshal peak rose in a series of sharp ridges. The chorten that marks this sacred birth of the Chenab river stood half-buried in snow. After a short rest on the new bridge, we started across the vast snowfield on the right bank of the Chandra river. It was getting warm and the snow had lost its early morning firmness. Footsteps sank in a foot or more and we floundered to get a firm foothold. Progress was slow.

At the end of the snowfield, there was a sharp climb. I remembered having gone up this bit in my jeep in summer in a series of slow zigzag turns. Now the road was nowhere to be seen. From the top of the seventeen thousand foot high ridge to the river bank, it was one vast avalanche-swept slope. Boulders, some clothed in snow, others bare, lay everywhere. Looking up, I noticed to my discomfort, that all the boulders had not come down yet. We plodded up the slope, talking turns to stamp out a path in the soft snow. We hurried along, anxious to clear this dangerous slope and come out on to a more open valley. In such places, you had to trust God and chance.

We were half way up the slope when the first avalanche came. Fortunately, it was not on our slope.

Across the river, a mass of snow, ice and boulders came pouring off one of the lower ridges of the Nilghar peaks, which are on the ridge that divides the Chandra valley from the Solang nullah valley on the Manali side. Thunder filled the air. A Himalayan avalanche from a high mountain is an awe-inspiring experience and spectacle—a sudden crack in the packed ice and snow on a steep slope, accompanied by a snow cloud formed by the pulverized ice blocks. The thunderous rumble of the avalanche is surely what must happen when the gods are on the move.

Fascinated, I watched this spectacle of nature's power. This seemed like a time signal. Soon avalanches were coming down with monotonous regularity. So far they were all on the opposite side of the river. But would our luck hold? The older men from Gondhla counselled speed. 'Sahib,' they said, 'we are on a dangerous slope. We have a long way to go, and it is getting late.' I could not have agreed more. We toiled up the slope, trying to get clear of the danger area. My two peons had begun to tire. They flopped down every now and then, gasping for breath. I hurried them on, knowing that it would be fatal to leave a straggler behind. We even shared their loads.*

At last, we were out on the flat Karga maidan. A short rest, a few photographs and we were off again. In single file, we struggled on through the soft snow. No one spoke because each of us was tired and concentrating on the path. The sun shone in a clear blue sky and the snow sparkled with the light of a million diamonds. White needles pierced my dark glasses and pricked my skin. The maidan seemed endless. At every step, I almost sank up to my knees in soft and melting snow. The unending walk was a torture, made in the glare of a pitiless sun. Gondhla appeared like a distinct mirage.

Near the journey's end, we ran into another bad patch. The route was dominated by an overhanging cliff, which bombarded the path with stones, rubble and snow. The danger zone was about a hundred yards. We sat down to rest and considered our course. I noticed that there was a distinct interval between falls. One by one, we dashed for safety, each carrying his own luck. At about 3 p.m., we climbed the last slope to Gondhla, after seven hours of continuous walking. Somebody produced hot tea and biscuits. The tea was a relief, but I had no appetite for food. I wanted only to lie in the afternoon sun. After I had rested for some time, I went out on the terrace and looked about at the

---

*'Avalanches fall in spring and summer, and occasionally cause serious loss of life. Many years ago, a glacier slipped and utterly buried a village in the mouth of the Yocha valley, not a soul escaping. An old man, who had gone up the mountain for some purpose a day or two before the catastrophe, is reported to have said on returning that his heart misgave him, that something was about to happen, as he had seen a band of strangely dressed people, dancing and holding high revel, at the top of the glaciers, who must have been fairies.' (*Kangra District Gazetteer*, 1897)

winter activity in the village. Some girls were taking straw from the roof to feed the cattle penned in the ground floor room; school children were sitting in the sun and parrot-learning their lessons; women sitting in twos and threes were spinning and gossiping on the sun-soaked terraces. The family produced the best meal they could for me of thukpa with mutton pieces and cauliflower, followed by a sweet pudding made of apricots, which are stored from the summer. I slept like a log that night.

The next morning, we were up at half past three as I wanted to make an early start. We were on the road at 5 a.m. The Gondhla peaks looked superb in the dawn light. As the first rays of the sun hit the top of the peaks with a golden shaft, I thought of the Omar Khayyam poem:

> The Hunter of the East has caught
> The Sultan's Turret in a Noose of Light.

Dropping sheer for five thousand feet to the Chandra river bed, this cliff, right in front of the village, across the Chandra river, is the most awe-inspiring mountain massif to be seen anywhere. General Bruce describes it thus: 'I have seldom seen such imposing and hopeless precipices, a magnificent piece of mountain sculpture, but not for the foot of man; some 8,000 feet of gigantic pitches, every little valley, being filled up with hanging glaciers, at the steepest angle, from whose ends, broke off continual small ice avalanches. The upper ridges seemed equally uncompromising, all of the boldest and steepest scale.'

As the dawn whisked away the night's dark mantle, a soft rosy flush seemed to spread over the mountain's finely-chiselled features. Unclimbed, they beckoned me, as they must have many other mountaineers passing that way. Who could be indifferent to such compelling beauty?

The snow was firm and crunched pleasantly under my feet, giving way an inch or two. The road was even and I discovered that walking in the snow could be fun, provided one did it in the early mornings when it had not begun to melt. On our left were beautiful snow slopes of all grades and I mused over the skiing possibilities of the area if it could be made accessible in winter. I believed in 1962 that one day, it should be possible to promote skiing and other winter sports in the Lahaul valley by lifting people with helicopters over the Rohtang pass into the valley. The sport would bring in rich tourists and income to the Lahaul people.*

Walking along, we came to a lonely house: a single brown cube on a field of white. Some girls were on the roof collecting straw from a stack. I stopped to take a picture and they obliged with blushes and giggles! When I finished, a request was made through Tshering Dorje for complimentary copies. So much for them being tribal!

A little short of Sissu, our halting place for the day, I heard some *chakors* calling on the slope below us. Rana went to look for them. He comes of expert shepherd stock—the famous Gaddis of Kangra. Glissading down the slope, he made for a

---

*Today, in the twenty-first century, this is very much a possibility that should be promoted by the state and central governments. There are plenty of slopes of varying degrees of difficulty in the Lahaul and Pattan valleys. The long winters and frequent snowfalls offer conditions for a fairly long skiing season. The Lahaulas can be encouraged to take up a bed and breakfast type of business. They are very clever people; with cheap government loans, they could provide excellent accommodation for tourists. Western people would love the cultural experience of close contact with a local family. Europeans are tired of the standard skiing resorts. A skiing experience in a remote Himalayan Shangrila would be welcomed by many. Electricity is available in the valley now and ski lifts can be serviced. I would not encourage the building of any hotels as they violate the architectural ambiance of the valley and take income away from the locals to the rich in Delhi and beyond. Helicopters are used every winter in Manali to ferry rich westerners up the Solan valley for skiing on the southern slopes of the Gondhla ridge. It is time to encourage them to take tourists into Lahaul.

clump of willows. We heard the shot and counted nine startled birds heading down the river. I had conjured up visions of fresh roasted chakors, but our luck was out. Rana rejoined us and we trudged on our weary way to Sissu.

In Lahaul villages, the houses are clustered together to provide easy inter-communication in the winter. Since the roofs form a series of terraces, it is possible to walk over from house to house. We climbed on to the nearest roof (in winter, the snow piles up in the narrow lanes and forms natural ramps). Thakur Duni Chand made us feel welcome. Kalimpong rugs were spread out in the sun and we relaxed over tea and cream biscuits. The schoolmaster was holding classes on one of the adjoining roofs. I walked over to have a look. I again noticed how the textbooks were all plains-oriented. The lessons were about trains, houses, cities, electricity—all things alien to Lahaul.

I asked the children, 'Have you seen a train?'

'No.'

'A bus?'

'No.'

'Electric lights?'

'No.'

'A plane?'

'Yes!' they all answered eagerly. Planes flew overhead daily. There goes one now!

I then asked about Maharaja Ranjit Singh and Rana Pratap. Blank looks.

'Tenzing?'

'Yes, he climbed the Everest. A mountaineer.'

Were they not all children of the mountains living in the oppressive shadow of the giant peaks?

A little later, a hot bath was followed by lunch with fresh meat and curd—luxuries all. In the morning, we were off before sunrise. The sky was clear and held the promise of a fine sunny day. A little beyond the village, we came to the Sissu nullah, which flows down a narrow gorge from the Gephan peak glaciers. There was no water, only a mass of snow, boulders and rubble. Avalanches had evidently hurtled down the tunnel, sweeping everything before them. The sides of the gorge appeared to have been sliced with a giant butter knife. The end of the funnel, the broad river bank, was piled high with ice seracs, boulders and loose snow. It seemed as if hundreds of giant earth moving machines had been at work. We had to keep going down, down to the very bed and then climb up the opposite slope. There was no road now, no jeep, and no other way to go. Avalanches do not stick to any regular time schedule. They are creatures of whim and fancy. I prayed that Gephan devta, the lord of the mountains, would let us pass. We went down the slope, our hearts in our mouths, praying feverishly. We hurried across the nullah bed and up the other side, our lungs straining for air. We dared not rest till we were out of the danger zone.

We reached Khoksar at about ten. Even by Lahaul standards, it was hardly a village—only four or five houses clustered together for warmth and security. The village lay on the right bank of the Chandra, on a maidan, safe from avalanches. The rest house on the left bank of the river and on the road to Rohtang was nowhere to be seen. It had disappeared under a mass of snow, roof and all. The chowkidar who lived in the village welcomed us. A few girls were beating straw for *poolas*, straw shoes, near the spring. The Lahaulas keep barley straw and during the winter, girls wet the straw and beat it with round wooden hammers to make it malleable. They then knit the hay into snow shoes for the family. These are worn to walk on the snow. They give fine insulation and keep the feet warm in missionary-woollen socks. The schoolmaster stood on the nearest roof with his seven nervous wards in their Sunday best. All the children had crude red nail polish on, evidently the baneful influence of Manali. I heard their lessons and distributed sweets among them. The deputy commissioner's inspection of the little Khoksar school in the winter was the first ever, and probably, the last.

The schoolmaster had a small, but neat room. I spread my sleeping bag near the fire and relaxed while Tshering Dorje prepared our dinner. It is amusing that in every village it had been the school master's house of one or two rooms that had been my rest place for the night.

The Rohtang pass dominates this little village and the lives of its people. In summer, the pass lets in a flood of visitors, engineers, labour gangs, tourists, mountaineers, officials and others. Tents, tea-shops and labour huts sprout around the rest house. The villagers do brisk business selling chhaang. Jeeps scream up the thin ribbon to the pass and mule trains jingle along the way to Kyelang. With the first hint of winter in September, the visitors depart, and all is silent, save for the moaning wind that howls down from the pass like some demon in agony. The first snowfall drapes the bare rugged mountains in white. The flakes float down till the sharp jagged outlines of the mountains becomes blurred and all is soft and rounded. Avalanches thunder down the slopes, choking up the river and piling masses of snow on the fields. For a couple of months, the little village is left completely to itself. As the winter abates, people begin to come in ones and twos. Khoksar is the spring-board for those who must go out and a haven of safety, warmth and security for those who come from Manali. The village is hospitable, and all are welcome here. Crouched over fires, with cups of chhaang, the travellers discuss their chances for the crossing, seeking information from those who have just come over. Everyone knows of the whimsical, cruel, capricious Gephan devta who broods over the pass. Each crossing is a kind of rebirth. To the travellers and the people of Khoksar, the great mass of the Rohtang pass is a brooding, almost malevolent giant that casts a heavy shadow over their land, and occasionally, brings great tragedies. All conversation is about the jote and the chances of survival of men and mules.

In the morning, we were up at 3 a.m. Tshering Dorje brewed

tea and cooked some parathas while I struggled into my many pairs of socks and sweaters. When I went out on to the veranda to brush my teeth, I found clouds banked upon the Spiti mountains. The wind whistled through the willows and the temperature was well below freezing point. We ate our breakfast and packed our rucksacks, hoping for a break in the weather, but the dawn was grey and murky. By about six, it began to snow. Disappointed, I unpacked my sleeping bag and prepared to spend the day in the little cell. The snow continued to fall with a maddening steadiness. Each time I went out, there were wisps of snow floating gently down. Soon, snow lay a couple of inches thick on the flat roofs. How much more snow must be on the pass above us! I brooded over the possibility of being snowbound in tiny Khoksar.

Manali seemed a world away. Tshering Dorje, however, did not fret. The Lahaulas are attuned to their environment. They know, that one must be patient with mountains. He went out and returned a little later with some local men. Sitting down near the fire, they began to play *chullo*, a dice game played with a hollow wooden cup, a pair of brass dice and twigs and grain as markers. The dice are rattled vigorously in the cup, which is banged down on a cloth pad. Simultaneously, the player shouts 'Chull'. This is supposed to help the dice fall the right way. The Lahaulas play chullo with gusto—banging the cup down with vigour and shouting lustily. How their faces beam when a player throws two sixes! They can be engrossed in this game for days. It is their barbiturate for the long winter hours, their bridge . . .

I watched them with an aloof disdainful air. Bureaucrats do not play chullo. Good heavens, no! In any case, what a childish game! I leaned over to have a closer look. I asked a few questions . . . just to find out. Well, no harm in having one throw, I suppose. At two o'clock, I insisted that Tshering Dorje prepare lunch, while the rest of us continued to play! In the evening, the sun broke through the clouds for a little while and gave hope for the morrow. After dinner, I called the three dak runners to decide the plans for the morning. They were poor people from a village in the Pattan valley, who were undertaking this hazardous journey to earn a little extra money. All three were tipsy, their eyes bloodshot. I asked them if they would advise a crossing in the morning in view of the fresh snow. Their leader, a lean man with deep set eyes and long locks hanging down to his shoulders, replied, 'We will go as sahib orders. We will lead. We will beat a path in the soft snow and risk the avalanches. Sahib can follow.' As he spoke, his mental censor seemed to drop away. He forgot my identity and saw in me only the privileged, whose paths through life must be smoothened out by others. His eyes burned through me as he leaned forward and continued, 'Yes sahib, we will go. Does it matter if we die? This is not our first crossing. It will not be our last. We must cross and recross for the hunger in our stomachs. Some crossing will be the last. Maybe it will be the snow, destroying and preserving; maybe stiffness in the joints. But for you it is different. Tomorrow we will cross, and we three will lead, beating out a path.' I lay awake long after the three had left, thinking.

We were up at three. The sky was a dull grey and the wind moaned through the willows. We held a counsel of war. Topdan, the old PWD chowkidar, veteran of numerous crossings, told us that we could go as the sky would most probably clear. The dak runners, stone sober now, said no. The weather was uncertain. The fresh snow was likely to avalanche. They had families to support. It was risky. I thought, considered, and hesitated. Finally, I put down my rucksack and decided to wait and watch. At about eight, the sky cleared, the wind dropped and the sun appeared. I decided to move. Topdan intervened and said that it was too late to start and that it was advisable to wait a day after a snowfall to let the fresh snow avalanche. Besides, it was considered inauspicious to cancel a move and then to start again—the core of his objection. I chided them for their superstitions, but they would not budge. Reluctantly, I took out my sleeping bag and spread it near the fire. After about ten, the avalanches began, the result of the fresh snow. Our decision to wait seemed to be a wise one after all.

I spent a long day of waiting in great boredom. I had not brought a book as it would have added to the unnecessary weight. I could not step out, except on to the small balcony of the room. All day I shuffled about in my sleeping bag, thinking of tomorrow. For the third successive morning, we were up at three. I went out to have a look. Millions of fireflies seemed to be floating in the dark void above. The false dawn, reflected by the snow, bathed the sleeping village in a soft soothing light. The willows were at rest, no wind tearing at their limbs. The peaks stood around like silent sentinels. All was peaceful. God seemed so near. Elated, I went in and began to pack my rucksack. Action at last . . . and the thrill of the unknown. My blood tingled with expectation.

We were out at about five. Topdan was ready, waiting. I can not forget his face even today, fifty years later—a powerful, high cheeked, crinkled-eyed, bronzed Sherpa. That is Topdan etched in my memory. He might have been anything up to fifty summers old. He led the way out of the silent sleeping village and down the ridge to the river. It was still dark and the slope was steep. We picked our way down with care, for a slip could have nasty results. The new snow had not packed properly yet, and gave way easily. It had also obliterated the path beaten out by previous parties. We were in for a strenuous day.

For about three furlongs, Topdan led the way upstream along the river. The river was choked with snow and one could cross it anywhere, but Topdan was looking for a really safe snow bridge. Probing cautiously with his stick, and choosing his steps with meticulous care, he led the way across. We were now at the foot of the climb. The ridge rose in a series of steep slopes, with occasional bumps just sufficient to break the line of ascent.

Gallantly, Topdan tackled the first slope. Leaning into the slope for balance, he probed the snow with his stick and moved forward sinking in up to his thighs. Then another step, and another, and another . . . up, up, up. His breath came in short gasps, and his chest heaved with the pressure on his lungs. Slowly, the slope receded below us. Near the top, there was an awkward bit of rock, with a thin film of ice on it, slippery and dangerous. Topdan tackled it with the instinct of a born mountaineer.

We followed a line of climb, well to the left of the bridge and the rest house. The route was possible only in the winter because continuous and repeated snowfalls had filled in the gullies and covered awkward rock features. It was a shorter walking route up towards the pass, and this was known only to experienced Lahaul hands like Topdan, who had made many winter ascents of the pass in years past.

We halted for a breather. The scene was superb. The sun, still hidden from view, was lighting up the distant Spiti mountains. There was a touch of gold on the three Gephan peaks. We continued to climb steadily, taking turns at the lead. At each step, the leader sank in up to the thighs. We halted every hundred yards or so, panting for breath. Our line of climbers, walking up the snow slopes, looked like a long centipede. The long line of dark human figures against the whiteness of the snow and with the three Gephan peaks in the background is scene that I photographed many times (and one that has been used on the cover of this book), for I knew that I would not pass this way again. Traversing one particular slope was a terrifying experience. The land fell almost sheer for a thousand feet below my steps. I dared not look down. Using my walking stick as an ice axe, I inched my way across, balancing carefully in the steps made by the leader. We did not use any ropes as mountaineers do. My companions had no mountain training, but they had a God-given unerring gift of climbing the steepest of mountains.

In one or two places, we noticed fresh avalanche tracks. These had evidently come down yesterday. If we had decided to venture out to climb to the pass yesterday . . .

At about nine, we were at the foot of the Harchu gully. Above us towered masses of ice and snow, balanced precariously on the ridge line. Who could say when these would come hurtling down in a river of destruction? I was scared and prayed silently. Gone was my agnosticism. Topdan chanted a Buddhist prayer in a low, sing-song voice. The scene was so dramatic that every now and then, I would stop the snaking line of climbers to take dramatic pictures against the great background of the Lahaul and Spiti mountains, which came more and more into view as we climbed higher.

The climb up the Harchu gully to the top of the pass was very steep. We had to go almost straight up. The snow here was deep and soft and each step required an effort. But I urged the party on, for every time I looked up at the mass poised on the ridge, it made my flesh creep. It seemed the climb would never end. And then the snow lessened, and rocks appeared, firm, dry, a beautiful brown, so soothing to the eyes. Suddenly, we were on top, a huge snowfield sloping gently towards Manali. Behind us were the three Gephan peaks, guardians of the pass. Other peaks of superb beauty, hitherto hidden, now came into view. We walked forward to the middle of the level ground and sat down on the rocks to eat something and to drink some tea. I felt no hunger. I wanted only to devour the beauty around us, to carve out mountains in my memory for the day when the step will no longer be light nor the muscles firm. On one side to the north of the pass, we could see the snow-filled Lahaul valley all the way to the Baralacha La; on the other, down the Manali-Kulu valley, to a mass of green forest and the shining tin roofs of habitations.

By the time we started again, the much-feared Rohtang wind had sprung up. It blew off the pass towards Lahaul, driving tiny granules of snow into our faces with such force that they stung like needles. I had to lean into the wind to keep my balance. We were in good spirits for we had passed most of the dangerous spots, except the Rani nullah. But we still had to get down to a safe height of about 9,000 feet near Marhi. The group of travellers now broke up into individuals. Everyone hurried forward at the maximum speed, anxious only to get to safe lower heights. Rank and status were ignored. All of us wanted to run down the slopes to Rahla. Being hardened mountain people, the others could go at a great speed. Most of them just ran off and very soon became distant dots. Only Tshering Dorje and Rana, my two staff officers, stuck by me to shepherd me down to safety. They walked at my speed. I was becoming somewhat careless, thinking that the dangerous bit had past, but Dorje knew it was not so and we had a long way to go through the dangerous Rani nullah, where one had to pass under overhanging snow masses. We had to get down the long slopes to Marhi and finally, further on to Rahla. The long climb down became strenuous and difficult. Gently, Dorje urged me to greater speed. As we started going lower, the green valleys visible in the distance beckoned to us and gave us heart.

The winter route is different from the jeep track that winds up to the pass in summer. We had to go down to the source of the Beas and then walk along the slopes on its right bank. The scale of the Himalayas can only be understood when one is walking among these giant mountains. The simple shoulder of a peak, takes ages to get around, though it seems so manageable and near. We knew we had many many miles yet to cover, not only down to Rahla, but further on to Manali, since there would be no transport waiting at the foot of the pass.

We raced downhill; occasionally, the new snow gave way and I sank in deep, floundering and laughing at my predicament. And then we came to the Rani nullah. It cuts across the route before joining the Beas. As at Sissu, we had to climb down into its bed, walk across, and climb up the other side. The nullah was well known for its sudden and fearful avalanches. Once, when Tshering Dorje was going to Lahaul with a party, they decided to halt for a little rest on one side of it. Suddenly, an avalanche hurtled down. The air blast flung Dorje a considerable distance away. When he recovered from the shock, he found that some of the party had disappeared, while others had been flung about the slope like him. They looked for their lost companions, but found none. Their courage gone, they returned to Manali.

We picked our way gingerly down the slopes to the nullah bed. The upper crust of the snow was firm, and Dorje had a brilliant idea—sliding down on our trouser seats! A little distance beyond the nullah, we found a stick stuck in the snow. It was the type which a villager carries on such journeys. We poked about in the snow, but found nothing. Yet, why was the stick stuck upright in the snow? Who knows? Rohtang is a cruel pass.

At Marhi, we rested for a while. The stone enclosures, which served as tea shops in the summer, were full of snow. I longed for a hot cup of tea, but we plodded on as Rahla, the foot of the pass, was still five miles away and Manali was another fifteen. I began to tire. With the crest of the pass behind us, the excitement had abated, and the monotony of a long walk remained.

Rana suggested that we glide down to Rahla, like the Gaddi shepherds. Being one himself, he showed me how and then glided off down the slopes beyond Marhi. Dorje suggested that I follow Rana. I sat down on the snow slope with my feet straight out and my sharp pointed walking stick held firmly, ready to dig into the snow and break my speed if needed. I then pushed forward a few times, and soon, I was sliding downhill. I gathered speed and it was fun. Dorje followed. Laughing and shouting, we tumbled down the slope. Surprisingly, the Lahaulas cannot glissade. Old Topdan and the rest of the party continued to plod on through the snow. Within minutes, we were safely down in Rahla. There was only one casualty: the seat of my trousers!

When I stood up and casually passed the hands down my back, I found that the intense friction had worn my trouser through and there was nothing left. I had no choice but to march on.

Rahla was desolate, save for a tiny tea-stall under a rock ledge. We went into the smoky interior. The warmth was very comforting. Dorje took command immediately, ordered tea, helped the owner with the oil stove, and was soon handing us hot mugs of tea. As it was the custom, Topdan collected contributions from each of the party for a thanksgiving offering to the Gephan devta. Usually, bright pieces of cloth are bought in Manali and prayers are printed on them. These flags are then tied to the ones already fluttering on the Rohtang top cairn. Occasionally, a party which has had a narrow escape will offer a goat or sheep in thanksgiving. The animal is slaughtered ceremonially and eaten. The heart and horns are taken and left on the cairn on the top of the pass.

After about an hour's rest, we hoisted our packs and pushed off down the jeep road to Manali. For some distance, the cruel white landscape continued. But as we descended, the trees appeared—pines, cedars, larches, and deodars; the snow lessened and then we saw patches of lovely chocolate-coloured earth. We squelched through little trickles of snow water on the road. After months of a harsh white landscape, it was good to see the beauties of bountiful and rich creation. We thanked God for the majestic cedars, the lovely moist green grass and the rich mud slithering about under our feet. We thanked the Gephan devta for a safe crossing and walked on our eager way to the warmth of Manali.

The Reason Why

I will find a way or make one.

—Hannibal

What was the reason for our presence in these remote Himalayan valleys on the Tibetan frontier? Why had the Punjab government created a separate district for a population of less than 20,000 people, spread over an area of more than 5,000 square miles of high mountains, glacier-filled valleys, and vast barren stretches, of what has been described as a cold Himalayan desert?

After the first Anglo-Sikh War in 1846, the British, under the treaty of Bharowal, took away the entire Kangra province from the Sikhs. This effectively cut off the mutilated Sikh kingdom from contact with Ladakh and Tibet, and also gave to the British the rich Pashmina-wool trade of these areas. The district of Kangra, as created by the British, had an area of almost 10,000 square miles, approximately half of the total area of present-day Himachal Pradesh. The deputy commissioner had his headquarters at Dharamsala, a short distance from Pathankot in the Beas river valley. Nearly 200 miles up the valley lay the headquarters of the assistant commissioner at Kulu. Lahaul-Spiti, which lay across the 13,000-feet-high treacherous Rohtang pass, formed part of the assistant commissioner's charge.

As elsewhere in India, the British were content to leave their subjects alone, so long as the Empire was upheld and maintained. The remote valleys of Lahaul and Spiti were, therefore, left more or less to their own devices. At the pleasure of the Punjab government, exercised through the Assistant Commissioner, Kulu, the hereditary tribal chiefs of the area, the wazir of Lahaul and the nono of Spiti, were allowed to hold total sway. The Lahaul wazir was one of the jagirdar families of the area and claimed a hereditary link with the ancient Kulu Rajas. The nono of Spiti, on the other hand, claimed royal links with Ladakh and Tibet.

The assistant commissioners, who were invariably English ICS officers, made the most of the pro-counselship of the scenic Kulu valley that had a most equable climate. The valley had a temperate climate and was rich in all that nature could bestow— pine forests on the hills leading up to the snow line, a fast-flowing river of clear blue water with numerous streams full of trout, and hill slopes dotted with orchards of apple, pear, plum and apricot. The men of Kulu were gentle and handsome, and the women are astoundingly beautiful. Naturally enough, the assistant commissioners spent most of their time in this pleasant paradise. In the summer, they made an annual visit to Lahaul-Spiti, when the wazir of Lahaul, and the nono of Spiti paid formal obeisance to the British government. The shadow of the Raj confirmed, the commissioners hastened out of these harsh, high valleys to the salubrious climate of Kulu, leaving the two local potentates to their own ways. The only contribution some of the assistant commissioners made during their annual visit to Spiti was to make some adventurous crossings of the high ridge dividing Spiti from the Parbati valley of Kulu. Kangra gazetteers record crossings made through the Pin-Parbati pass, and even more difficult ones, through the Gyundi nullah beyond Rangrik, and over into the Dibbibokri nullah, going down into the Parbati valley and to Bhuntar in Kulu.

The wazir and the nono were the magistrates, police, jailers, revenue and forest officers, all rolled in one. They knew and applied little of the law as accepted by the British, and largely trusted their own instincts and ways to administer the areas under their charge. Justice G.D. Khosla, in his book *Himalayan Circuit*, has vividly described the ways of the then nono of Spiti. This gentleman used to lock up malefactors in a dungeon at the ancient Dankhar fort, high above the village of Kaza. The noble judge of the High Court who was on a tour of Spiti, accompanied by the commissioner of Jalandhar, was horrified at the nono's total indifference to Indian penal and civil codes. The nono, of course, like many Indian rulers, saw his system as far more intrinsically just than the lawyer and litigation-burdened system of the British. So, while the assistant commissioner enjoyed himself in the happy valley of Kulu, the wazir and nono ran the administration of Lahaul and Spiti according to their best abilities. Life went on along this frozen pattern right up to 1947 and later.

The deputy commissioner at Dharamsala was remote enough, but the commissioner at Jalandhar was even further away. Once in a while, the commissioner made a ceremonial visit to the valleys, but most of the time, they were left in peace. Though the people were left largely to their own devices, they still retain memories of some of the assistant commissioners of Kulu. H.L. Shuttleworth, Arthur Lall, Azim Hussain, and Harcourt, all assistant commissioners of Kulu, are remembered for their sympathetic ways with the people. Shuttleworth, in particular, continued in folk memory long after he completed his second term in the early 1920s. He was a man of total dedication and great scholarship, who knew all the dialects of Lahaul. He could never get over his attachment to his charge, which he kept visiting, long after he went back to England. After Lahaul-Spiti became a separate district, Shuttleworth made his last visit. The chowkidar of the Sissu rest house took him for one of the stray foreign tourists and refused him accommodation. Luckily, an official of the PWD recognized him and extended hospitality. Shuttleworth, by then an old man, chatted with the children in the village, distributed sweets, and went back over the Rohtang, after one last lingering look at the valley. He died on his way home.

Arthur Lall, an Indian member of the ICS, and after independence, one of India's most successful diplomats, was unlike the image of a traditional administrator. He mixed freely with the people in a way that must have been frowned upon by the conservatives among his brotherhood. He was the first to encourage education among the people and personally paid the expenses of a few students from Kulu and Lahaul. He was also known, after fining people in court, to pay these from his own pocket in order to save these simple-minded folk from a stretch in prison. Lall was the first man to recommend to the Government of Punjab, a change in the set-up. The Pattan valley, at that time, was in some ferment against the wazirate. Arthur Lall visualized very early the kind of set-up that was eventually going to come about. He wrote a beautiful note in his own hand, which Tandon, the deputy commissioner of Kangra, forwarded to the commissioner. Unfortunately, the suggestion was dismissed in a couple of curt sentences. Azim Hussain, another Indian member of the ICS who was to make his mark as a diplomat after independence, also left a vivid impression in the minds of the Lahaul people.

However, of all the odd characters that served in Kulu, the ones that left the most stories about themselves were Fairly and Emerson. Fairly belied his name in every way. It was the practice, under the prevailing protocol, for the wazir of Lahaul to receive the assistant commissioner on top of the Rohtang pass. Thakur

Mangal Chand, who was officiating for his mentally infirm brother Thakur Abhay Chand, was unable to go up to the pass on account of indisposition. He sent a respectful letter, apologizing for this, and said that he was waiting for the sahib at the Khoksar rest house, on the other side of the Rohtang.

Fairly was annoyed, and by the time he trekked down to Khoksar, was quite ready to be publicly rude to the wazir. However, as they met, Fairly's eyes fell on the expensive and beautiful pair of shoes that Mangal Chand was wearing. Immediately, he ordered him to take off one shoe and tried it on, while the assembled dignitaries looked on in baffled silence. The shoe fit. Fairly demanded and put on the second. For a moment, he strutted about, obviously pleased with the excellent fit. Having decided that he liked them, he calmly asked his orderly to deliver his own pair of old road masters to Mangal Chand, and get from the wazir a receipt for Rs 30, a big sum in those days.

Mangal Chand felt humiliated, but so great was the terror of authority that he could not tell anyone about it. After a three-day trek, the party reached Kyelang, where the unsuspecting village headman hosted a tea for the assistant commissioner in a gold and silver set. At the end of the tea, Fairly, with complete aplomb, directed his orderly to collect the tea set from the headman along with a receipt for Rs 40.

The procession moved on to Kolong, the seat of the wazir. The Buddhists had the same view of the English as the orthodox Hindus, namely, that they were *mlechhas*. They considered themselves polluted by the touch of an Englishman. So as the entourage moved to Patseo and Baralacha, Mangal Chand asked his porter to remain at a safe distance from the 'Stant Saheb' as the assistant commissioners were locally known. Fairly was, however, too sharp to miss anything, and the attractive wicker basket containing the Thakur's lunch caught his fancy. He wanted to have a look at it. However, every time he approached the porter, the man ran away. Fairly was intrigued by this odd behaviour. In exasperation, he directed Thakur Mangal Chand to produce the porter with the wicker basket. Poor Mangal Chand had no choice. The basket was produced. Fairly fingered it to judge its worth and rejected it. While the basket was luckily saved, the wazir had to go through a long day's march without his lunch as it had been polluted.

Emerson, the deputy commissioner of Kangra, and therefore of Lahaul-Spiti, was a self-willed crank, who went about his job as his whims dictated. His father, at that time, was the Governor of the Punjab. On one occasion, Governor Emerson was visiting Kulu and deputy commissioner Emerson, who was on a tour of Spiti, was expected to return in time to receive his Excellency. Emerson Junior, who was accompanied by his pretty wife, took it into his head to try an entirely unknown route across a pass above the Rangrik valley from Kaza. He wanted to cross the unknown pass into the Parbati valley and then find his way back to Kulu. The route had never been done before. All advice against attempting the pass was forcefully dismissed by the young Emerson.

The party went up the Rangrik nullah. They suffered great hardship, and at the head of the glacier, the horses had to be abandoned. Since they did not arrive in Kulu on the expected date and by the normal route, there was anxiety for their safety. There was no wireless then, nor any other means of locating the deputy commissioner. His Excellency, the Governor was annoyed and worried. Emerson Junior, however, persisted in his efforts, and did manage to make the first crossing from the Rangrik nullah into the Parbati valley of Kulu, via the Dibbibokri nullah. Peter Holmes of Cambridge University and later Chairman of Burma Shell, with his wife and a friend, made the second crossing in 1956, and wrote a book about it. I climbed to the top of this pass from the Kulu and Dibbibokri side in 1963 with a mountaineering expedition. Emerson subsequently wrote a detailed account, which finds mention in the *Kangra Gazetteer.* While he may have enjoyed the climb over unchartered mountains, he lost his job. His Excellency felt that his son was too unbalanced to be a deputy commissioner. The instance speaks volumes of the British ethics of administration. Sons, no matter how beloved of their fathers, received the same treatment as any other officer where administration was concerned.

However, with their policy of laissez-faire, the British administration, made no effort towards development. This vacuum was filled to an extent by the Moravian mission which was in Lahaul from 1854 to 1940. The mission had little success by way of gaining converts to their faith. They found it hard to come to grips with the easy ways of the hill people and the mild humanitarian philosophy of Buddhism. While the mission failed to spread Christianity, it showed impressive results in improving and developing the economy of Lahaul. The German *padris* introduced the growing of potatoes, cabbage, tomatoes and other vegetables, set up schools, and taught the women knitting and other handicrafts. They improved the architecture of the houses, combining beauty with utility. The Moravians also gave Lombardy poplars and smokeless hearths and tandoors to Lahaul.

There were only five priests, all of them extraordinary men, in the ninety-year life of the mission. The founding priest, Reverend Hyde, had put in fifty-one years of service in the mission by 1905, when he left for his home in Prussia, where he died two years later. Hyde did remarkable work on the Tibetan language, publishing a grammar and also a Bhoti translation of the Bible. The mission was closed down in 1940, and the last pastor, Reverend Peter, interned in Yule camp in Kangra. With that went their Bhoti printing press and the valuable research material the missionaries had collected. Their house was bought by Thakur Pratap Chand of Lahaul and is now the deputy commissioner's residence. Below it, in a small yard, lie buried the Hyde children; their graves shaded by pink and yellow rose bushes. It is said that the ghost of the gentle Elisa Hyde can sometimes be seen walking along the house's veranda.

While Lall's proposals were not taken seriously in his time, conditions changed over the years. The realization began to dawn on the government that they needed an effective and objective administration in Lahaul-Spiti. In 1942, a *naib tehsildar* and a forest ranger, were posted in the area. The wazir was not formally displaced, but his functions were reduced. This arrangement continued after independence, right up to 1960. The year 1958 saw the beginnings of tension between India and China on the northern frontier. Clashes of Indian and Chinese patrols took place at the Chip-Chap river, and beyond Daulat Baig Auldi, in north-western Ladakh. The Government of India got more and more concerned over its northern border. Sardar Partap Singh Kairon, the then chief minister of Punjab, immediately realized the need for an effective Indian presence on the border. It became necessary both to show India's continued presence in these remote areas and to rapidly develop them economically. The old set-up became totally inadequate under the circumstances. The strategic importance of Lahaul-Spiti was recognized and in June 1960, it was broken off from the district of Kangra. It gained a set-up of its own consisting of a deputy commissioner at Kyelang in Lahaul and separate sub-divisional magistrates for Lahaul and Spiti. All other administrative structures that go with the district were also organized. Kairon insisted that the men appointed to the frontier region were to be young, energetic, and of course, from the first day, were to live in the area. Offices were set up in a school hostel and the staff, including officers, lived in hired rooms in local houses in the small village of Kyelang. The deputy commissioner alone had the semblance of a house. This was made possible by hiring the old mission house from Thakur Partap Chand. P.H. Vaishnav became the first deputy commissioner with Das and Kapila as his sub-divisional officers. All three were young and were bachelors.

One was a Gujarati, the second a Bengali, and the third, Punjabi.

Life at that time was extremely hard in these valleys. The road over the Rohtang hardly existed and was closed in any case for six months. People were locked in the valley with no links with the outside world for long periods. Today, in an emergency, a patient can at least be picked up by a helicopter. At that time, one relied on God's mercy! A practical and understanding man, Kairon realized the necessity for creating enthusiasm among the officers who had to work under such hard conditions. The pay of those posted to the area was increased by one-third and they were given other financial benefits. But even more than this, Kairon made the Lahaul-Spiti officers feel important and wanted.

Whenever a meeting was held, he fussed over each and every one of them like a hen over her brood. He treated their personal problems as his own, and it was made clear to everyone in the State Secretariat that these boys were important to him. During meetings, he encouraged them to speak up boldly, be it against the chief engineer, the finance secretary, or even the chief secretary. Invariably, he sympathized with their point of view, for like the British administrators, he always felt that more often than not, the man on the spot knew best.

In this attitude, he was helped by his Chief Secretary, E.N. Mangat Rai, one of the most liberal-minded civil servants that India has produced. He was as unconventional in his ways as the chief minister and took Lahaul-Spiti and its administrators under his special care. A priority slip marked 'Lahaul-Spiti' was introduced in the Secretariat. It was considered as important as the 'day and night' slip that was used for matters of utmost urgency. Kairon and Mangat Rai made this tribal area their special concern, and this fact was made clear to the slow moving Secretariat hierarchy in Chandigarh. Delay in any other matter was forgivable, but not in those relating to Lahaul-Spiti.

Kairon realized that if the development of the area was to be speeded up, the local officers, and above all, the deputy commissioner, must have full powers. He recognized the distance and remoteness of Lahaul-Spiti from Chandigarh. For half the year, wireless was the sole means of communication. Even in the summer, it was not easy to get to the area. Kairon was clear, therefore, that little could be achieved if all matters had to be referred to Chandigarh for a final decision. Accordingly, when the district was set-up, special financial and administrative powers were conferred on the deputy commissioner. He was made the head of department of every agency working under him.

Thus, for the police, the deputy commissioner was the inspector general, while for the civil surgeon the deputy commissioner was the director of health services. In this way, he was in a position to give the necessary sanctions and to keep development moving. I remember telling the civil surgeon jokingly once that if I so chose, I could in my capacity as the Director of Health Services, insist on performing operations in his hospital. Of course, in those early years, there was nothing called a hospital, or even basic emergency services, in Kyelang. We relied on luck and our youth and good health.

To ensure the enthusiastic participation of the people in development work and to give them an effective say in the administration, Kairon also created the Tribes Advisory Council. It consisted of elected representatives from the entire district and was presided over by the chief minister himself. The chief secretary acted as the secretary of the council. Important ministers of the state government, and all the secretaries were required to attend its meetings. The Council met twice a year and Kairon insisted that it meet in Lahaul-Spiti. Though Kairon was a man carrying the burden of many illnesses, including diabetes and asthma, he travelled regularly on horseback or on foot across the Rohtang pass to preside over the Council meetings that were held alternately in the Lahaul and Spiti valleys. Kairon went because he was determined to take the ministers and senior civil servants to the area, so that they could better appreciate the needs and problems of the tribal people. One wishes that the Government of India too adopts this simple stratagem in order to bring home to the Central Secretariat gnomes the hardships and the needs of people living on India's frontiers, be they Nagas, Mizos or Andamanis. It is so frustrating to see the Delhi babus in the finance and planning ministries quibble over petty grants that mean so much to these remote regions, while not batting an eyelid over the wastage of hundreds of crores on the pet whims of the central ministries.

The meeting, when it took place, was invested with special significance. During the trip, the Secretariat at Chandigarh was empty, with most of the ministers and secretaries puffing up the sharp slopes of the Rohtang pass. Today, I can recall Sarla Grewal, at that time the first woman in the Punjab cadre, and later principal secretary to Rajiv Gandhi, and Sukhchain Grewal, cabinet secretary with Morarji Desai, all trudging up the Rohtang slopes to attend the chief minister's meeting. Sukhchain and Sarla later got married and their romance undoubtedly blossomed on the slopes of the great pass, encouraged by the chief secretary and his wife. While the exercise brought a slight touch of colour to the sallow cheeks of civil servants, it also gave them an opportunity to know each other as well as the ministers better. The evenings spent under canvas tents and the common dining and wining helped to promote a spirit of camaraderie. At Kaza, the headquarters of Spiti, Kairon once famously organized a *gully-danda* match between the ministers and the secretaries!

The Tribes Advisory Council had unique powers. Since the chief minister presided and all senior ministers and Secretaries were present at these meetings, Kairon insisted that its decisions were to be treated as final. He did not allow the finance department the privilege of a separate examination of a proposal at a later date; nor would he allow the chief secretary to insist on taking such matters to the Cabinet. He bluntly told everyone that they had to make their objections and project their views at the meeting only. Decisions were thus taken quickly and what is more important, they were final. The deputy commissioner and his team of officers, therefore, came to each Council meeting fully armed with facts and figures to fight the objections of the Secretariatwallahs. More often than not, with a sympathetic wink from Kairon, they got the better of the Secretariat babus. The tribal members were shown special consideration by the chief minister at these gatherings. He personally made sure of their comfort, and in discussions, their views were allowed to prevail against those of the civil servants.

Kairon was a generous and large-hearted man who realized the value of gaining the goodwill of the tribal leadership. In achieving this objective, unlike many in the Government of India, he did not count his pennies. Sadly, in my long experience in the Government of India, I have rarely seen such wisdom and generosity, which Kairon displayed in dealing with the frontier people. We continue to have problems with sub-nationalities in our remote areas, which a Kairon-like administration could easily solve. Little problems are allowed to fester and small requests are denied, leading to grievances, which take long to fade. The young officers who administered Lahaul-Spiti from 1960 to the end of 1966, when the area was given away to Himachal Pradesh, all worked with a rare zeal and keenness. The work of providing schools, dispensaries, irrigation from the glaciers down to the village flats, bringing drinking water in polythene pipes from high mountain springs to the village lanes—all these and many more—were taken up in the short summer working seasons with great energy. I remember crawling along a narrow three-foot wide kuhl cut into the ledge of a steep cliff to check the water source. I was frightened and I dared not look down. But I did the crawl because the local people did. We had the arrogance and the will to match these mountain people. I will give only one example of our development work as it transformed the economics of the valley.

The Moravian missionaries had introduced potatoes and other vegetables to the region. They brought kuth from Kashmir and introduced it into Lahaul. This herb benefited the people and had a great market in China. Unfortunately, after the 1962 war with China, the export of kuth to Singapore and China stopped. Prices fell from Rs 800 per *maund* to Rs 200. Lahaul was in distress.

In 1965–66, Kamaljit Singh Bains was the deputy commissioner. He was from Jalandhar and knew much about potato cultivation in that area. It occurred to him that Lahaul, locked in by the Rohtang, Kunzam, and Baralacha passes, was virus-free. It could therefore be used for the cultivation of seed potatoes for the rest of the country. He invited Dr Sikka, deputy director of the Potato Research Institute in Simla and Sikh farmers from Jalandhar to Kyelang. Meetings were held and assessments made, and finally, the mother seed was obtained from the Potato Research Institute. During the winter of 1965, farmers, both men and women, were educated in this new project. In April and May 1966, while the Rohtang was still shut and the valley was under snow, fields were cleared and the potato seeds were planted. By October 1966, totally disease-free potato seeds were produced for the first time outside controlled research farms. A miracle had happened. In November 1966, Punjabis left Lahaul forever, but Lahaul has not looked back since then and remembers to this day the contributions of Kairon and the officers of the Punjab cadre.

The Lahaul Potato Growers Cooperative Society today handles the transportation and marketing efficiently. It has offices in Manali and recorded a turnover of more than a hundred crore rupees. They own marketing yards, petrol pumps and trucks, and have even built a hotel in Manali called Chandramukhi after one of the varieties of potato introduced in the valley.

In 1992, when I was secretary of the Agriculture and Cooperatives ministry, I once called Tshering Dorje in Kyelang to ask of the welfare of the valley. When he told me that the Lahaul Potato Growers Cooperative was in some financial distress, I immediately ordered substantial financial assistance to the society. I knew that though I had been the valley a long long time ago, my affection for the people there will always remain.

When the Punjab was taken over by the British in 1846, they put together a young and enthusiastic band of district officers under Sir Henry Lawrence to run this difficult frontier province. They realized that to successfully rule this turbulent land, they needed an administrative attitude, which was different from that followed in the settled Presidencies of Madras, Bombay, and Bengal. On this unsettled frontier, it was essential to trust the man on the spot and to back him with all the powers at the command of the state government. Thus was born the Punjab School of Administration.

Kairon, to my knowledge, never read the administrative history of the Punjab. But when he chose to set up an administrative arrangement for the new frontier district of Lahaul-Spiti, he instinctively applied the same principles. The success of his vision was immediate and immense. The proof of it is before us today. Since 1966, Lahaul-Spiti, along with the rest of the Kangra valley, forms part of Himachal Pradesh. The Himachal people have a natural rivalry with Punjab. They cannot, in the background of the political history of the region, be expected to praise any achievements of the erstwhile Punjab administration. And yet, one afternoon, at a luncheon party in Simla, a leading Himachali politician said to me, 'You know, we cannot say this in public for obvious reasons, but the tribal people of Himachal Pradesh miss Kairon.'

The commitment of the then Punjab officers to Lahaul-Spiti was complete and unequivocal. Today, in 2009, as I write and look back over my public life, I see that I never gave up my emotional bond with Lahaul. Again and again, I took my family on visits to Kyelang. I remember one visit when I took my wife and three young girls to Kyelang. We went up the valley and then came back to Khoksar towards the third week of September. I had long dreamt of visiting the Chandrataal. I asked people in Kyelang, but they cautioned me against going there at this time of the year. At the Khoksar rest house, a party of geologists too tried to dissuade me from going there. I proposed to motor up to Batal, the foot of the pass, sleep the night in the one-room hut there and early the next morning, go up to the top of the pass with Tara, my old peon, who had now become a driver. I then planned to walk from there with my wife and a Lahaula young man along the ridge northwards, going slowly down to the lake. I directed Tara to come back down towards Batal and wait for me in the afternoon at the fifth loop of the road. We three would get to the snow lake, spend a little time there, and walk along a narrow Gaddi path, just above the Chandra river towards Batal. I did not realize that I was no longer fit and acclimatized and had come for a sudden holiday at this altitude. The geologists could not believe that we could go to the lake and back in such a rush. But I brushed aside their worries.

Leaving my three girls with their grandfather, we raced off in the jeep one morning to Batal. We slept the night there and early in the morning, drove up to the Kunzam. At sunrise, we were at the chorten and the colour prayer flags of the pass. It was a magic moment and I took many photographs of the Mulkila range. Then, after carefully instructing Tara, we started the angled walk down the ridge, towards the Chandrataal. This region had risen from the Tethys Sea millions of years ago. These mountains are largely composed of sediment mud of the ocean floor, with boulders and fish embedded in them. They are dusty and unstable and walking on them is not pleasant. As the day came up, the glare and dust bothered us a great deal. But we did get to the Chandrataal. It was a glorious site. The still lake mirrored the Mulkila peaks and golden brahmani ducks dotted the waters. We sat down to enjoy the scene and have some lunch. But I had a tremendous headache and could not eat. I also realized that I had taken on far more than I could handle. The afternoon was fading and we had a long walk back down on a steep muddy slope above the Chandra back to the road, where we expected to find Tara and the jeep. Anything could go wrong.

We hastily left the lake and started the trek back. The path became more and more difficult: a narrow footpath on a steep unstable hill, with rocks and round boulders rolling down into the river every now and then. The afternoon wind of these valleys blew strong on our faces, raising dust to make walking difficult. One could be easily hit by a fast rolling stone coming down the slope. The walk became a test of our will and stamina. I was worried for my wife, just as she was for me. For long stretches, all three of us, holding hands for notional courage, inched forward, careful not to lose balance. Any slip and one would roll down into the river. Holding my wife's fingers, I really could not protect her if she stumbled. The walk became a nightmare, but it had to be finished. We struggled up the last few kilometres to the road loop. Darkness had come and I worried about finding the jeep.

Finally, we crawled and stumbled up to the road parapet. God bless Tara. He was sitting there, looking for us. We quickly drove downhill. Tara, a boy from the Mahendergarh desert in Haryana, whom I had taken to Lahaul with me, had now become a driver of the district staff. After long years on the road, he knew every bend, and he drove fast in the night to get us back to Khoksar. While my headache was gone, Vinnie suddenly had a severe attack of altitude sickness. She felt she was choking. The valley was empty, darkness had come, and we had to get to Khoksar.

We raced. There was not a soul anywhere in that empty wilderness. Only at one place we saw a light on an outcrop above the road. We stopped, and Tara ran up to the lonely tent of a Tibetan. He obtained some hot water, which we carried on feeding Vinnie as we drove back. The journey was unending, as it is always in a crisis. Finally, we reached Khoksar, but Vinnie was in poor shape. She had to get to a lower altitude, but that could only be the next day, over the pass. I was worried, but the ever present geologists, who were on their way back from the Shigri, offered us hope. They said they always carried Coca-30 homoeopathic pills, which they used for altitude problems high on the Shigri. They fed her these pills every hour, and remarkably, by late night, she was fine and normal. We had had our adventure and had survived it!

In 2008, my family and I went for one more visit to Kyelang. But even in Delhi, all through my life, I had stayed in touch with Lahaul. When I became the secretary of the Petrochemicals Ministry in 1988, I called the chairman of the Oil and Natural Gas Corporation and asked him to supply cooking gas to the small population in the valley. I felt that just as the whole country got cooking gas cylinders, these few thousands in Lahaul too were entitled to them. There was little wood and other fuel in the valley. I am happy to say that the ONGC did organize the supply of cooking gas cylinders to the Lahaul and Spiti valleys. Today, as the sports minister of India, I make sure that the young people of Lahaul-Spiti have equal opportunities to go on youth tours to different countries. Recently, Rs 5 lakhs were assigned to the deputy commissioner to procure equipment for a proposed skiing club in Kyelang. No wonder then that when I am sick or in trouble, it is the Lahaul lamas like Paljor and others who say prayers for me.

Having travelled to the corners of this vast country, the wisdom of Kairon's policy for the frontier regions keeps coming back to me. I will mention only one instance—that of the Andaman and Nicobar Islands. Lying more than a thousand miles away from the coast of India and more than 2,000 miles from Delhi, they are indeed on the very periphery of the country. The government, in its wisdom, has appointed a very senior officer as chief commissioner of the chain of islands. One would imagine that the man on the spot would be trusted to do his best for the development of these islands. It also seems obvious that the men in Delhi, particularly the Secretariat babus, can hardly be expected to contribute to the development related decision-making of this remote region. Most people have never been there and some have barely heard of it. Few ministers take the trouble of even visiting these islands.

I was horrified, therefore, to find in 1973 that the chief commissioner had to refer every little matter to the relevant ministry in Delhi, which, of course, makes further references to the ministries of law, finance and home before they deign to send back an answer. This takes years! Such a policy of distrust of the local administration can hardly aid development, and so, while the men in the Andamans fret and fume and wait for sanctions from Delhi, the men in Delhi do not even betray an awareness of the problems of the people of this forgotten corner of the country. In their scheme of things, these territories and their petty problems rate low. A man who is busy sanctioning Rs 1,000 crore for oil exploration could not be bothered by a demand of a crore for a sea jetty on an obscure island. He leaves such matters to an under secretary, who promptly turns these requests down. Parkinson's theory, that men in their ignorance will pass vast atomic projects while haggling over cycle sheds for workers, is repeated every day in the offices at South Block in New Delhi.

Today, things have changed somewhat. There is a lieutenant

governor and there are deputy commissioners in Car Nicobar and elsewhere. Due to defence concerns, the armed forces have a presence there, and of course, jet planes ensure contact with the mainland. When I went there in 1973, the chief commissioner had a hundred and fifty tonne ancient tub as his means of communication. The islands hardly had any communication with Port Blair. As managing director of the National Cooperative Development Corporation, I remember twisting rules and buying a small ship to create some contact for Campbell Bay and other far off islands with the headquarters. In the recent past, great havoc was caused by the tsunami in the Andamans. I tried hard to pursue relief measures through the local administration, but I found it wooden. It did not have the ethos of Kairon or of the Lawrence brothers.

I sometimes wish that Kairon had been the home minister of the Government of India for a while. He might have given a new deal to the people of such remote and forgotten lands as the Andaman and Nicobar Islands, Arunachal Pradesh, Lakshadweep, Mizoram, Ladakh and Manipur. Even more important, he might have made them feel wanted and trusted. Alas! Lahaul-Spiti remains Kairon's only experiment in frontier administration. Fate never willed that he would paint on a larger canvas.

Glossary

ashram	hermitage
bagthidpa	the substitute for the bridegroom in the marriage party
Basant	Hindu spring festival
bhatt	Hindu priest from the Pattan valley, an expert in curing sickness
bhojpatra	skin of the birch tree used as paper
bhoot	spirit, ghost
chakor	hill pheasant
chela	disciple
chhaang	homemade barley beer
chham	devil dance
chomo	female Buddhist nun
chorten	Buddhist stupa built to house the remains of famous lamas
chulha	hearth
churu	cross between a yak and a cow
daang	a kind of grass
dahho	enemy
dambargya	a Buddhist religious ceremony

dambargyee kilkhur	wooden altar used in Buddhist religious ceremonies
dange	a mound of roasted barley flour, prepared for prayers
delu	bell
demo puja	ceremony for driving away witches
dergot	a powerful spirit
devi	goddess
devta	god
dontsar	ceremonial bowls of water
dorje	thunderbolt
garpon	official of the Chinese monarchy sent to Tibet
gatpo	revenue official
geling	pipe instrument of the lama band
gewa	food offered to villagers at a death ceremony
ghee	clarified butter
gompa	monastery
goor	disciple through whom a local deity manifests itself and answers people's queries about their future
Gotsi	Lahauli festival of thanksgiving for male children born during the year
gully-danda	a game commonly played in the plains of north India
gyadung	long trumpet of the lama band
Halda	festival of light
havan	Hindu worship of fire
havan kund	vessel or spot for conducting the havan ceremony
jadoo	magic, bewitchment
jadoogar	magicain
jagir	feudal landholding
jagirdar	feudal landholder

jhula	swing
jogini	witch
jote	pass
kalchorpa	beautifully dressed and bejewelled beauties who carry chhaang in ceremonial goblets with each of the family processions during Gotsi
Kam Gotsi	Gotsi festival in a year when no sons have been born in the village
kangling	pipe instrument of the lama band
karipa	the carriers of offerings during Gotsi
Khampa	Tibetan tribe
khang-chung	smaller house in which the monks of a family live
khultsi	stuffed lambskins used for the priest to shoot at during Gotsi
kuhl	water channels
kuth	aromatic herb used in Chinese religious ceremonies
labdagpa	priest of the Gotsi festival
Lakshmi	Hindu goddess of wealth
lambardar	feudal landholder
laupa	assistant of the labdagpa
Laxmanrekha	the mythical line that Laxman drew to protect Sita; Sita subsequently crossed the line and was adbucted by the rakshasa Ravana
lohaar	men of the blacksmith caste who also act as drummers at all ceremonies and festivals in Lahaul
Lonchhenpa	a special caste to which the Gotsi priest belongs
mai-baap	literally 'mother and father', refers to those who hold absolute power

maidan	flat open ground
maund	an Indian unit of weight of about forty kilograms
mithugpa	one of the prayers offered after a death
mitsab	the 'in exchange for man' ceremony performed to avert death
mlechha	a person of an unclean caste
naib tehsildar	junior revenue official
nga	flat drums
nullah	water course, such as a river bed or ravine
padri	padre
pagsgormo	bronze bowls
Panchayat	the village-level governing body in India
patwari	the keeper of land records at the village level
phurpa	ceremonial dagger used by lamas during prayers
pothi	prayer book
prasad	holy food distributed after a prayer
rakashasa	demon
rakashasani	she-demon
rimpoche	a lama who has achieved salvation
robdagpa	the carriers of the dead at funerals
rolance	an evil spirit that has entered a dead body
sadhu	a holy man in India
sarpanch	headman of a village
sarua	metal cup with handle for pouring offerings into the havan kund
sattu	roasted barley flour, the most popular food item in Lahaul
shamla	the flowing part left loose out of a turban
shringa	amulet which protects a person
shringaar	the bells and decorations on a pony or mule

subedar	the highest position that an Indian could gain in the colonial British India Army
tagpo jinsrang	a ceremony to remove bewitchments
tana mana	a common Buddhist prayer
tangrol	ibex (*Capra sibirica*)
Tangyur	two hundred and sixteen books containing commentaries on the Kangyur (one hundred and three books containing all the writings of Buddhism) and the translation of the Hindu *Shastras*
tapasya	meditation
tehsildar	revenue official
thanka	religious painting on silk or canvas
thotpa	hollowed out human skull used as a cup or bowl
tsadam	long green grass
tshog	sweets used at prayer ceremonies
umzad	chief priest at a funeral ceremony, invariably the abbot of the local monastery
Vividh Bharti	a popular music programme on All India Radio
Yamraj	the Hindu and Buddhist god of death
yangkhug	one of the funeral ceremonies

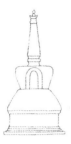

APPENDIX I

Major Monasteries in Lahaul and Spiti

LAHAUL

Lahaul is surrounded by different cultures. In the north, near Kyelang, the Buddhist influence is stronger with monasteries like Karding. There are also many small temples to local deities like Gephan.

To the west, at Udaipur, is the prime temple of Lahaul, Triloknath—perfect mixture of Hindu and Buddhist traditions. There is also a temple of Durga in Udaipur called Mrikula Devi. Beyond this, the Chandrabhaga enters the Kishtwar area and is called the Chenab, after which the Islamic influence predominates. Most important villages have temples for various local deities.

SPITI

Kye	Has a 12-kilometre-long motorable approach from Kaza. Kye is a large monastic complex of the Gelukpa sect standing on a hill.
Tangyud	A monastery about 4 kilometres above Kaza; patronized by the nonos of Spiti. A large complex is under construction. Tangyud is situated near Hikim monastery of the Sakyapa sect.
Dankhar	An ancient monastery built in the twelfth century over a ridge. A new structure is under construction. Dankhar can be reached by a motorable road (6 kilometres) from Sichling monastery of the Gelukpa sect.
Tabo	Founded in AD 996, this is a beautiful monastic complex of the Gelukpa sect built on a plain with unusual structures, caves and rare wall paintings. It is situated on the main road to Kaza.
Gungri	The main monastery of the Pin valley founded by Padma Sambhava. It is also one of the oldest monasteries in Spiti. Situated in the Pin valley, it is located about 18 kilometres from Attargo on the Kaza road and 4 kilometres from Sagnam, the principal village of the Pin area.

In addition to the major monasteries, there are several village-level monasteries. Listed below are some of the significant monasteries in north and south Spiti

North Spiti

Losar	On the way to Kunzam la
Hansa	A newly-built monastery with a temple of Jamlu devta in the basement
Kibber	Situated in the highest village in India

Kaza	A small monastery of the Sakyapa sect
Komik	A village monastery
Langja	A village monastery

All the above monasteries, except the one at Kaza, belong to the Gelukpa sect.

South Spiti

Lalung	A beautifully-located village monastery with a three-cornered Buddha statue. 12 kilometres off the main road to Kaza
Mane	Two village monasteries in the lower and upper villages
Gue	A small monastery in a village of the same name, which has a beautiful silver statue of Buddha, with gold gilding
Kaurik	A village monastery overlooking Tibet; located above the Parechu gorge as the river re-enters India

All these monasteries belong to the Gelukpa sect.

Pin valley

Sagnam	A rich monastery in the largest village of the Pin valley
Todnam	A village monastery
Tiling	A village monastery
Mud	A large monastery situated above the village. It overlooks the entire valley

All the monasteries in the Pin valley belong to the Nyingmapa sect.

APPENDIX II

Major Peaks in Lahaul and Spiti

LAHAUL

The valleys of Lahaul can be classified into the following sections.

Bara Shigri glacier is a long and complicated glacier with a number of peaks, including:

Kulu Pumori (6563 metres)
Parbati (6633 metres)
Shigri Parvat (6526 metres)
Central Peak (6285 metres)
Lion Peak (6126 metres)
Snow Cone (6309 metres)
Lal Qila (6349 metres)
Lalana (6265 metres)

Papsura (6451 metres)
Dharamsura (6446 metres)
Cathedral (6100 metres)

The Chandra-Bhaga Region comprises of all the peaks between the Chandra and Bhaga rivers. There are a host of peaks here known only by numbers: CB 14, CB 13, CB 11 and so on. Most of these range from around 6000 to 6200 metres, and many of them have already been climbed.

The higher peaks belong to the 'M' or Mulkila Group and include the Mulkila IV (6517 metres). The other peaks numbered I to X are in the range of 6000 to 6300 metres. In the Koa Rong group, also known as the KR peaks, the highest peak is KR I (6157 metres) and the remaining seven peaks are between 6000 to 6160 metres. The Tela group are numbered with the prefix 'T'. There are ten of these peaks, all of which are close to 6000 metres.

The Pangi valley in western Lahaul consists of several high peaks and forms a major climbing area in Lahaul. It consists of the Miyar nullah and other smaller valleys such as:

Phabrang (6172 metres)
Menthosa (6444 metres)
Jambu (5105 metres)
Munda Jote (5130 metres)
Baihali Jote (6280 metres)
Duphao Jote (6100 metres)
Jatham Jote (6294 metres)
Shivu (6142 metres)
Shib Shankar (5850 metres)
Gangstang (6163 metres)

SPITI

Peaks in the Eastern Valleys

Shilla (6132 metres)
Chau Chau Kang Nilda (6303 metres) [earlier referred to as
Guan Nelda or Blue Moon in the Sky]
Chau Chau Kang Nilda II (6158 metres)
Kanamo (5964 metres) [formerly known as Kanikma or the
White Hostess]
Rock Tower (c. 6100 metres)
Zumto (c. 5800 metres)
Tserip (c. 5980 metres)
Kawu (c. 5910 metres) [near Shilla Jote above Langja]
In the lower Lingti valley:
  Lagma (5761 metres)
  Sibu (5700 metres)
  Tangmor (5900 metres)
  Sisbang (c. 5250 metres)
Lama Kyent (6040 metres) [on the Lingti-Rupshu divide]
Labrang (c. 5900 m) [east of Shilla]
Runse (6175 metres)
Geling (c. 6100 metres)
Gyadung (c. 6160 metres)
Parilungbi (6166 metres) [in Rupshu, across the Lingti valley]
Lhakhang (6250 metres) [north of Shilla]
Gyagar (c. 6400 metres) [north of the Chaksachan la]
Gya North (6520 metres)
Gyasumpa (6480 metres)
Gya East (6680 metres)

Peaks in the Western Valleys

Manirang (6593 metres)
Parahio (5920 metres) [on the Parahio-Ratang divide]

Khamengar (5760 metres) [on the Khamengar-Ratang divide]
Ratang Tower (6170 metres)
Other peaks in the Ratang valley:
  Fluted Peak (6139 metres)
  Num Themga (6024 metres)
  Khangla Tarbo I (6315 metres)
  Khangla Tarbo II (6120 metres)
  Khang Shilling (6360 metres) [also known as the 'Mountain with Four Ridges']
  Ramabang (6135 metres)

APPENDIX III

Major Trekking Routes in Lahaul and Spiti

LAHAUL

The valleys of Lahaul, rather unfortunately for trekkers, are well connected by several roads. Almost any valley of any size has a road to it. Moreover, the main Manali-Leh highway passes through the centre of Lahaul and many smaller roads bifurcate from this main artery. Thus, most trekking routes approach the centre of valleys after two or three days of walking, like the Bara Shigri, the Chandrataal lake, Sersank valley and Miyar valley, which is motorable till Urgus village, almost halfway up the trek.

The main trail leading from Darcha (in northern Lahaul) to Padam starts at a beautiful point, but after two days of trekking, it leaves Lahaul and enters Zanskar. Thus options for a long trek within Lahaul are limited unless you trek from Lahaul to the Zanskar, Kullu or Spiti valleys.

On the Bharmour-Kyelang route via Kalicho pass
  Bharmour to Badgam (by road)
  Badgam–Bhadra (10 kilometres)
  Leundi (15 kilometres)
  Bansar (12 kilometres)
  Alyas (9 kilometres)
  Kalicho pass (3 kilometre descent to Triloknath)
  Kyelang (by road)

On the Bharmour-Kyelang route via Chobia pass
  Katheru Temple (20 kilometres)
  Alyas (13 kilometres)
  Chobia pass (8 kilometres)
  Alyas (10 kilometres)
  Bhayali (12 kilometres)
  Udaipur (6 kilometres)
  Udaipur–Kyelang (by road)

On the Bharmour-Kyelang route via Kugti pass
  Bharmour–Hadsar (by road)
  Kugti (12 kilometres)
  Duggi cave (13 kilometres)
  Alyas (13 kilometres)
  Kugti Pass (6 kilometres)
  Khodu Temple (6 kilometres)
  Rappe (8 kilometres)
  Udaipur–Kyelang (by road)

Sural valley
  Killar (by road)
  Dharwas (9 kilometres)
  Sural (13 kilometres)
  Shib Shankar la (6 kilometres) [here the trail crosses to Zanskar]

Batal to Baralacha pass
    Manali to Batal (across the Rohtang pass by road)
    Chandrataal (8 kilometres)
    Topko Yongma (12 kilometres)
    Topko Gongma (14 kilometres)
    Baralacha la (10 kilometres)
    Darcha–Kyelang (by road)

SPITI

On the route to western Spiti from the Pin-Parbati pass
    Manikaran (1697 metres)
    Pulga (2220 metres)
    Khirganga (2920 metres)
    Tundabhuj (3400 metres)
    Pando Seo Thatch (3780 metres)
    Bara Dwari
    Thatch (3920 metres)
    Mantalai (4150 metres)
    Pin-Parbati Pass (5400 metres)
    Chhochhoden (4000 metres)
    Mud [connected by a motorable raod from Mud to Sagnam
    Attargo and Kaza] (4000 metres)
    Sagnam (3680 m)
    Attargo

On the route over the Manirang pass
    Sichling (3365 metres)
    Mane village (3600 metres)
    Saponang (4500 metres)
    Manirang pass (5550 metres)
    Liti Thatch (4150 metres)
    Thatang (4100 metres)
    Ropa (3300 metres)
    Siasu khad (3200 metres)

On the route from Spiti to Karzok, Tso Moriri in Ladakh via
Parang la
  Kaza (3680 metres)
  Kibber (4400 metres)
  Thalda (4570 metres)
  Borogen (5180 metres)
  Dutung (4880 metres)
  Umdung (4880 metres)
  Narbu Sumdo (4670 metres)
  Kiangdom (4540 metres)
  Karzok (4540 metres)

On the route from Sagnam-Mud to Larang la and across Tari
Khango to Kafnu
  Sagnam (3680 metres): by road from Kaza-Attargo.
  Mud (3700 metres): by motorable road from Sagnam (14
  kilometres).
  Larang nullah (3850 metres): 9-kilometre walk on flat motorable
  road along the Pin river.
  Killung la (5175 metres): in the Larang nullah. This pass leads
  to the Khamengar valley at Thango. [Thango-Sagnam is a 12-
  kilometre-long trek.]
  Baldar (3850 metres): from Larang nullah bridge, on motorable
  road; camping is possible on the right bank of the Pin river.
  Chaphale: reached after a walk along the bank and a turn into
  the Tari Khango nullah. The motorable road goes south to the
  Bhaba pass (4200 metres).
  Tari Khango pass (4865 metres): climb over almost flat glacier
  and final scree to the pass.
  Fustirang (3950 metres): a good trail that descends towards
  Kinnaur.
  Mulling (3250 metres): trek past great meadows of Pasha and
  across the river to walk along the Bhaba valley where camping
  is possible.

Kafnu (2390 metres): steep descent to the valley to meet motorable road at Kafnu, which is connected by road to Wangtu (20 kilometres) on national highway no. 22.

APPENDIX IV

A Note on the Weather in Lahaul and Spiti

Spiti is a land of extremes. In winter, it is extremely cold with temperatures dipping to -40°C in the higher reaches and at least -20°C in the valleys. While the summer can be quite hot, it is the pure and direct sunlight that causes severe dehydration. But evenings, nights and mornings are generally pleasant. Spiti gets hardly any rainfall. Lahaul has better weather with milder winters. But the roads are blocked once snow falls on the Rohtang pass.

The season for visiting these regions are dictated by the opening of these passes and roads. The valley road from Simla to Kinnaur to Spiti is open for most of the year. Travelling in winter can be a challenge as many nullahs freeze over and it is difficult to drive safely across these streams. During summer, some of the nullahs flood and the water's force washes away roads. 'The Malling Block' caused by a nullah of the same name is notorious for traffic stoppages.

The northern approach road via Manali crosses two high passes—Rohtang for entering Lahaul and the Kunzam la. Thus the road has to be cleared of snow on both these passes before one can drive into Spiti. Rohtang is well maintained by army engineers and is open by late May or mid-June. The Kunzam la is open from mid-July till early-August. Though Lahaul has the Baralacha pass to its north, it is not the preferred route as it links with Leh.

With global warming and changing weather patterns, one can never be sure of these timings, but go prepared for any eventualities.

June to mid-September are the best months for trekking, depending on how high one wishes to trek. High passes are generally open from late June to mid-September. Many villages and valleys in Lahaul and Spiti are cut off during winters as road transport gets suspended and hotels and rest houses close. During the summer months, however, one can view green carpets of grass near villages, flowery meadows and clear views of peaks as there is no rain or haze.